PEACEMAKING IN
A DIVIDED SOCIETY

CASS SERIES: ISRAELI HISTORY, POLITICS AND SOCIETY
Series Editor: Efraim Karsh
ISSN: 1368-4795

This series provides a multidisciplinary examination of all aspects of Israeli history, politics and society, and serves as a means of communication between the various communities interested in Israel: academics, policy-makers, practitioners, journalists and the informed public.

Peacemaking in a Divided Society

Israel After Rabin

Edited by
SASSON SOFER

FRANK CASS
LONDON • PORTLAND, OR

First Published in 2001 in Great Britain by
FRANK CASS PUBLISHERS
Newbury House, 900 Eastern Avenue
London, IG2 7HH

and in the United States of America by
FRANK CASS PUBLISHERS
c/o ISBS, 5824 N.E. Hassalo Street
Portland, Oregon, 97213-3644

Website: www.frankcass.com

British Library Cataloguing in Publication Data:

Peacemaking in Israel after Rabin. – (Cass studies in
Israeli history, politics and society; no. 12)
1. Arab–Israeli conflict – 1993– – Peace 2. Israel – Politics
and government – 1993– 3. Israel – Foreign relations
I. Sofer, Sasson
320.9'5694'09049

ISBN 0-7146-5010-2 (cloth)
ISBN 0-7146-8064-8 (paper)

Library of Congress Cataloging-in-Publication Data:

Peacemaking in Israel after Rabin / edited by Sasson Sofer.
    p. cm. – (Cass series–Israeli history, politics, and society)
  Includes bibliographical references (p.) and index.
  ISBN 0-7146-5010-2 (cloth) – ISBN 0-7146-8064-8 (pbk.)
    1. Arab–Israeli conflict–1993–Peace. 2. Israel–Politics and government–1993– 3.
Israel–Foreign relations. 4. Arab–Israeli conflict–1993–Peace–Public opinion. 5.
Public opinion–Israel. 6. Civil–military relations–Israel. I. Sofer, Sasson. II. Series.
DS119.76.P43 2000
956.9405'4–dc21   00-057003

Typeset by Vitaset, Paddock Wood, Kent
Printed in Great Britain by
MPG Books Ltd, Bodmin, Cornwall

Contents

List of Tables

List of Figures

Notes on Contributors

Yaacov Bar-Siman-Tov is the Giancarlo Elia Valori Professor of International Relations at the Hebrew University and Director of the Leonard Davis Institute for International Relations. He is the author of *Israel and the Peace process 1977–1982: In Search of Legitimacy for Peace* (Albany: SUNY Press, 1994).

Abraham Diskin is professor of Political Science at the Hebrew University and the chair of the Israeli Political Science Association. He is the author of *Elections and Voters in Israel* (New York: Praeger, 1991).

Hillel Frisch is lecturer in the Department of Political Science at the Hebrew University. He is the author of *Countdown to Statehood: Palestinian State Formation in the West Bank and Gaza* (Albany: SUNY Press, 1998).

Reuven Hazan is lecturer in the Department of Political Science at the Hebrew University. His most recent book is *Centre Parties: Polarization and Competition in European Parliamentary Democracies* (London: Pinter, 1997).

Menachem Hofnung is senior lecturer in Political Science at the Hebrew University, specializing in constitutional politics and management of political finance. He is the author of *Law, Democracy and National Security in Israel* (Aldershot: Dartmouth Publishing, 1996).

Victor Lavy is professor of Economics and chair of the Department of Economics at the Hebrew University. His most recent book is *Foreign Aid and Economic Development in the Middle East: Egypt, Syria, and Jordan* (with E. Sheffer) (New York: Praeger, 1991).

Moshe Lissak is professor of Sociology (emeritus) at the Hebrew University. He is co-author of *Origins of Israeli Polity* (Chicago:

University of Chicago Press, 1978) and *Trouble in Utopia* (Albany: State University of New York, 1989), both with Dan Horowitz.

Chanan Naveh is lecturer in the Department of International Relations at the Hebrew University and in the Department of Political Science, Tel-Aviv University. He serves also as a senior editor at the Voice of Israel, Israel's Public Radio Station.

Sasson Sofer is chairman of the Department of International Relations at the Hebrew University. His recent book *Zionism and the Foundations of Israeli Diplomacy* was published by Cambridge University Press (1998).

Ehud Sprinzak is professor of Political Science at the Hebrew University. His most recent book is *Brother Against Brother: Violence and Extremism in Israeli Politics* (New York: The Free Press, 1999).

Introduction

This volume presents the results of an interdisciplinary effort to study the domestic sources of Israeli foreign policy, in particular those related to the peace process. Although most of the salient perspectives are presented, no claim is made for completeness. The research was conducted during 1995–97, under the auspices of the Leonard Davis Institute for International Relations (the Hebrew University of Jerusalem), and was supported by a generous grant from the Konrad Adenauer Foundation. The fact that there were three different governments in Israel during this period is a testimony to the volatile nature of Israeli politics and the unpredictable setting of its diplomacy.

If it was never accurate to regard states as unitary actors, the dichotomization into external and internal structures is no more evident or exact. Indeed, in recent years, foreign-policy analysis has undergone profound changes. The political system; the fabric of political elites; leadership; the role of mass social movements; shared meanings, norms, and ideas; public opinion; historical roots and national identities—all are considered legitimate variables in the study of foreign policy and understanding its intricacies. James Rosenau coined the concept of the 'frontier' as the new political space, where 'issues are contested and the course of events configured'. It is among a host of diverse frontiers, the meeting points of the domestic and the international, that foreign policies are formulated.

The 1990s were critical years in Israel's history. The deep and severe rifts of its society found their ultimate manifestation in the assassination of a prime minister. Israeli society was subject to uncontrolled upheavals in the political, economic, and demographic spheres, making it less tolerant and more distant from universal issues.

The development of Israel's political tradition exhibits a close link between the character and structure of the society on the one hand and its foreign policy on the other. The fragmented political order imposes a heavy burden on the conduct of diplomacy. Although

Israelis display a high level of political involvement, they also have one of the lowest levels of faith in government efficiency. A new electoral system has further fragmented the body politic, weakening the Knesset and the major political parties alike. The Israeli statesman must constantly deal with a divided constituency, hampering his ability to achieve solid public support and legitimacy for his policy. The convulsions of recent years should be understood in this light; forging ahead with the peace process entailed struggling with the Israeli public's deep-rooted fears about the consequences of peace, particularly territorial concessions. Peace did not speak for itself during Rabin's government; a slow adaptation to what peace entails came only in the aftermath of his death. The period of his tenure offered striking and unmistakable proof that even the best-crafted statesmanship can fail on the internal front.

The interplay between the domestic and the external provides the theme of Yaacov Bar-Siman-Tov's chapter. It examines peacemaking with Arab states in terms of the interaction between the two factors, using Putnam's two-level game. Although in most cases peace initiatives began externally, domestic factors determined the boundaries and the legitimacy of what was achievable in negotiations. Formal notification of a peace agreement does not signal the end of the internal struggle but, rather, the beginning of a search for legitimacy, ranging from efforts at persuasion among parties and factions to a possible referendum. This has been the pattern for all peace settlements over the past three decades, from the end of the War of Attrition in the summer of 1970 to the Oslo accords.

Territories and the future of settlement, a central ethos of Zionism, became the main impediments to attaining peace and to consolidating public support for it. Beginning with the first partition plan of 1937, territorial issues have always brought about shifts in alliances in Israeli politics. There were other domestic factors that affected the course of peace negotiations, including personal animosities among political leaders, particularly those between Rabin and Peres and, more recently, Netanyahu and Mordechai; extraparliamentary groups, with their radicalizing influence on the political scene; and, most importantly, terrorist acts. On the positive side, it should be stressed that the Israeli public has supported each and every peace agreement once it became a fact. The essential lesson is that finding the right balance between external and internal factors is crucial to the outcome.

Abraham Diskin provides an overview of the electoral attitudes toward the Arab–Israeli conflict and voting behavior of the Israeli public, at a time when a new electoral system has crystallized the 'Americanization' of Israeli politics. Diskin's findings corroborate the accepted view that foreign and defense policies are the dominant factors for Israeli voters; this appears to be decisively the case for the Jewish voters in particular. He also finds that voters tend to adapt themselves to election results, which is a less common perception.

The designations 'left' and 'right' are devoid of socioeconomic significance, and mainly correspond to degrees of dovishness and hawkishness. Strongest among the voters are centrist positions, notwithstanding the failure of centrist parties in Israeli politics. Israeli society appears to be polarized mainly along the ethnic divisions between Jews and Arabs. Although the peace process caused deep divisions within the Jewish public, Jews and Arabs are sharply divided on the issues of Jerusalem and of the mirror image of the enemy. Since 1992, there has been solid support for peace, but with a substantial percentage of the public still not ready to accept the territorial concessions that it entails. This may allay puzzlement over the 1996 elections, in which the electorate, despite its support for the peace process, favored a candidate who was regarded as less qualified, but who promised to move at a slower pace.

Ehud Sprinzak's chapter maps out the fragmented domain of the Israeli right. It explores the politics of the right in the wake of Rabin's assassination and Binyamin Netanyahu's extraordinary rise to dominance in the Likud. Sprinzak categorizes the right into four groups: parliamentarians, moderates, extremists, and terrorists. The Israeli right does not advocate a socioeconomic platform: it mainly comprises the 'national camp', that is, the loyalists of the Greater Land of Israel. Territories, security, and settlement are the main elements of its program. The right also seems less supportive than the left of pluralist democracy. However, the main reason for its radicalization was Palestinian terrorism.

The Oslo accords had a stunning and disorienting effect on the right. It returned to power, by the narrowest margins in Israeli history, only in the aftermath of brutal acts of Islamic terrorism, and ultimately failed to win over the Israeli public to its cause.

The right's struggle against the Oslo process turned into a vicious confrontation between the normally reserved and aloof Rabin and the messianic fundamentalists. The ruling of prominent rabbis to actively resist the evacuation of settlements openly violated the sanctity of Israeli law, dangerously shifting the struggle from its legitimate confines. The most radical attempt to stop the peace process was Baruch Goldstein's massacre at the Cave of the Patriarchs in Hebron, which triggered counterviolence by Islamic fundamentalists and, along with other acts by Israeli right-wing extremists, severely damaged the cause of Greater Israel. Political realities have marginalized the radicals and accorded a more central role to the pragmatists, who have proved to be more politically effective.

In 1995, the extreme right began to monopolize the struggle against Rabin and the Oslo process. Netanyahu's decision to ride the wild tiger of radicalism propelled him to power, but limited his room for maneuver after he took office. Netanyahu's victory culminated, indeed, in an improbable result: a tacit acquiescence to the Oslo process by the majority of the right.

The Israeli left has always been a grouping of factions. In his chapter, Reuven Hazan carefully scrutinizes the effects of the protracted peace process on the Labor Party. He first elaborates the propositions that parties are not unitary actors, and that cohesion or division within a party can considerably influence foreign-policy formulation. This point sheds further light on how domestic politics influences foreign policy, and is particularly pertinent to cases of a radical change in policy. Intraparty divisions hamper the building of public support and legitimacy for a government's policy, and may ultimately endanger a peace process. From a historical perspective, it is clear that the Labor Party leadership, particularly Rabin and Peres, failed to foresee the extent and intensity of the internal opposition to territorial concessions. After the departure of the Orthodox religious Shas Party from the coalition and the resignation of the Labor politician Haim Ramon, Rabin was forced from autumn 1993 to rely on a precarious minority government.

The Labor Party was plagued with infighting, not necessarily on issues related to the peace process, and was disintegrating at the very moment its support was needed. The party had already lost its traditional power bases, the kibbutz movement and the Histadrut. Although Rabin received the backing of the Peres camp, he never enjoyed his party's solid support. Both leaders reached their decisions on the peace process in solitude, with no apparent need for counsel and advice, and moved dangerously ahead of the party's Knesset faction.

Both terrorism and the fear of electoral defeat took their toll on the party. When the possibility of a peace treaty with Syria emerged, it began to split. There were calls for Rabin's resignation from within

Labor itself. In a critical period, his last year in office, Rabin was abandoned by many within the Labor Party, despite his diplomatic achievements. The benefits of peace did not alleviate the internal divisions. The Labor Party had, indeed, lost touch with the people and lacked support for excessive territorial concessions.

Although it is commonly assumed that Israeli Arabs play only a marginal role in politics and in Palestinian affairs, Hillel Frisch disputes this viewpoint. Because of coalition politics and the fragmentation of the Israeli body politic, the Arabs are likely to play an increasingly important role. Israeli Arab leaders have already become unofficial go-betweens of Middle Eastern diplomacy. In 1995, Rabin appointed the first Israeli Arab to an ambassadorship. Frisch analyzes the Israeli Arabs' role within the context of ethnic and diaspora groups, pointing to the similarities of strategies employed by African-Americans. Indeed, ethnic groups are most effective in a democracy. Not being a secessionist ethnic group, the Israeli Arabs will undoubtedly benefit from peace agreements between Israel and its neighbors. Peace will also resolve their main inner dilemma, that of conflicting national identities. Israeli Arabs have already shown some capability to influence Israeli foreign policy, despite their espousal of positions that are unacceptable to the Jewish public. Thus, in 1996 they took such a position on the Kafar Kanna incident, and reduced their support for the Labor Party at a crucial juncture. They have also pressured Israeli actors in the territories to respect Palestinian civil and human rights.

The Arab influence on Israeli politics reflects a change in strategy. By working within the system instead of outside it, Israeli Arabs went from being powerless outsiders to influential insiders. They legitimized their actions and rhetoric by framing them in terms of the Israeli national interest. We are undoubtedly witnessing only the beginning of a slow process in which Arab political power will increase substantially.

Shifting the focus to the economic sphere, Victor Lavy investigates the relationship between country risk and foreign direct investment. Economic fluctuations both influence and reflect social and political changes in Israeli society. The peace process, together with the immigration from the former Soviet Union, has contributed to the economy's rapid growth. In the context of the region, the Israeli economy's much larger size and high level of modernization have major implications for the prospects for peace. For the first time, international political economy has become an integral part of

Middle Eastern diplomacy, and of shaping a new regional order for the future.

The positive effects of the peace process on the Israeli economy included the forging of ties with Arab countries and the opening of new channels for Israeli trade, particularly into Asia. There were additional benefits, such as the lifting of the Arab boycott, a US loan guarantee of US$10 billion that allowed the investment needed in infrastructure, the beginning of important reforms such as the reduction of trade barriers, and the signing of free-trade agreements with the European Union.

Indeed, the peace process transformed Israel's standing in the international business community. It improved Israel's country risk rating, and foreign firms were attracted to invest in its markets. Israel was, at last, considered a developed country. In 1995, direct investment in the country came to a record US$2 billion.

The chapter by Menachem Hofnung deals with the legal implications of the peace process. He highlights the paradoxical situation of possessing the doubtful privilege of extended authority over occupied territories in a state of transition. The agreements with Jordan and the Palestinian Authority have created internal constraints on Israeli legislation. That is, because certain measures may amount to a breach of their stipulations, these agreements imposed new limitations on the range of options available to the Knesset, mainly in economic matters. Attempts to unilaterally ratify or implement policies in disputed areas are no longer regarded as internal matters by the international community.

The agreements with the Palestinian Authority contain provisions that, if fully implemented, will foster situations that are closer to the relations between states and a federal government. Yet, because the arrangements of the Oslo agreements are complicated, both parties are impelled to cooperate in implementing them. Essentially, the peace accords opened new venues for cooperation that were non-existent in the past. This growing interdependence has given Israel's internal legislation a new dimension of reference and consideration; the Israeli *Book of Laws* reveals the extent of such consideration.

Chanan Naveh explores the intricacies of the media's mood-setting, informative, and mobilizing roles in the peace process. Despite the fact that legitimacy became increasingly important for achieving peace, the media's role was somewhat ignored by the government. Naveh also finds that the media did not help much in consolidating support for the peace process during Rabin's tenure.

The Israeli media has undergone drastic changes: it is now pluralist, highly privatized, and strongly motivated by profit and business calculations. This has affected the media's role in projecting possible outcomes of foreign policy, in gaining public legitimacy, and in the domestic politicization of foreign policy.

The preferred medium for garnering public support in Israel seems to be television, particularly in times of crisis. Despite its high exposure to news, the Israeli public holds the media in low esteem and has little trust in it. This attitude is stronger among supporters of the right who resist the peace process, weakening the media's influence on this sector.

During the critical months before Rabin's assassination, the anti-Oslo groups received almost equal coverage to the supporters of peace. The right-wing media demonized both Rabin as an individual and his government's policy. The inevitable, intensive coverage of terrorist acts further delegitimized both the Rabin and Peres governments.

It is striking, then, to find that many Israeli decisionmakers ignore the media's role in the peace process. In any case, it is still difficult to assess the media's ability to change public attitudes. Any attempt to mobilize the media in support of the government's policy in the peace process would encounter many impediments, since the process remains controversial to this day.

Finally, Moshe Lissak carefully delineates the interactions between the military and civilian sectors. In this regard, Israeli society has developed a unique tradition where the military has substantial influence on politics, particularly in areas related to national security. There is also a growing involvement of the military establishment in diplomatic negotiations, national intelligence evaluation, and the military industry. Nevertheless, Israel has never become a 'garrison state': the senior military staff is ideologically pluralist, and the supreme authority rests in civilian hands.

Still, there is mounting evidence of the blurring of the boundaries between the civilian and military sectors, and in certain cases the military acquired a veto power over political decisions, particularly those linked to security matters. Lissak argues convincingly that the boundaries between the two sectors are varied and complex; compared with other countries, the meeting points between the two sectors are more intense. He points, however, to a socialization of high-ranking officers who, in increasing numbers, are assimilated into the civilian realm after retirement. There has also been a weakening of the national consensus about the use of military force, and a relative decline in the status of the military establishment.

The military was given an important role in negotiations with the Palestinians. Indeed, Rabin and Peres were sharply criticized for the excessive involvement of generals in diplomatic talks. The military's participation in national security affairs, however, has integrated it into the democratic framework. Following peace settlements, we should expect a reduction of the military's role in civilian matters.

This book has the merits of a collective effort. It is a special pleasure for me to thank all my colleagues who contributed to this volume. Moreover, this project could not have been initiated or sustained without the support and encouragement of the Konrad Adenauer Foundation.

The research was conducted while I served as director of the Leonard Davis Institute. Its success would not have been possible without the support and goodwill of the Institute's staff, and I express my gratitude. In particular, I would like to thank Robin Twite, the indefatigable coordinator of the project. Robin inspired us with his courteous manners, diplomatic experience, and deep belief in peace and cooperation in the Middle East. Special thanks also go to David Hornik for his kindness and expertise as editor. I would like to thank all those at Frank Cass Publishers, who helped in the preparation of this book. I am particularly indebted to Sally Green for her excellent editorship and for her kindness. Lastly, I would like to record my deep indebtedness to Laura Wharton, the indispensable executive manager of the Leonard Davis Institute. One could not imagine a more talented and generous person.

SASSON SOFER
The Hebrew University of Jerusalem

1 Israel in the World Order: Social and International Perspectives

SASSON SOFER

As the century winds down and the state of Israel prepares to celebrate 50 years of independence, it is fair to say that triumph and perseverance characterize the course of its history. For the first time, Israel is a full and legitimate member of the international community. Promising and unparalleled frontiers have opened to Israeli diplomacy, bringing an unprecedented expansion in external relations; the bonds of the Arab–Israeli conflict are loosening, though no sign of a decisive end to the conflict is apparent so far.

Israel faces these challenges as a critically divided society. New social forces have gained a pivotal political position, introducing fundamentalist beliefs and a vague historical vision, which usually hamper the emergence of the realism and pragmatism that a prudent diplomacy requires. Indeed, the prospects for reaching an end to the Arab–Israeli conflict, and for fashioning a new regional and international role for Israel, adaptable to the realities and norms of the post-Cold War era, remain obscure.

DIPLOMACY OF A DIVIDED SOCIETY

Diplomacy, in most cases, is socially bounded. More than in any past period, overlapping divisions—ethnic, religious, social, and political—have gained substantial sway over the formulation and conduct of Israeli foreign policy. Uncontrolled demographic fluctuations, the weakening of social solidarity, and an acute crisis of leadership have made the foundations of political legitimacy fragile.

These factors, coupled with a crisis of national identity, have kept Israeli society distant from the universal trends that are shaping a new world order.[1]

The cleavages in Israeli society are deepening. Its income inequality and rate of poverty are the highest among Western societies. Ethnic, class, and generational inequalities, manifested in terms of education, occupation, and income, have persisted and sometimes widened.[2]

The secular–religious rift is, perhaps, the most fundamental one in Israeli society, and will remain so even after peace is achieved. The ultra-Orthodox cult of separateness, and the radical nationalism of a significant proportion of religious Zionists, have created an entrenched enclave with no desire to accommodate to a civil society based on equality, claiming privileges not accorded to any minority in a democracy.[3] The secular–religious division may well determine Israel's national identity, its democratic fabric, the essence of its relationship with the Diaspora, and to a certain extent its international orientation and role in the Middle East. The recent tendency toward nationalism among the ultra-Orthodox constitutes one of the most dramatic changes in Israeli Jewish society, the full consequences of which we have not yet witnessed.

The right–left cleavage is no less complex. The Labor Party remains fully associated with the establishment and the peace process; the recent rise to power of the right looks like a revolt of the underprivileged, and of those threatened by modernity and progress. The right was stunned by the accelerating peace process, and even after electoral victory finds it difficult to adjust to the new political realities of the Middle East.

Israeli politics is undergoing radical changes. A new system of elections, where the Knesset and the prime minister are separately but simultaneously elected, has kept the situation unbalanced. A fragmented political body is in the making, with the roles of parliament, parties, and political leaders in a process of redefinition. Although the makeup of coalitions is still important, questions regarding the prime minister's role and his authority vis-à-vis the government, the Knesset, and his party have not been settled. A weaker party system will likely facilitate a stronger pressure-group system. Arabs, traditionally not included in the national discourse, are struggling for full equality, and will become more influential in Israeli politics.[4]

The divided nature of Israeli politics, the inconsistencies in political attitudes, and the rampant skepticism of the public are well reflected in all public surveys conducted in recent years, including the survey that the Leonard Davis Institute conducted in 1996, before and after the elections of that year.[5]

Issues related to foreign and defense policies, particularly those associated with the Arab–Israeli conflict, are dominant in determining political attitudes. There is solid support for peace, but also high skepticism about the prospects of achieving it. The public is divided between left and right, secular and religious, concerning the extent of territorial withdrawal, the establishment of a Palestinian state, and the very definitions of peace and of democratic norms.

Significantly, whereas an overwhelming majority wants the government to make all efforts to achieve peace, and a surprisingly solid majority wants Israel to be an integral part of the New Middle East, Israeli society is sharply divided on the question of whether territorial compromises will lead to peace. The same inconsistency is apparent in the tendency to support idealistic worldwide goals, such as universal human rights and arms control, whereas the same norms are not applied in regard to the Palestinians and Arab countries.[6]

The divisions in Israeli society are reflected in real or imaginary profiles of the two dominant parties, which may provide an explanation for political stagnation. The majority believes that the Likud Party is likely to be better at safeguarding the territories and fighting terror, and, at the same time, regards the Labor Party as better at securing democracy and achieving a true peace.[7]

These divisions in society have grave consequences for diplomacy. A divided political order places a heavy burden on the conduct of foreign affairs, and factional struggles make systematic planning or consensual national policy difficult to achieve. Any change of political hegemony also entails change at the conceptual and cognitive level, affecting the ways in which international reality is understood and analyzed. Israel's situation may well be termed a case of diplomatic discontinuity. A new ethnonational component has been introduced into Israel's governance and national policy, reflecting the widening cleavage between the nationalist right on the one hand and the Labor Party and its left-wing supporters on the other. Israel has, indeed, two distinct foreign policies with different regional and international perspectives.[8]

Israeli statesmen must deal, then, with a fragmented constituency, and encounter enormous difficulty in achieving solid support and legitimacy for a given policy, whether of the left or the right. The Israeli public is highly political, yet has no trust in politicians and no belief in its own ability to influence policy. This public is marked by a narrow attitude toward international affairs, focusing almost entirely on war and peace in the Middle East and the future of the occupied territories; interest in global issues, such as international political economy, human rights, and environmental problems, is very limited.

Not surprisingly, from the beginning Israeli diplomacy inclined toward a fait accompli approach. When making crucial decisions, Israeli statesmen tend almost to ignore the public. Diplomatic achievements have never been made in the public domain. This is true of the Partition Plan of 1947, the Camp David accords, and the Oslo agreements: all were introduced as faits accomplis, the parties and the Knesset only being asked to approve formally what already had been agreed upon with foreign governments.[9] In the case of the Oslo agreements, there was almost a flagrant neglect of the domestic front, leaving a significant proportion of the public out of touch with the peace process and its ultimate implications; peace did not speak for itself. Whatever the policy, it involves the diplomacy of a divided society, where a cynical and skeptical populace faces preoccupied and often manipulative politicians.

The Course of Israeli Diplomacy

Summing up a lifetime of diplomatic experience, Abba Eban wrote:

> There is no doubt that the pervasive theme of Israel's performance is triumph. And yet the victorious state of Israel has more unresolved marks of interrogation hanging over it than most other political units in the modern world. Israel's structure, dimensions, boundaries, human composition, political regime, Jewish vocation and moral quality all became uncertain once the underlying principles of the early years were abandoned.[10]

As a small nation, a democracy, and the only Jewish state, Israel is a unique international actor. There has always been a certain exclusiveness about its place in the world. Israel has difficulty maintaining a single international identity, wholly consistent either with its own national values or with world norms at large.[11]

A lack of strategic depth, numerical inferiority, and exposed frontiers have induced a sense of insecurity, not completely warranted by either the realities of world politics or the actual balance of power in the Middle East. A constant preoccupation with the Arab–

Israeli conflict has resulted in a conspicuous discrepancy between the aspiration to meet universal norms and the necessity to resort to realpolitik vis-à-vis neighboring countries.

No major issues seem to be conclusively settled. Israel is one of the few states that are not formally affiliated with any regional bloc. Even the natural partnership with the Diaspora communities is destined for changes, and the alliance with the United States has yet to pass the tests of a longer period of history.

It is customary to blame Israeli diplomacy for many lapses and deficiencies, such as a lack of foresight and long-range planning, a susceptibility to impulse and crisis exigencies, a paucity of originality and inventiveness.[12] In fact, Israeli diplomacy has scored some remarkable achievements. Most notable are the special relationship with the United States; the early, solid association with the European Community; the peripheral strategy involving Turkey, Iran, and Ethiopia; the peace settlements with Egypt and Jordan; and Israel's foreign aid and cooperation program in the Third World. Israel's diplomacy has always retained a streak of idealism.

All of the achievements came about despite the burden of domestic politics, and Israeli prime ministers' strong penchant for summitry, backstage diplomacy, and covert actions. Moreover, there is a sense prevalent in Israeli society that international frameworks and standards are unreliable; Israeli governments have never invested much of their time, or of the national budget, in foreign affairs.

The Israeli Foreign Ministry is rather small, with a yearly allocation of about 0.5 per cent of the national budget.[13] It is still the least political of the government ministries, providing a continuity in planning and policy where a legacy of confusing traditions is the norm. The Foreign Ministry also helps to balance Israel's foreign policy by paying attention to such neglected aspects of diplomacy as international organizations, cultural relations, human rights, international cooperation, and global aspects of economy.[14]

Israeli diplomacy is facing a challenge from the unprecedented expansion in the number of diplomatic missions and the range of its responsibilities. This unforeseen expansion has not been matched with the elevation of diplomacy to its proper place on the national agenda. Israeli foreign policy also needs to fashion an adequate response to global patterns, particularly in the commercial and technological spheres; and it needs to develop a more explicit commitment to universal standards of behavior.

THE NEW MIDDLE EAST

The New Middle East is both an idea and metaphor, which both converges with and departs from reality. The Middle East is enjoying the mixed blessings of the post-Cold War era: on the one hand, relative stability and distance from great-power intervention; on the other, continued economic and political lack of development compared with most other regions of the world. It is still a region of scarcity and turbulence, marked by unprecedented population growth, food dependency, and water shortage. In all probability, the fiercest competition over freshwater anywhere in the world will be in the Middle East.[15]

The profound economic gap between Israel and the Arab countries is not a promising basis for regional cooperation. In the Middle East, history tends to progress by fait accompli. Strategic surprises, diplomatic as well as military, are common. Although Israel has always taken part in the region's machinations, a more overt integration into Middle Eastern politics may prove more complicated than the covert dealings of the past. There no longer exists, however, an implacable and monolithic Arab adversary, and Israel will need a more refined regional diplomacy.

Bernard Lewis notes that the Middle East has been left on its own, with no great-power tutelage: 'currently the countries of the Middle East face a challenging and, for some, frightening prospect: the prospect of having to take responsibility for their own affairs'.[16] The region has yet to emerge from the status of a no man's land between North and South. Although pan-Arabism has declined, fundamentalism must be contained and the threat of nonconventional weapons urgently addressed.

At present, a shadowy struggle for hegemony is taking place, aimed mainly at preventing Iran and Iraq from becoming dominant.[17] The revival of Turkish–Israeli strategic cooperation has introduced a new, key element into the shaky Middle Eastern balance of power. The growing ties between the two countries reflect their similar geostrategic predicaments, and the fact that both are seeking a viable international orientation.[18] This development is another indication of the weakness of the Arab world, as well as being a by-product of Europe's refusal to grant Turkey entry into the European Union.

It was the resourceful Israeli statesman Shimon Peres who publicly articulated, perhaps prematurely, the vision of a New Middle East. It has since become a metaphor for the prospective progress of the entire region. Peres mainly invoked a functionalist model, based on the European example; essentially a prudent, rational, businesslike approach that was cut short by the fears and suspicions of too many on both sides of the barricades. In Peres's vision, a spirit of commercial cooperation and economic interdependence would lead to regional regrouping, multilateral security agreements and, possibly, federative arrangements between Jordan, Israel, and the Palestinians.[19]

The idea of a New Middle East has introduced a completely new balance of risks and benefits, together with an image of stability and progress that has strongly appealed to economic and political elites. For a short time, it was thought that the Middle East would merge with world globalization, ceasing to be a unique and incorrigible case. Inadvertently, however, the idea of a New Middle East ignited the suspicions of Arab statesmen, particularly in Egypt, who feared that its ultimate outcome, sweetened by economic incentives and the blessings of the United States, would be Israeli hegemony. These fears ebbed, however, with the election of a new Israeli government that ridiculed the very notion of a New Middle East, and was viewed by Arab governments as less likely to make any diplomatic headway.

History unfolded differently from what was envisaged. Peres, an 'unpaid dreamer' as he called himself, was replaced by Binyamin Netanyahu, who aspired to a 'reversal of causality' where peace with security would be achieved behind an iron wall. It is puzzling to see Prime Minister Netanyahu advancing the Kantian logic of eternal peace among democracies, embracing lofty but unattainable goals, while forfeiting the unprecedented opportunities of the present.[20]

The political future of the Middle East rests on a delicate balance. The dual containment of Iraq and Iran, together with the international effort to isolate both countries, is not working. Saddam Hussein continues to challenge the United States and, indeed, the collective will of the international community. The Gulf remains a focus of possible conflict, levels of military spending are as high as ever, and the production of weapons of mass destruction is continuing almost unchecked.

The end of the Cold War can have only a limited impact on the future of regional conflicts. If the peace process does not progress further, another Arab–Israeli war is inevitable, as has always been the case in the past.[21] Egypt and Syria are the two pivotal states in terms of signaling the direction—whether toward war or peace—that the Middle East will take.

Israel's main, most pressing security dilemma now involves non-conventional weapons and arms control. China, Russia, and North Korea, all short on cash earnings, have been drawn into questionable arms deals with the radical countries of the Middle East, particularly Iran, Iraq, and Syria. It is also unclear what strategic aims are being served by Israel's nuclear option at present. If Iran and Iraq come closer to developing nuclear weapons, it may be prudent for Israel, for the first time, to move beyond its traditional strategy of opacity.

Nonproliferation, though a necessity, is unlikely to be achieved before a political solution to the Arab–Israeli conflict is reached. Verification procedures are extremely difficult, if not impossible, in the Middle East. The current multilateral talks cannot produce a conclusive solution until national leaders agree on a political settlement. Israel may consider joining the Non-Proliferation Treaty, and establish a nuclear-weapons-free zone, only after a comprehensive Middle Eastern peace is established.[22]

The stakes remain high in the Middle East; skepticism, or at best reserved optimism, prevails. Recent events may portend a long and possibly violent period ahead. Discrepancies, normative as well as structural, between Israel and Arab states make US involvement a necessity. Direct negotiations have seldom, if ever, produced lasting settlements in the Middle East. Trust is a key factor, but a scarce one. In the short run, self-governance and political autonomy for the Palestinians may be the only viable option, ultimately developing, in stages, into statehood, a third partition, or possibly a tripartite confederation between Israel, Jordan, and the Palestinian Authority. Such solutions would mean the achievement of the ultimate aim: the acknowledgment and honoring of the territorial integrity, sovereignty, political independence, and national identity of every state in the Middle East.[23] We should not, however, expect final and perfect solutions, or be tempted to think in absolute terms of the peace that will end all wars.

ISRAEL'S PLACE IN THE WORLD

The question of Zionism's international orientation was a major preoccupation of the founding fathers. For a long period it defined the essence of Zionist diplomacy—the effort to secure the support of at least one great power for which the Middle East was an important sphere of influence. The concept of international orientation also entailed decisions with moral and ethical dimensions. Although at times it strove for universal ideals, Zionism settled, under the mounting pressures of Arab hostility and a turbulent international arena, for more utilitarian and realistic approaches.

Neither part of the East nor the West, yet a country that cannot afford to dwell alone, today Israel faces, for the first time in its history, considerable international room to maneuver. It still faces, as well, the question of its future international identity. Both its left-wing and right-wing governments have wavered between realism and internationalism, accommodating with difficulty to a world of greater interdependence where global issues of nonproliferation, international political economy, environment, and human rights predominate. The dualism of a regional realpolitik policy on the one hand, and an orientation toward Western liberal democracy on the other, is precarious, and may prove nonviable in the future.

Relations With the United States

The partnership with the United States is essential to Israel and utterly dominates its foreign policy. Israel's special relationship with the US rests on solid foundations: shared democratic values and considerable complementary interests. When one takes into account the vastly disparate size and power of the two countries, and the fact that no formal alliance exists between them, this is a unique case in modern history. Total US assistance to Israel has reached the fabulous sum of US$90 billion by the end of the twentieth century.[24]

This partnership, however, will face the test of history in the coming years as a new world order takes shape, ultimately altering the United States' strategic and international posture. For the time being, it seems that the US is capable of maintaining its imperium in the Middle East at about half the price that was required of it during the Cold War era. In the short run, Israel remains the United States' most reliable ally in a region that contains most of the world's known oil reserves.

Questions are often raised about the durability of this special relationship. As Garfinkle remarks, 'intuition alone tells us that no relationship so distinctly intense can remain tranquil for very long'.[25] For all appearances, this relationship remains stable, though presumably it will become less intense. Unparalleled military cooperation and multifaceted, overlapping economic and political interests provide a strong anchor in the uncertain waters of the Middle East. The cooperation between the two countries has even, lately, been enhanced, in the form of joint air and naval exercises, institutionalized strategic consultations, and extensive military and intelligence cooperation; the first free-trade zone established by the US was with Israel.

There are, of course, negative ramifications as well. A by-product of the peace process has been the equipment of moderate Arab states with sophisticated American weaponry. There are also ongoing disagreements about nonconventional weapons in the Middle East and in Israel itself.[26] In the long run, shared values and moral commitments based on the Judeo-Christian heritage may prove more reliable than the strategic considerations often stressed by Israeli leaders. Strategic doctrines and international interests of great powers are destined to change, and with them the passing attachments to small nations. Israel should strive to help keep the US the predominant power in the Middle East—although isolationist public opinion at home, more pressing items on its international agenda, and the expected marginalization of the Middle East will ultimately change US policy in the next century.

Relations With Europe

Strategically and diplomatically, Israel prefers its alignment with the United States, though it may well face a need to balance it with closer ties to Europe. The giant merchants of the Old World are closer to the Middle East than are either the United States or the Asian powers. The decline and rise of Europe in world politics is indeed a matter of historical wonder. For the time being, however, the Middle East and the Mediterranean are among the few arenas where Europe could play a significant role.

There is still much anger and mistrust toward Europe in the Middle East, particularly in Israel, where the calamities of the past have left scars. Indeed, for most Israeli statesmen, reflecting a general consensus, to leave the fate of Israel in European hands is an ominous prospect. A continuous effort to distance Europe from any critical role in the peace process has been an integral part of Israeli diplomacy.

Yet Europe is the birthplace of Zionism, culturally closer to Israel than any other civilization. Britain was the first great power to grant Zionism international legitimacy. The Middle East will permanently remain Europe's backyard, and in fact, Israel's commerce with the European Union already surpasses that with the United States.[27] An implicit, large-scale partnership in the strategic, political, and economic spheres—not reflected in the declaratory sphere—has served both Western Europe and Israel well. Both sides also share the goal of transforming the Middle East into a zone of peace and prosperity.

Traditionally, the Middle East has always been more important to Europe than to the United States. Europe is more dependent on energy supplies and capital imported from the region. European diplomacy, though tending to the crafty, rests on a delicate balance. Europe's forwardness in endorsing the Arab cause, reluctance to support the US dual containment policy, and cultivation of economic ties with Arab states under almost all circumstances have not endeared it to either the US or Israel. The relative benefit of this approach remains questionable. Europe plays only a marginal role in the peace process; the Venice Declaration of 1980 notwithstanding, it lacks a coherent policy. Having a permanent European representative to the Middle East and pressuring Israel through trade relations have not been effective so far.[28] Europe can potentially contribute much, however, by limiting the transfer of weapons and high technology to the Middle East.

Another European initiative, the revival of the Mediterranean idea, may prove more important. The Euro-Mediterranean programs were inaugurated at the Barcelona Conference of November 1995.[29] The Mediterranean, however, is an area with no definite boundaries, reflecting conflictive international identities. The disparities in income and wealth between Europe and most of the Mediterranean countries may prove insurmountable. Europe does not have a united approach to the Mediterranean front; Italy, Spain, and France play the major roles. Most European states, despite the vested interests they have in North Africa and the Middle East, are not determined to play a role in the Mediterranean.

Israel, too, so far lacks a clear Mediterranean policy. The Middle Eastern sphere and the Mediterranean sphere have separate geostrategic, cultural, political, and economic identities, not necessarily compatible with each other and, in the case of Israel, clashing with its strong American orientation.

Two European powers, Russia and Germany, are playing increasingly important roles. Germany is emerging as the dominant power in the continent, and it remains the most important European state for Israel, balancing less favorable attitudes within the European Union.

Russia, it seems, will return to Middle Eastern diplomacy not far in the future. The Middle East has become almost the only area where

Russia can benefit by opposing the United States and project the image of a great power. Despite Russia's decline in world politics, it is capable of disturbing the Middle Eastern balance of power to Israel's detriment. Russia has been courting Iran, and exploiting Washington's failure to resolve the situation in the Gulf.[30] Islamic fundamentalism, however, has become a major concern for Russia; it is, moreover, incapable of competing economically with either the US or Western Europe.

The Israeli–Russian relationship has known only short periods of grace—during the first years after Israel's independence, and at the present time. Israel, no doubt, is one of the beneficiaries of the decline of Russia's power in the Middle East. Despite diplomatic normalization and expanding economic ties that include the former Soviet republics, the future of this relationship is highly unpredictable.[31]

Relations With Non-Western States

Israel's relations with non-Western states occupy a unique place in its diplomatic history. In particular, Latin American countries played a crucial role in the birth of Israel, supporting it in the historic United Nations vote on the partition of Palestine in November 1947. This fascinating chronology began not without idealistic aspirations, which turned into utilitarian approaches, before the relations collapsed in the 1970s. Over the past decade these associations have revived, though they will never recapture the old élan.

Although in the early 1950s Israel made an attempt at non-alignment, this tendency never gained momentum in Israeli diplomacy. Nevertheless, Israel was remarkably successful in forging connections with Third World countries, particularly in Africa and Latin America, through which Israel gained considerable diplomatic support for international organizations. Israel's development co-operation with non-Western countries constitutes a unique experiment that still preserves its idealistic spirit. As of 1996, about 10,000 trainees from 55 countries have taken part in courses initiated and conducted by Israel.[32]

The military component of Israel's relations with Third World countries has always been problematic, both politically and morally. In particular, the self-interests and ambitions of despotic leaders have often determined the course of these relationships. Generally, Israel has done better in bilateral ties with Third World countries than it has in multilateral forums, particularly the United Nations.

Since the mid-1980s, Israel has managed to restructure its diplomatic relations with most non-Western states, including Islamic countries in Asia and Africa. Many of these non-Western states believe Israel can enhance their relations with Washington. These relationships, however, are now on more solid ground than was the case in the past.

Among Israel's major diplomatic challenges are Far East Asia and Pacific-rim countries. There has been steady progress in relations with China, Japan, and the Asian 'tigers', though no real breakthroughs. Early in this decade, after an alienation that had lasted over 40 years, China and Israel normalized their diplomatic relations. As China has opened itself to the world, Israel has developed close and clandestine military ties with it. Even though China remains a main military exporter to Middle Eastern countries hostile to Israel, there is considerable strategic cooperation between the two countries. As for Japan, having eased its once-severe dependence on Arab oil, it has improved its economic and diplomatic relations with Israel, though the potential cooperation between the two countries is far from exhausted.

Relations With World Jewry

The weight of Jewish history always rested heavily on Zionist diplomacy. Today, the relationship between Israel and the Diaspora communities is approaching a historical crossroads. On the one hand, Israel has become less dependent on Jewish support; on the other, there is growing autonomy among the Diaspora communities. Indeed, it was never evident that Israel could serve as the sole guarantor of the Jewish people.

For Israeli diplomacy, Diaspora communities remain a source of power and inspiration, yet are also a constraining factor. The relationship with Russia represents, perhaps, the most complicated case.

As international diasporas burgeon, the Jewish structure of center and periphery no longer constitutes a unique historical phenomenon. It still involves, however, the most audacious and successful case of diaspora diplomacy. Yet, with the Diaspora communities of the West apparently in demographic decline, this center–periphery structure is destined for dramatic changes. In numbers, the Jewish people have never recovered from the Holocaust: from about 18 million before the outbreak of World War II, at present they total no more than 12–13 million. By the beginning of the next century, the Jewish community of Israel will be the largest in the world.

In the Diaspora, the American Jewish community remains dominant. Jewish involvement in American life, including donations for political purposes, continues to be disproportionately large. Despite a relative decline in the influence of the Jewish lobby, it remains among the strongest in Washington.[33] There are limits, however, to Israel's partnership with this community. The American Jewish community is becoming fragmented along the lines that divide Israel politically. Indeed, in a mood of mutual disenchantment, Israel's centrality to Jewish life may diminish.

CONCLUSION

Toward the beginning of the third millennium, Israel is facing new diplomatic opportunities, more promising than at any other time in its history. The most important challenges facing Israel are: to conclude the peace process with Syria and the Palestinians; to fashion an adequate role within the Middle Eastern state system; to explore further the Mediterranean option; to address the mounting non-conventional threats in the Middle East; to balance Israel's international orientation between the United States and Europe; to expand its international reach, particularly in East and Central Asia; and, overall, to act as a progressive force in international politics, while adhering to the new international norms and global covenants.

There is a need to restore the delicate balance of the past between realism and idealism, between national goals and attentiveness to the external world. Both Israel and the Middle East as a whole are, after all, dependent on the structure and normative evolution of international society. Unfortunately, these dimensions are flagrantly neglected by Middle Eastern governments and leaders. If peace is achieved, Israeli society will face the challenge of redefining its national identity, and that has always been interconnected with Israel's place in the world.

NOTES

1. See also A. Arian, *The Second Republic* (UK: Chatham House, 1997), pp. 1–18; M. Lissak and D. Horowitz, *Trouble in Utopia* (Tel-Aviv: Am Oved, 1990), pp. 69–141 (in Hebrew). The population of Israel is 5.5 million, 81.2% of Jewish origin; half of the population is native-born, while the other half came from 70 different countries. It is a relatively young society (median age 26.4 years), urban (90%), with a GNP of about US$17,000 per capita.
2. C. Goldscheider, *Israel's Changing Society* (Boulder, CO: Westview, 1996), pp. 19–37, 61–81, 129–46; Arian, *Second Republic*, p. 71.
3. See also T. Hermann and E. Yaar (eds), *Israeli Society and the Challenge of Transition to Co-Existence* (Tel-Aviv: Tel-Aviv University, 1997), pp. 47–54; S. Sandler, *The State of Israel, The Land of Israel* (Westport, CT: Greenwood, 1993), pp. 235–58.
4. M. Hofnung, 'The Unintended Consequences of Unplanned Constitutional Reform: Constitutional Politics in Israel', *American Journal of Comparative Law*, 44 (1996), pp. 585–604; H. Frisch, 'The Israeli Arabs and Israeli Foreign Policy: Minority Participation in Ethnonational Politics', in *The Role of Domestic Politics in Israeli Peacemaking* (Jerusalem: Leonard Davis Institute for International Relations, The Hebrew University, 1997), pp. 40–64; Hermann and Yaar, *Israeli Society*, pp. 55–73; Arian, *Second Republic*, pp. 237–323, 351–82.
5. The surveys were conducted by Professor Abraham Diskin as part of the Leonard Davis Institute research project at the Hebrew University on 'Internal Changes, The Peace Process, and Israeli Foreign Policy'. See also A. Diskin, 'Voters' Attitudes on the Arab–Israeli Conflict and the 1996 Elections', in *Role of Domestic Politics*, pp. 25–33.
6. The following are findings of the Leonard Davis Institute surveys conducted in May and July 1996:

Table 1.1: Findings of the Leonard Davis Institute Survey, May and July, 1996

Extent of support	May (N = 1064)	July (N = 1087)
The peace process	904	902
Importance of Israel's security	1,038	1,065
Importance of state's Jewish character	745	764
Importance of democratic values	1,013	1,022
Being part of the New Middle East	618	609
Balanced orientation between Europe and the United States	518	491
Greater efforts (human rights)	842	828
Greater efforts (arms control)	622	602
Negotiations with Syria	711	707
Negotiations with Palestinians	745	748
Prospects for peace in the Middle East	311	312
Comprehensive peace will bring security	504	503
Ceasing nuclear option after peace	305	301
Arab world favors Israel's annihilation	623	651
Foreign and security issues as main reason for political support	487	509

See also Arian, *Second Republic*, pp. 9, 12–13, 215, 223, 225, 310, 312, 365–66, 377; A. Arian, *Public Opinion on National Security Affairs* (Tel-Aviv: Tel-Aviv University, 1997) (in Hebrew). Arian finds solid support for negotiations with the Palestinians and less suspicion of the Arabs' ultimate aims, but also a strong feeling of personal insecurity.
7. Arian, *Second Republic*, pp. 234–6.
8. Sandler, *State of Israel*, pp. 235–58, 263–73.
9. See also S. Sofer, *Begin: An Anatomy of Leadership* (Oxford: Blackwell, 1988), pp. 189–200.
10. A. Eban, *Personal Witness* (New York, NY: Putnam, 1992), p. 653.

11. See also M. N. Barnett (ed.), *Israel in Comparative Perspective* (New York, NY: State University of New York Press, 1996), pp. 3–21.
12. On Israeli diplomacy, see A. Eban, *An Autobiography* (New York: Random House, 1977), pp. 590–610; G. Rafael, *Destination Peace* (New York, NY: Weidenfeld and Nicolson, 1981), pp. 3–20, 376–87; A. S. Kleiman, *Israel and the World After 40 Years* (Washington, DC, Pergamon-Brassey's, 1990), pp. 107–27, 143–51, 233–48.
13. As of 1997, the Foreign Ministry's budget was US$230 million and it had 850 personnel. See also Kleiman, *Israel and the World After 40 Years*.
14. See also A. Kleiman, 'Israel Rejoins the World', *Israel Studies Bulletin* (1994), pp. 11–14. During the 1990s, the Foreign Ministry underwent a modest organizational reform. A planning section was established, as well as divisions for human rights, arms control, and the peace process. Israel maintained diplomatic relations with 155 countries. Cf. Brecher's view of Israel's foreign policy during the first 20 years of statehood, in M. Brecher, *The Foreign Policy System of Israel* (Oxford: Oxford University Press, 1972), pp. 542–65; also M. Gazit, 'The Role of the Foreign Ministry', *Jerusalem Quarterly*, 18 (1981), pp. 3–13.
15. See A. Richards, 'Economic Roots of Instability in the Middle East', *Middle East Policy* (September 1995), pp. 175–87. The population of Iraq, Syria, and Turkey is expected to grow by 50% over the next 30 years; *New York Times*, 15 December 1997.
16. B. Lewis, 'Rethinking the Middle East', *Foreign Affairs*, 71 (1992), p. 105.
17. See also W. B. Quandt, 'The Middle East on the Brink: Prospects for Change in the 21st Century', *Middle East Journal*, 50 (1996), pp. 9–17.
18. See also J. M. Nomikos, *Looking Back to See Forward: Israel–Turkey Defense Relations* (Athens: Research Institute for European Studies, 1997); *Turkey and Israel in a Changing Middle East* (Ramat Gan: BESA Center for Strategic Studies, 1996).
19. S. Peres, *The New Middle East* (New York, NY: H. Holt, 1993), pp. 33–60, 155–75; see also E. Inbar, *An OEEC for the Middle East?* (Jerusalem: The Hebrew University of Jerusalem, 1997); T. Sadeh, *Middle Eastern Monetary Integration* (Jerusalem: The Hebrew University of Jerusalem, 1997); M. Hirsch, *Environmental Cooperation in the Economic Commission for Europe and the Future of the Middle East: Regional Cooperation in Asymmetric Settings* (Jerusalem: The Hebrew University of Jerusalem, 1997). Initial programs for infrastructure projects and for the establishment of the Middle East Development Bank were agreed upon at the Casablanca summit (1994) and at the Amman summit (1995).
20. B. Netanyahu, *A Place Among the Nations* (New York, NY: Bantam Books, 1993), pp. 238–55. Indeed, to devise better systems of governance is still among the major challenges facing the Middle East; see also R. W. Murphy and F. G. Gause, 'Democracy and U.S. Policy in the Muslim Middle East', *Middle East Policy*, 5 (1997), pp. 58–67.
21. See also B. Rubin, *The New Middle East: Opportunities and Risks* (Ramat Gan: BESA Center for Strategic Studies, 1995); E. Inbar, 'Contours of Israel's New Strategic Thinking', *Political Science Quarterly*, 111 (1996), pp. 41–64; A. Shlaim, *War and Peace in the Middle East* (London: Penguin Books, 1995), pp. 104–46.
22. See G. M. Steinberg, *Strategy in the Era of Non-Conventional Weapons* (Tel-Aviv, 1997), pp. 120–8 (in Hebrew); S. Feldman, *Nuclear Weapons and Arms Control in the Middle East* (Cambridge, MA: MIT Press, 1997), pp. 95–113; S. Aronson and O. Brosh, *The Politics and Strategy of Nuclear Weapons in the Middle East* (Albany, NY: State University of New York Press, 1992), pp. 1–16, 271–96.
23. See also R. Lapidoth, *Autonomy* (Washington, DC: United States Institute of Peace, 1997), pp. 152–67.
24. See also A. Garfinkle, 'The United States' Imperial Postulate in the Mideast', *Orbis*, 41 (1997), pp. 15–29; B. Reich, *Securing the Covenant* (Westport, WA: Praeger, 1995), pp. 1–13.
25. A. Garfinkle, 'US–Israeli Relations After the Cold War', *Orbis*, 40 (1996), p. 558.
26. See also E. N. Luttwak, *Strategic Aspects of American–Israeli Relations* (Washington, DC, 1994); E. Watkins, 'The Unfolding U.S. Policy in the Middle East', *International Affairs*, 73 (1997), pp. 1–14; L. T. Hadar, 'America's Moment in the Middle East', *Current History*, 95 (1996), pp. 1–5; Y. M. Makelberg, 'The Future of U.S.–Israeli Relations', in E. Karsh and G. Mahler (eds), *Israel at the Crossroads* (London: British Academic Press, 1994), pp. 185–97.

27. See also R. Hollis, 'Israeli–European Relations in the 1990s', in Karsh and Mahler, *Israel at the Crossroads*, pp. 218–30.
28. See also A. Ahiram and A. Tovias (eds), *Whither Europe–Israeli Relations?* (Frankfurt: Peter Lang, 1995), pp. 1–20.
29. See also A. V. Lorca, 'The European Union and the Mediterranean: Is an "Us" vs. "Them" Situation Inevitable?', *International Spectator*, 31 (1996), pp. 51–69; C. Echeverria Jesus, 'The Mediterranean Security Dialogue', Institute for Security Studies, no. 18 (October 1996); R. Hollis, 'Europe and the Middle East: Power by Stealth?', *International Affairs*, 73 (1997), pp. 15–29.
30. S. J. Blank, 'Russia's Return to Mideast Diplomacy', *Orbis*, 40 (1996), pp. 517–35.
31. See also R. O. Freedman, 'Israel and the Successor States of the Soviet Union: A Preliminary Analysis', in Karsh and Mahler, *Israel at the Crossroads*, pp. 198–217. Israel made successful diplomatic and economic advances in the Ukraine and in Central Asia, particularly in Kazakhstan and Kyrgystan.
32. See S. Amir, 'Israel Development Cooperation', mimeograph (Jerusalem, 1996). As of 1996, 3,628 trainees in Israel and 6,262 abroad took part in Israeli programs. The Foreign Ministry's budget for development cooperation for 1996 came to US$31 million.
33. See also Reich, *Securing the Covenant*, pp. 65–90.

2 Peace Policy as Domestic and Foreign Policy: The Israeli Case

YAACOV BAR-SIMAN-TOV

Domestic and foreign policies are sometimes linked. However, we do not know much theoretically and empirically about how and when they are linked or under what conditions they influence each other. Much of the literature neglects the interactions between the two domains, instead focusing on the impact of one on the other. We do have some knowledge about the interactions between domestic and international conflicts,[1] and between external factors (adversary relations or regional and global developments) and conflict reduction and resolution.[2] We know very little, however, about the relationship between domestic politics and peacemaking.[3] Nor do we know much about why, how, and when the interactions between international and domestic politics influence peacemaking.

International and domestic politics may be treated as conditions or manipulable elements in a strategy to bring about conflict reduction or resolution. International politics in this regard refers mainly to adversary relations or regional and global interactions. A damaging stalemate following a war or crisis, or regional and global pressures, may be regarded as external constraints that may influence the parties in a conflict to consider its reduction or resolution.[4] By domestic politics we refer, as Kriesberg and Husbands suggest, to the basic political structures and processes that involve such political actors as leaders, political elites, interest groups, and even the public, as well as the political interactions between and among them.[5]

Although external factors are sometimes necessary conditions for initiating a peace policy, domestic factors may encourage or even pressure decisionmakers to initiate conflict reduction or resolution;

they may also inhibit leaders from doing so. In democratic states, external factors are not sufficient to produce an agreement without domestic acceptance. Peace initiatives may create or exacerbate domestic opposition that can endanger or even foil the peace efforts. Understanding the interactions between domestic politics and peacemaking is necessary, not only for determining the ripeness or the timing for conflict reduction or resolution, but also for assessing the chances that peace efforts will culminate in an agreement.

Here, as Putnam suggests, a two-level game may develop: bargaining between two rivals or enemies that aims at reaching a peace agreement (Level 1) is connected with domestic political bargaining about whether to accept and ratify an agreement (Level 2). Each decisionmaker, as Putnam maintains, plays 'at both game boards' and cannot ignore either one of them. At the international level, as his duty to the national interest, the decisionmaker has to play so as to maximize his chances to reach the best agreement; this also involves pacifying domestic opposition and minimizing negative domestic reactions. At the national level, he has to build a coalition for the agreement among the relevant political and interest groups. Failure to do so may mean forfeiting the opportunity for an agreement.[6]

Efforts to resolve an international conflict may lead to a domestic conflict when the concessions that are made are not acceptable to parts of the political elites, interest groups, or even the general public. In this two-level game, decisionmakers on both sides who aim for a peace agreement should take into account their own, as well as the other, side's ability to acquire domestic legitimacy for it. Particularly in democracies, domestic legitimacy may be necessary for conflict reduction or resolution.[7]

ISRAEL AS A CASE STUDY

This study aims to examine Israel's complex peacemaking with Arab actors in terms of interactions between external and domestic factors.

Until the Six Day War, peace was regarded by the Israeli political system as a lofty ideal, unattainable because of the Arab refusal to recognize Israel and conclude a peace agreement with it.[8] These perceptions underwent their first partial modification in response to the outcomes of the war, particularly Israel's gaining control of the Sinai Peninsula, the Gaza Strip, the West Bank, and the Golan Heights. Different conceptions began to develop in the political system about the possibility of obtaining peace in exchange for all, most, or even some of the occupied territories. The trade-off of 'territories for peace' became the focus of an internal political debate between 'hawks' and 'doves' that crossed the political spectrum of coalition and opposition parties.[9]

Furthermore, differences of attitude arose as to whether the benefits of peace were worth its security, ideological, and historical costs. Not only were most of the territories regarded as vital in security terms, but some were perceived as important for religious, ideological, and historical reasons. Although the Sinai and the Golan were mainly regarded as strategically valuable, the West Bank or Judea and Samaria, in addition to strategic importance, had special religious and historical associations. The building of settlements in the territories was aimed at consolidating Israel's control of them, and only enhanced their importance by adding to the picture the central Zionist value of land settlement. Thus, the dismantling of settlements came to be perceived as a threat, if not a betrayal of Zionist ideals,[10] and the settlement of the territories increased the difficulty of trading territories for peace.

The value of peace not only contradicted other values, such as territory, security, ideology, and religion, but was incommensurable with them. Territory is a real, tangible asset; peace is a largely abstract, elusive, and uncontrollable entity that is dependent on the future development of relations between the two sides. The question was how to create a reasonable and acceptable trade-off between the value of territory (overall) and the value of peace.

In the aftermath of the Six Day War, Israeli decisionmakers realized that any peacemaking process that would involve territorial concessions would be regarded, not only as a foreign policy issue, but also as a domestic one, and this could pose real problems both in peacemaking and in domestic politics. However, because the Arabs were perceived as uninterested in resolving the conflict with Israel, the question remained hypothetical and an issue in the domestic debate rather than a real foreign policy issue. However, when conflict reduction or resolution became a viable option, the relationship between international and domestic politics in peacemaking turned into a concrete problem that the political system had to cope with.

This chapter argues that:

1. External rather than domestic factors were responsible for initiating conflict reduction or resolution; however, the role of domestic factors increased during the negotiations.

2. Every Israeli peacemaking effort that involves territorial concessions immediately and automatically becomes a two-level game
   because it creates a value conflict.

3. A lack of consensus arose in the political system about making
   territorial concessions for the sake of peace, not only between
   coalition vs. opposition parties, but sometimes even within the
   coalition itself.

4. Decisionmakers need to acknowledge that peacemaking requiring territorial concessions is not only a foreign-policy issue but also
   a domestic one, and therefore requires wide domestic legitimacy.

5. A tacit domestic understanding developed that every territorial
   concession needed to be legitimized by different forums: the
   party, the cabinet, the government, the Knesset, and even by a
   referendum or elections.

6. A formal ratification or approval of a peace agreement does not
   constitute an end to a domestic debate when the agreement
   remains unacceptable to some of the political elites and groups.

The first serious case of a two-level game that entangled external
and domestic factors in peacemaking occurred in the attempts to end
the War of Attrition in 1970; the most recent one took place in January
1997 with the concluding of the Hebron agreement with the
Palestinians.

The considerable historical record of conflict reduction and
peacemaking efforts made by Israeli leaders that we have today
enables a comparative inquiry into the following cases:

1. The US initiative to terminate the War of Attrition (June 1970).

2. The first disengagement agreement with Egypt (January 1974).

3. The disengagement agreement with Syria (May 1974).

4. The second disengagement agreement with Egypt (September
   1975).

5. The peace agreement with Egypt (1977–1979).

6. The Oslo agreements with the Palestinians (September 1993,
   October 1995).

7. The peace agreement with Jordan (October 1994).

8. The Hebron agreement with the Palestinians (January 1997).

DISCUSSING THE CASES

Ending the War of Attrition (June 1970)

The first real crisis that involved external and domestic factors in conflict reduction attempts occurred at the end of the War of Attrition. External factors dominated these efforts. Although the initial US proposal of a cease-fire was rejected by Israel, the bargaining that developed with the United States led Israel to comply. New US assurances were most important in changing Israel's position. The Egyptian acceptance of the US initiative and the increased danger of Israeli–Soviet military confrontation also constituted important external pressures on the Israeli government.[11] In addition to the cease-fire, the US initiative called on Israel to declare its readiness to withdraw on all fronts, including Judea and Samaria, within the framework of Security Council Resolution 242 and with the aim of reaching a contractual peace agreement between Israel and Arab states. Although that demand was only declaratory and not operational, since it was not yet clear whether the Arabs would agree to negotiate a peace treaty with Israel, it triggered an immediate domestic crisis. Menachem Begin, the leader of the Gahal Party that was part of the National Unity Government (which had been formed on the eve of the Six Day War), refused to have any part in a governmental policy to redivide the land of Israel. Although not everyone in Gahal fully shared Begin's outlook, they supported him in his stance against accepting the US initiative. Attempts by Prime Minister Golda Meir to dissuade Gahal from leaving the National Unity Government failed to change Begin's position.[12]

On 31 July 1970, the government decided to accept the US initiative, despite the opposition of Gahal ministers; the vote was 17:6. At Gahal's insistence, two votes were taken; on the second, concerning the cease-fire, the government was unanimous. Gahal wanted to distinguish between the cease-fire on the one hand and the US demand for territorial concessions in the West Bank on the other.[13] The government's decision was approved by the Knesset on 4 August by a vote of 66:28 with nine abstentions.[14] The acceptance of the US initiative enabled the termination of the war, but caused the collapse of the National Unity Government.

Thus, the government fell because of a foreign-policy issue, and this made the question of territorial concessions in the West Bank a central and controversial issue. The majority of the government preferred the costs of domestic crisis to the costs of continuation of war, which could include an escalation of the military confrontation with the Soviet Union, and a political confrontation with the US. The domestic political conflict remained relatively moderate because of the three years of cooperation in the National Unity Government, which softened personal and policy antagonism.[15]

The two-level game, which combined interstate bargaining (with the US) and intracoalition bargaining, was influenced by the fact that the government could survive without Gahal. This created, as Brecher maintains, 'greater self-confidence among those in power and a potential for more flexibility in foreign policy initiatives'. At the same time, the development of a domestic conflict, in the form of Gahal's opposition to the government's decision, created a concern among the top leadership that 'flexibility might be interpreted in Israel as a concession to external pressure; and that, in turn, would reduce the Government's credibility in the eyes of the mass public. In addition to that restraining factor, many members of the Coalition had been persuaded that a hard line was just and sound.'[16]

In sum, the Israeli decision to accept the US initiative was mainly influenced by external factors rather than domestic ones. The leading elite in the coalition, the Labor Party, accepted not only the costs of the collapse of the National Unity Government, but also the requirements of: withdrawal from occupied territories; implementing all the provisions of Security Council Resolution 242; and mediation of the conflict instead of direct negotiations. However, since not much was really achieved by the mediation attempts until the Yom Kippur War, no real problems developed from reciprocal relations between domestic and external factors. Nevertheless, while the government failed to exploit the domestic constraints in order to reach a better agreement, it succeeded in bargaining with the US to secure guarantees as well as military and economic support.

The First Disengagement Agreement With Egypt (January 1974)

The attempts by the United States following the Yom Kippur War to reduce the Israeli–Egyptian conflict again involved a mix of domestic and external factors. This occurred because the idea of conflict reduction was based on the principle of territorial disengagement between the Israeli and Egyptian armies, which necessitated a limited Israeli withdrawal in the Sinai. That, in turn, negated the Israeli principle that no territorial withdrawal would be made for the sake of conflict reduction but only for its resolution.

Again external factors dominated the decisionmaking process, although domestic factors were very significant. Important external constraints included US political pressure, Soviet military threats, and military instability along the cease-fire lines, which carried the danger of a new war. In addition, the high rate of casualties in the war, the need to release productive manpower from military tasks, and the crisis of national morale led to severe domestic pressure on the government to stabilize the cease-fire.

Nevertheless, the government perceived that the proposed agreement on disengagement of forces amounted to no more than a unilateral Israeli withdrawal. Israel alone was asked to pull back, both from the west bank of the Suez Canal and from positions that it occupied on the east bank. Moreover, it was feared that not only would this weaken Israeli militarily, but that if Israel once yielded to pressure it would invite an unending process of pressure. In addition, there was a bitter sense that Israel was being asked to award a prize to those who had attacked it.[17] Although the government was essentially interested in an agreement with Egypt, the domestic political constraints meant that it was in no position to make territorial concessions, especially with elections imminent. The Alignment party expected that such concessions would be politically exploited by the opposition or even by coalition partners.[18] The Alignment's victory in the elections in late 1973 did not necessarily eliminate its domestic political constraints. Not only had the party lost some of its power (five Knesset seats), but it now faced a unified right-wing opposition party, the Likud, which had increased its power in the elections (seven Knesset seats) and blamed the Alignment for the debacle of the war. The victory in the elections, however, signaled more than anything else that the people still wanted the Alignment to find a way to stabilize the military situation. Nevertheless, to the militant opposition in the Knesset and outside of it, the government had to prove not only that it emphasized Israel's security concerns, but that it could bargain effectively without making concessions that would endanger Israel's security. It had to make, as Kissinger maintains, 'a show of bravado for domestic consumption'.[19] The government, indeed, preferred to be perceived as coerced by the United States 'to release its prey rather than relinquishing it voluntarily'.[20] It was easier to justify the concessions as an acquiescence to the United States than to the Arabs.

Thus, the government struggled between the need to conclude an agreement and the need to avoid domestic criticism. The withdrawal would be Israel's first on any front since 1957, and the need to legitimize it was paramount. Indeed, throughout the disengagement negotiations the Likud and extraparliamentary groups organized demonstrations warning the government about Kissinger's evil intentions and about making concessions that would endanger Israel and betray its interests. Later, the opposition denounced the agreement as an apocalyptic disaster for Israel. Begin and Ariel Sharon blamed the government for relinquishing territorial assets for which Israel had paid in blood, while gaining little in return. Moreover, Israel had conceded territories while remaining in a state of war.[21]

On 17 January 1974, the government unanimously approved the disengagement agreement. The next day it was signed with Egypt. Although Egyptian President Sadat wanted the agreement to read that Israel was 'retreating' to an agreed-upon line, the Israeli government refused to accept that term because of its sensitivity in Israel and instead accepted only the term 'deploy'.[22]

Although the Israeli Basic Laws did not require the government to submit the agreement to the Knesset for approval, the government was most interested in legitimizing it, because of the precedent of its including a territorial concession, because of the domestic constraints, and probably because of the government's need to enhance its own confidence in the agreement. The government informed Kissinger, and asked him to inform Egypt, that the agreement would need to be ratified by the Knesset. On 22 January, following a stormy debate in the Knesset, the agreement was supported by 76 Members of Knesset (MKs), with 35 voting against. Because of the power differential between the coalition and the opposition, there was no problem in legitimizing the agreement with a large majority. The government's decision to submit the agreement to the Knesset for approval became a precedent for future agreements involving territorial concessions.

This case demonstrated for the first time not only that conflict reduction or resolution entailed the intertwining of external and domestic factors, but also that the dominance of external factors over domestic ones in the government's calculations did not eliminate or diminish the problem of legitimizing agreements that involved territorial concessions. Indeed, the government's concerns about domestic constraints weakened its self-confidence and influenced its style of negotiation. On the other hand, the government was able to exploit its domestic weaknesses to attain a better agreement, or at least to secure US guarantees and military and economic support.

The Disengagement Agreement With Syria (May 1974)

The disengagement negotiations with Syria in May 1974 again combined external and domestic factors. Again Israel was asked to make concessions that included part of the territory it had captured in the Six Day War, in addition to the territory it had captured in the Yom Kippur War, in return for a disengagement agreement with Syria. However, the convergence of external and domestic factors was this time totally different, not only from the case of the negotiations with Egypt, but also from future cases, because an interim government handled the negotiations.

Golda Meir, who established her new government on 10 March 1974 (following the elections of 31 December), resigned on 11 April, mainly as a result of her realization that her government lacked domestic legitimacy because of its responsibility for the devastation of the Yom Kippur War. The victory in the elections had been illusory; the protests against the government, especially against Defense Minister Moshe Dayan, only intensified following the publication of the Agranat Inquiry Commission's report, which blamed the military leadership for the debacle and actually whitewashed the role of the political leadership.[23]

Although Yitzhak Rabin was elected by the Alignment as the designated prime minister, the establishment of a new government was delayed until the conclusion of an agreement with Syria. It was accepted that the interim government, because of its experience as well as its responsibility for the war, should serve until the end of the negotiations with Syria.[24] This rare situation minimized the role of domestic political constraints, since there was no way this government could be toppled. Moreover, the Likud, which strongly opposed the negotiations and the agreement, surprisingly accepted as legitimate the fact that an interim government was responsible for negotiating such a crucial agreement.

The fact that this was its last mission made the government, and especially Meir, feel even more beholden to conclude an agreement that would in some way compensate for the debacle of the war. Indeed, Meir told Kissinger that 'this agreement was her way of drawing a line under the last war. She could then say that she finished her task'.[25]

The government's decisionmaking calculations were dominated

by: an intensified war of attrition with Syria that created strategic instability; the need to moderate Syrian enmity so as to avoid endangering the process of conflict reduction with Egypt; and US pressure. There were, however, domestic nonpolitical considerations. Kissinger felt that the need to secure the release of Israeli prisoners of war was the most important factor affecting Meir's behavior: 'I thought I detected a sense of relief that she would be the Prime Minister who brought back the last Israeli prisoners from a war for which she would never cease blaming herself.'[26]

Nevertheless, the long history of conflict with Syria, the mistrust, and the objective situation on the ground (involving a small stretch of territory that was close to Israeli population centers and that contained settlements) made the negotiation of a disengagement agreement with Syria even more difficult than that with Egypt. Kissinger, in fact, concentrated most of his efforts in Israel, holding 23 meetings with the Israeli negotiating team and only 14 with President Assad of Syria.[27] The negotiating team was made more effective by its representing an interim government. The resolution of the domestic political crisis by the resignation of the government enabled it to concentrate all its energies on the negotiations. 'The negotiations were their last hurrah and they were determined to go out with the right agreement.'[28] The Israeli team was tougher and more ready than during the negotiations with Egypt.[29]

On 29 May 1974, the government unanimously accepted the disengagement agreement with Syria. A day later the agreement was presented for the Knesset's approval, according to the new tradition that began with the agreement with Egypt. Although the government portrayed the agreement as the best that it could obtain, the Likud again objected and argued that not only had the government violated its own principle of not making any territorial concessions without concluding a peace agreement, it had conceded strategic assets in return for a mere cease-fire. Nevertheless, the government had wide support: 76 MKs voted in favor of the agreement, 36 opposed it, and three abstained.[30]

The Second Disengagement Agreement With Egypt (September 1975)

The second disengagement agreement with Egypt of September 1975 again involved a mix of external and internal factors, mainly because it included new territorial concessions in the Sinai that were regarded as strategically and economically important. However, the inter-action between the two domains was different this time, for the following reasons:

1. The coming to power of a new Israeli government headed by Yitzhak Rabin as prime minister, Shimon Peres as defense minister, and Yigal Allon as foreign minister.
2. The choice of another disengagement agreement with Egypt as a preferred policy, not only as a preemption of external constraints, but also as a response to domestic constraints.
3. The crisis in the negotiations in March 1975, which preceded the agreement of September 1975.

Even without US or Egyptian pressures, Rabin wanted to ensure the continuation of political negotiations with Arab factors in order to stabilize the conflict-reduction process: 'I did not want us merely to respond to outside initiatives—be they American or Arab.'[31] He was concerned that without renewed momentum in this direction, a military deterioration would occur. He preferred another disengage-ment agreement with Egypt because it was the most important Arab party and an agreement with it had greater potential to stabilize the Arab–Israeli conflict than would a first disengagement agreement with Jordan or a second one with Syria. Such an agreement might also break the Egyptian–Syrian alliance, and minimize the prospects of a new Arab war against Israel.[32] No less important was the assess-ment that territorial concessions in this agreement would be less costly than those with Jordan or Syria, and therefore more acceptable by domestic factors. Another aim of concluding a new agreement with Egypt was to minimize Kissinger's pressure to conclude a disen-gagement agreement with Jordan. Rabin realized that an agreement with Jordan that would include territorial withdrawal in the West Bank would cause the collapse of his government, mainly because his coalition partners (the National Religious Party) and even promi-nent members of his own party, especially Peres, would not accept such terms. The personal tensions and rivalry between Rabin and Peres constituted another obstacle to greater flexibility on the Jordanian front. Rabin even adopted Meir's commitment to submit any agreement on the future of the West Bank to the approval of the public via elections to the Knesset.[33] Rabin's lack of experience in domestic politics, and probably his sense of political insecurity, also contributed to excluding Jordan from the negotiations and enabled a second disengagement agreement with Egypt.

With respect to the negotiations with Egypt, coalition pressures, especially those coming from the young leaders of the National Religious Party, whose views were identical to those of the Likud, also became a domestic constraint. The competitive relationships among the 'triumvirate' (Rabin, Peres, and Allon) also influenced the negotiations with Egypt.

In contrast to the previous agreements, which were more reactive to external constraints, the new agreement with Egypt was an Israeli initiative aimed at coping better with both external and domestic constraints. The initial Israeli proposal made by Rabin himself was that in return for Egypt's acceptance of an end to the state of belligerency, Israel would withdraw its forces another 30–50 km, which would mean relinquishing the Gidi and Mitla passes (except for their eastern parts) and the Abu Rodeis oil fields.[34] Alternatively, if Egypt could agree only to stabilization of the cease-fire and some political improvements, Israel's withdrawal would not include the passes.[35] Rabin, however, was most interested in an agreement with Egypt and was prepared for a withdrawal in the Sinai even 'without getting a substantive political concession from Egypt'[36]—this being despite the sharp criticisms already given voice in Israel.

Kissinger's interventions in March 1975 failed, however, to forge an agreement on the depth of Israel's withdrawal, the extent of the Egyptian advance, and the duration of the agreement.[37] Israel refused to concede on the issue of the depth of its withdrawal, especially since this was to include the passes. Although the government's considerations were mainly strategic, it seemed it also could not domestically justify such a concession, except in return for the termination of the state of war.

The United States blamed Israel for the failure of the negotiations and adopted a policy of reassessment that had a punitive element against Israel.[38] The increased external constraints triggered a reaction of domestic solidarity in Israel. The opposition parties, headed by Begin, promised unconditional support for the government's position.[39] Indeed, in a Knesset session on 24 March 1975, 92 MKs supported the government's position, while only four opposed it and six abstained.[40] Nevertheless, the US reassessment policy led Israel to reconsider its stance. Again external constraints dominated Israeli calculations. Israel was now ready to withdraw from the eastern entrances to the passes if in return the US would take over all the early-warning installations in the area of the passes and operate them on behalf of both Israel and Egypt.[41] This enabled Kissinger to renew the negotiations and to reach an agreement. The new agreement was not really much different from that of March; nevertheless, the US constraints and inducements were what persuaded Israel to change its position.[42]

On 1 September 1975, the government unanimously accepted the agreement. However, this provoked unprecedented opposition. For the first time, three prominent members of the Alignment, among them Dayan, joined the opposition in voting against the agreement in the Knesset.[43] Among the other coalition parties, two MKs from the National Religious Party voted against, and one from the Independent Liberals abstained.[44] In the Knesset debate held on 3 September, the opposition speakers accused the government of making concessions that endangered Israel's security. They maintained that there was no reason to change the stance it had taken in March which had been supported by the opposition, especially when Israel had not gained anything real that could justify the change. The acceptance of the agreement, they claimed, constituted surrender to the US, and would only increase Israel's dependence on the Americans. They also criticized the government for poor handling of the negotiations that had damaged Israel's bargaining power. Because of the importance of the issue, the government was asked to call for new elections. At the end of the discussion, only 70 Knesset members voted for the agreement, 43 against, and seven abstained.[45]

In addition to the opposition in the party, in the coalition, and in the Knesset, Gush Emunim, which became the main right-wing interest group, organized demonstrations and riots against Kissinger and the government, indicating that the power of extraparliamentary groups was greater than ever before.[46]

The Peace Agreement With Egypt (1977–1979)

An unprecedented convergence between external and domestic politics occurred in the peacemaking process with Egypt, mainly for the following reasons:

1. This was the first conflict-resolution event between Israel and an Arab party.

2. Making peace with Egypt required total withdrawal from the Sinai, dismantling of settlements, and establishment of autonomy for the Palestinians in Judea, Samaria, and Gaza.

3. The conflict-resolution process was handled for the first time by a

right-wing leader who had opposed the conflict-reduction agreements with Egypt and Syria.

4. The interaction between domestic and external factors varied at different stages of the peacemaking process.

5. Domestic opposition to making peace came mainly from the ruling party and the coalition, whereas support came mainly from the opposition parties.

6. Extraparliamentary groups mounted the strongest opposition to the peacemaking process, particularly in its implementation phase.

Begin, like Rabin before him, oriented Israel's peacemaking toward Egypt. Like Rabin, he realized that the Egyptian–Israeli conflict was territorial and strategic, rather than ideological and emotional, and that if Egypt could be persuaded to remove itself from the Arab–Israeli conflict, wars would cease and other Arab states might be encouraged to negotiate with Israel. However, Begin believed that only a comprehensive approach to negotiations could lead to a contractual peace treaty—'comprehensive' meaning a fully fledged peace with one country, even if only a separate peace. Begin also believed in going into peace negotiations directly from a state of war without any military or political interim agreements, since he did not think Israel would get enough in return for partial withdrawals or other such concessions. He sought to achieve two seemingly contradictory goals: keeping Judea and Samaria under Israel's control, and creating the conditions for an Egyptian–Israeli peace agreement. Although the ambition to incorporate Greater Israel reflected a strong passion to gain ideological legitimacy, the search for peace served as a means of gaining domestic and international legitimacy. It was important to him to prove to his opponents that he could be a statesman, a leader who could bring Israel to a new and better situation.[47]

Personal and domestic factors rather than external constraints, such as US political pressure and actual or potential Egyptian threats to resume the war, motivated Begin to signal to Egypt his desire to reach a peace agreement. Begin preferred direct negotiations with Egypt so as to avoid an active US role; he feared that any external mediation would aim to impose unfavorable conditions on Israel. A direct approach toward Egypt also preempted US constraints aimed at reaching a comprehensive peace via an international conference under US–Soviet auspices.[48] Sadat's decision to carry out his initiative was made only after he had become convinced, through direct and indirect exchanges with Israel, that it would receive a positive response.[49]

Sadat's visit to Jerusalem was welcomed, not only by the entire government, but also by an overwhelming Knesset majority of 83:3 and more than 90 per cent of the public. Domestic factors encouraged the advancing of the negotiations with Egypt. However, the prolonged deadlock in the negotiations following Sadat's visit and Begin's visit to Ismailia increased both the external and the domestic constraints on the government. The US and Egypt agreed upon a strategy for pressuring Israel: the US intensified its political pressures on Israel, while Egypt threatened to withdraw from the peace process.[50]

On the domestic level, two contradictory constraints emerged. On one side, MKs from the Likud and the National Religious Party within the coalition, as well as some from the Alignment, together with the extraparliamentary groups Gush Emunim, Movement for a Greater Israel, and the Sinai settlers, tried to coordinate their struggle against the government's peace plan. On the other side, the opposition parties and a new interest group, Peace Now, accused the government of squandering a rare opportunity for a peace treaty with Egypt because of inflexible positions.[51]

The government's peace policy now encountered opposition, not only in the Knesset and among the public, but within the government itself. The key dissenting figure was Defense Minister Ezer Weizman. Essentially, Weizman believed that Sadat was sincere in his desire to conclude a peace treaty quickly, and that Begin and Dayan were responsible for the breakdown of the negotiations.[52]

Begin's agreement to attend the Camp David summit greatly decreased the domestic constraints. Not only did Begin's decision easily gain the support of his own party, the cabinet, the opposition parties, and the Peace Now movement, but perhaps surprisingly, no opposition emerged at this point from among those who objected to the Israeli peace plan and even to the peace process itself. The general support may be explained by the fact that the Alignment and Peace Now perceived the conference as an important chance to revitalize the peace process, and Begin had promised his party and the Sinai settlers that under no circumstances would the Israeli delegation accept the removal of any settlement in the Sinai.[53]

At the Camp David summit, however, the interaction between external and domestic constraints reached a climax and confronted Begin with a severe value conflict. Begin was offered a peace agreement with Egypt, conditional upon relinquishing all of the Sinai, dismantling the settlements, evacuating the airfields in the Sinai, and altering his autonomy plan. Begin stood alone against a common US–Egyptian position that made the potential costs of resisting extremely grave: not only endangerment of the prospects of reaching an agreement with Egypt, but also aggravation of Israel's relationship with the US. On the other side, Begin faced pressures from his own delegation, especially Dayan and Weizman, to comply. Begin had, moreover, his own personal constraints, especially after having promised not to concede on the Sinai settlements. However, the rare symmetry of external (US and Egyptian) and domestic constraints proved effective in inducing Begin to prefer the peace agreement over the settlements.[54]

Begin's signing of the Camp David accords forced him to face new domestic constraints: from the party, the cabinet, the Knesset, and the public. Nevertheless, he continued to enjoy the support of the opposition parties and of Peace Now. In the cabinet, Begin won the support of 11 members, two voted against, one abstained, and the three National Religious Party ministers, as well as one other minister, decided not to participate in the vote. In the Knesset, 84 voted in favor of the Camp David accords, 19 opposed, and 17 abstained. Ten (seven from the Likud) of those who opposed the accords and 13 who abstained (nine from the Likud) came from the coalition. Without the opposition's support, Begin could not have won the Knesset's approval of the accords.[55]

The extraparliamentary opposition to the agreements—mainly Gush Emunim, the Movement for a Greater Israel, and the Sinai settlers—became active immediately after they were signed. However, they failed to exert any important impact on the Knesset or the public. Indeed, 75 per cent of the public expressed satisfaction with the Camp David agreements, affirming that the advantages exceeded the costs; 78 per cent justified the concessions made by the government; 70 per cent supported the possible removal of the Rafiah settlements.[56]

The balance between external and domestic constraints changed again following the Knesset's approval of the agreements. Serious differences between Israel and Egypt about the interpretation of the Camp David agreements prevented a speedy conclusion of the negotiations on a peace treaty and developed into a crisis that intensified external constraints on Israeli decisionmaking. Egypt, with the support of the United States, introduced new demands that Israel could not accept. Israel refused to make any further concessions beyond those in the accords, leading to a new deadlock.[57]

The cabinet's determination to 'bargain harder' was aimed not only at preventing any alterations in the accords, but also at easing the domestic constraints from those who opposed the agreements. Although the government's position in the new negotiations was backed by the opposition parties, domestic opposition to the agreements did not diminish.[58] New US constraints on Israel were what brought about the resumption of the negotiations, and President Jimmy Carter's visit to Israel and Egypt in March 1979 led to a breakthrough and conclusion of the peace treaty. With this, the role of external constraints ended.[59]

On 19 March 1978, the government approved the treaty, with two ministers voting against. In the Knesset vote, 95 voted in favor, 18 against, and two abstained (with five not participating). The increased support over the Camp David agreements (95:84, respectively) reflected the Alignment's decision to impose party discipline on its members, and decisions by five MKs from the Likud and three from the National Religious Party who had opposed or abstained on Camp David to vote in favor of the peace treaty. The government's main legitimacy problem remained with its own party: seven from the Likud opposed the treaty, two abstained, and two did not participate.[60]

The MKs' massive support for the peace treaty marked the end of the formal process of legitimizing the government's peace policy, which had begun after Sadat's visit. However, it did not end the domestic constraints. Moreover, the implementation stage proved much more difficult because it entailed carrying out tangible concessions: the return of territory, evacuation of residents, and dismantlement of settlements.

Domestic opposition to the peace implementation began immediately after the Knesset's approval of the treaty. The opposition was led by extraparliamentary groups: Gush Emunim, its offshoot the Movement to Stop the Withdrawal (MSW) in the Sinai, as well as some of the Sinai settlers. However, although the opposition to the withdrawal culminated in a violent confrontation between the army and the MSW, it never actually endangered the implementation of the peace treaty.[61]

In addition to these constraints, new domestic constraints emerged because of the government's settlement policy in Judea and Samaria, as well as its negotiating style in the autonomy talks. Not only was the cabinet sharply divided on those issues, which led to Dayan's and Weizman's resignation from the government, but also the opposition parties and Peace Now intensified their pressures on the government. Dayan, Weizman, and the opposition groups feared that the government's policy was aimed at foiling the implementation of the peace treaty. These domestic constraints, however, had only minimal impact on the government, mainly because its settlement policy as well as its negotiating style in the autonomy talks were aimed both at ensuring that the autonomy would not develop into a Palestinian state and at coping with the constraints that came from the right wing.[62]

In sum, the peacemaking process with Egypt constituted a particular and dynamic example of interactions between external and domestic constraints, with fluctuations in the interactions at each stage of the negotiations. The external constraints were again more influential than the domestic ones. The two different kinds of domestic constraints (from the left and the right) to some extent neutralized each other's influence on the peacemaking process. Nevertheless, the massive support of the opposition parties and groups for the peace policy enabled the approval of the peace agreements in the Knesset. In contrast, with the disengagement agreements, the opposition parties triggered domestic constraints against the agreements.

The Oslo Agreements With the Palestinians (September 1993, October 1995)

The interaction of external and internal constraints in Israel's peacemaking with the Palestinians has unique characteristics that differed from the peacemaking process with Egypt.

1. The peacemaking process was made by a homogeneous center-left government that had only a minimal majority in the Knesset.
2. Both external and domestic constraints were responsible for initiating the peace process.
3. This time the peacemaking was with the PLO, which was considered the most dangerous political and ideological enemy of the state of Israel.
4. The territorial concessions in this case were perceived as the most critical, not just in territorial, strategic, and security terms, but especially in political, historical, and ideological terms.
5. The domestic constraints became the most severe of any Israeli

peacemaking effort and even led to the assassination of Rabin.

6. The interaction between external constraints (terrorist actions) and domestic constraints led to the government's defeat in the 1996 elections.

External constraints played an important role in initiating the peace process with the Palestinians. These constraints were Palestinian and regional rather than American. Indeed, this marked the first time in Israeli peacemaking history that US constraints played so minimal a role. Rabin was impelled by the recognition that there was no military solution to the intifada, and hence a political solution was needed. Just before the 1992 elections, personal security had been undermined by a wave of fatal stabbings by Palestinians, and Rabin believed that the sole remedy to such violence was a separation between Israel and the Palestinians, which could be achieved only by granting personal autonomy to the latter. He therefore promised to implement autonomy for the Palestinians within nine months of the establishment of his government.

The deadlock in the Washington talks with a Palestinian delegation that Labor had inherited from the Likud government formed another external constraint that influenced the government. The concern that the PLO was on the verge of collapse, and the only alternative would be the radical Hamas, constituted another constraint. The escalation of the wave of stabbings, and the costly continuation of the Israel Defense Force's (IDF) presence in Gaza, strengthened the inclination to leave Gaza, but this could only be effectuated through an agreement with an authorized Palestinian body that could take responsibility for the area after its evacuation.

Another external constraint that contributed to Rabin's decision to negotiate with the PLO was the lack of a viable Syrian option. Rabin, who preferred the Syrian track, realized that it would be very costly because it entailed an immediate readiness for withdrawal from the Golan Heights, including the removal of the settlements there. Therefore, the Palestinian option became more attractive.[63]

The domestic constraints on Rabin came from his coalition partner, Meretz, and from his own party, both of which pushed for negotiations with the PLO. Rabin's promises throughout the election campaign to do his best to resolve the Arab–Israeli conflict, and particularly the Israeli–Palestinian conflict, also created a potential domestic constraint; Rabin felt obligated to carry out his commitment. There was also a personal factor: Rabin and Peres were both in their early seventies, and realized that this could well be their last opportunity to advance the peace policy they believed in. They felt they owed such peacemaking to their constituency and to history.[64]

The homogeneous nature of the government, which included only Labor and Meretz (following the withdrawal of Shas from the coalition), eased the government's legitimizing of the Oslo agreements; only two ministers abstained. However, the opposition parties and groups were totally opposed. Rabin and Peres realized that any negotiation with the PLO might trigger immediate domestic constraints, because such a policy would be perceived by many, especially the right-wing parties and groups, as a betrayal of Israel's national interest and national consensus. Both leaders realized that the opposition parties, as well as the right-wing interest groups, including the settlers in Judea, Samaria, and Gaza, would strongly oppose the peace initiative. It seems, however, that they did not foresee the extent and intensity of the opposition.[65]

Rabin and Peres had, indeed, great difficulty legitimizing the peace policy in the Knesset. Only 61 MKs supported the Oslo 1 agreement, 50 opposed it, eight abstained, and one did not participate in the vote.[66] The Cairo agreement was supported by only 52 MKs; the opposition boycotted the vote to show that there was no majority among the public in favor of the agreement. Only 61 MKs voted in favor of the Oslo 2 agreement, and 59 voted against, including two Labor MKs. Thus, all three agreements were supported by only minimal majorities in the Knesset. Moreover, without the support of the Arab party and the mostly Arab ex-communist party, which were not part of the coalition, the government could not have ratified the agreements in the Knesset.[67]

This was the first time since 1974 that support for the Arab–Israeli agreements was at such a low level. Neither the opposition parties nor the interest groups, led by the West Bank and Gaza settlers, recognized the Knesset's approval as legitimizing the peace policy. They argued that because of the agreements' crucial political and territorial significance—including recognition of the PLO and negotiation with it, as well as territorial concessions in Judea, Samaria, and Gaza—the government could not genuinely legitimize them by a minimal majority, especially when it had to rely on non-Jewish and non-Zionist support from the Arab parties. On issues so vital to the Jewish people, the opposition insisted, there was a need at least for a special majority that would neutralize the Arab vote in the Knesset, and for a referendum that would truly reflect the will of the Jewish people. Indeed, they preferred new elections as the best way to legitimize the agreements. There were also arguments from religious quarters that the government was not permitted to transfer any parts of Eretz Israel (Land of Israel) to foreigners, even if this was approved by the Knesset. From this standpoint, neither a national referendum nor elections could legitimize the exchange of territories for peace.[68]

The opposition parties were unable to foil the approval of the agreements by the Knesset, and the domestic constraints shifted from the Knesset to the 'political backyard'. The opposition parties were willing to cooperate with extraparliamentary groups, such as the Yesha Council (which represents the settlers in Judea, Samaria, and Gaza), in order to delegitimize the government and its peace policy. Other extraparliamentary groups that strongly opposed the peace policy with the Palestinians included the Yesha Rabbis Council, the Committee for Abolition of the Autonomy Plan, Zo Artzenu (This Is Our Land), and small ultraright groups such as Kach and Eyal. The main activity of the Yesha Council was to organize antigovernment demonstrations in cooperation with the opposition parties. Some of these demonstrations escalated into violence. In cooperation with the opposition parties, the Yesha Council acted to delegitimize the government by portraying it as having abandoned Israeli interests and values. Indeed, some groups and individuals not only referred to the government's peace policy as 'an act of national treachery', but called Rabin and Peres 'traitors' and 'murderers'. Some circles adopted illegitimate means to foil the policy, including traffic disruptions as well as threats of unrest, assassination, and even civil war. The actual assassination of Rabin was a direct outcome of the delegitimization campaign.[69]

Although the government failed to legitimize the peace policy among the opposition parties and interest groups, it gained majority support among the public, but not by a wide margin. In a poll taken in late August 1993, 53 per cent supported the Oslo 1 agreement, 45 per cent opposed it, and 2 per cent had no opinion. Oslo 2 was supported by only 51 per cent, with 47 per cent opposing and 2 per cent taking no position.[70]

The domestic constraints escalated from September 1993 and culminated in Rabin's assassination, and the external constraints did not diminish. The continuation of Palestinian terrorist actions (though not by the PLO), Arafat's negative declarations including calls for jihad, and the failure to expunge the offensive parts of the Palestinian National Covenant as stipulated in the Oslo agreement were all factors that constrained the government, because they indicated that the government had not properly assessed the conflict environment or the other side's peaceful intentions.[71]

The escalation of terrorist activity, mainly suicide bombings, was exploited by the opposition parties as evidence that the peace policy was mistaken. Thus, external constraints interacted with domestic constraints, the former intensifying the latter. The Oslo process has not strengthened tactical or personal security: more than 200 Israelis, including both soldiers and civilians, have been killed in terrorist attacks since the process began. This has been the most important factor in influencing the public, and apparently caused the defeat of Peres and the Labor Party in the May 1996 elections.[72]

The Peace Agreement With Jordan (October 1994)

The peace agreement with Jordan was totally different from the previous agreements with other Arab parties, mainly because it did not involve territorial concessions, only the exchange of territories. Nevertheless, the Jordanians' claims for territories occupied by Israel created external constraints on the government. Although the Israeli government recognized Jordanian claims as legitimate, it found them difficult to accept, mainly because they might endanger the existence of Israeli settlements in these territories and trigger domestic constraints. Only an agreement on exchange of territories avoiding the removal of Israeli settlements could prevent domestic constraints against a peace agreement with Jordan from emerging. Indeed, such a solution was found and prevented not only the emergence of domestic constraints, but also the convergence of external and domestic constraints.[73]

The government unanimously approved the peace agreement with Jordan, and an overwhelming majority of MKs also supported it: 105 in favor, three against, and six abstentions.[74] As for the public, 91.5 per cent supported the agreement. Overall, this amounted to the most overwhelming support for any agreement with an Arab party to that date. This support was a direct outcome of the lack of territorial concessions and, also, of the widespread sympathy for King Hussein in Israel.[75]

The Hebron Agreement With the Palestinians (January 1997)

The agreement with the Palestinians on Hebron signed by the Netanyahu government again reflected a mixture of external and domestic constraints. The interaction of the constraints, in turn, reflected certain factors. The Hebron agreement was part of the Oslo 2 agreement, which had not been implemented by the Labor government because of the election campaign and its loss of the elections. The agreement was signed by Netanyahu, who opposed the Oslo process and upon whom it was, in effect, imposed. Lastly, external constraints dominated the implementation of the agreement, while domestic constraints acted in contradictory directions, both for and against the agreement.

The fact that the Hebron agreement was part of the Oslo 2 agreement dominated Israeli decisionmaking. The Oslo and Hebron agreements in themselves constituted constraints. Netanyahu's government could not evade the Hebron agreement, mainly because he realized that its implementation was required and only a severe violation of the agreement could justify delaying or blocking its implementation. But, because he perceived both the Oslo agreements in general and the Hebron agreement in particular as negative developments, he tried to renegotiate the agreement as a condition of its implementation.

Netanyahu's government faced various external constraints favoring immediate implementation of the agreement—from the United States, the Palestinians, Egypt, and Jordan. Whereas the US, Egypt, and Jordan threatened, in one way or another, that avoiding implementation would harm or endanger relations with Israel, the Palestinians threatened to resume violent actions.

The domestic constraints were of two kinds. The opposition parties pushed for immediate implementation of the agreement as it had been concluded by the previous government; some in the Likud, the government, the coalition parties, and the right-wing extraparliamentary groups opposed the agreement and had hoped that the new right-wing government would refuse to implement it. For them, Netanyahu's claim that the agreement had been imposed on him by the previous government and that he had no choice but to implement it was not convincing.

Although the domestic constraints from his own party were significant, external constraints determined the decisionmaking on the Hebron agreement. The deterioration of Israel's relations with Egypt and Jordan, the jeopardising of relations with the US, and Israel's isolation in the world, were perceived as worse contingencies than anything the domestic constraints could cause. Still, Netanyahu could not ignore the constraints from his own party and government, so that renegotiation of the Hebron agreement became the only way to cope with such contradictory constraints. He sought to prove to domestic opponents of the agreement that he was trying his best to improve its terms in a very complicated situation. His knowledge that the opposition parties would support the agreement made it easier for him to cope with his own camp's constraints.

In fact, Netanyahu failed to convince considerable parts of his party and government. On 15 January 1997, only 11 ministers voted in favor of the agreement, and seven (three of them from his own party) opposed it.[76] This constituted the largest opposition within a government to an agreement with Arab parties since 1974. However, a day later, as expected, Netanyahu won massive support in the Knesset because of the opposition's backing: 87 MKs voted in favor of the agreement, 17 opposed it, one abstained, and 15 did not participate. Fifteen of the opponents came from the coalition (seven from the Likud). Some of those who declined to participate did so as an act of political protest (among them three ministers).[77] The public, too, decisively supported the agreement: in a poll taken on 29 January 1997, 66.7 per cent favored it, 26.8 per cent opposed it, and the rest took no position or did not know.[78]

CONCLUSIONS

Among the cases considered in this study, one was an agreement on ending a war, three were agreements on a conflict reduction, two were peace agreements involving conflict resolution, and three were interim agreements. Besides the agreement on ending the War of Attrition, which involved only willingness to make territorial concessions, all the others actually involved territorial concessions—in the case of the agreement with Jordan, an exchange of territories. One case (ending the War of Attrition) was handled by a National Unity Government, two by a Likud government, and six by a Labor (Alignment) government. The following findings emerge from these cases.

In most of the cases, external rather than domestic constraints were responsible for initiating conflict reduction or resolution. However, in two cases—the second disengagement agreement with Egypt, and the peace agreement with Egypt—initiatives by leaders, rather than external or domestic constraints, were what started the process. Nevertheless, in these two cases the role of external constraints increased throughout the process, and was crucial for a successful conclusion. Although US constraints were more influential than regional ones, concerns about a new war initiated by the Arabs, or about the instability of the strategic relationships, were also significant.

Although domestic political constraints played a minimal role in instigating or preventing peace initiatives, they became very important once the process got under way. They acted mainly as obstacles, but never succeeded in preventing the formulation or implementation of peacemaking.

Potential or actual territorial concessions triggered domestic constraints because they created value conflict. In all the cases discussed, domestic constraints against territorial concessions came mainly from the right wing. These constraints were more considerable when the agreements were handled by Labor governments than by Likud governments, mainly because the right-wing opposition parties managed and directed the opposition to the peacemaking initiatives. Moreover, the left-wing constraints were aimed, not against the peacemaking initiatives themselves, but against attempts to retard or stop them.

Decisionmakers acknowledged that peacemaking requiring territorial concessions should be legitimized by certain forums, especially the Knesset. Knesset legitimization was regarded as the best way to cope with domestic constraints. However, it was not sufficient to prevent or reduce them, and even encouraged the emergence of extraparliamentary constraints, since the Knesset ceased to be an effective venue for opposing a peace process once an agreement had been approved by it. Specifically, in three cases—the peace agreement with Egypt and the two Oslo agreements (1 and 2)—Knesset approval of the agreements actually increased the constraints.

Except for the peace process with Jordan, all of the cases took the form of a two-level game characterized by interaction between external and domestic constraints. The dynamic of the interaction was not necessarily linear: that is, the increase or decrease of external constraints was not necessarily followed by the increase or decrease of domestic constraints. But increased external constraints seemed to decrease domestic constraints when the government was led by the Labor Party (as in the case of the second disengagement agreement with Egypt) and to increase them when the Likud was in power (as in the peace agreement with Egypt and the negotiations on the Hebron agreement). Whereas the right-wing opposition tends to decrease its constraints to support a government facing external constraints, the left-wing opposition tends to increase its constraints when the government is perceived as foiling the peace process.

Aware of this two-level game, decisionmakers sometimes tended to manipulate it in order to cope with one kind of constraint or another. In negotiations, they tended to emphasize their domestic constraints so as to cope with external constraints; in coping with domestic opposition, they sometimes utilized external constraints, on occasion even preferring that the US pressure Israel in order to justify the concessions made. It is not clear to what extent this interplay between the contradictory constraints improved the different governments' bargaining power in coping with external and domestic constraints.

NOTES

1. See, for example, G. Blainey, *The Causes of War* (New York, NY: Free Press, 1973); J. Wilkenfeld (ed.), *Conflict Behavior and Linkage Politics* (New York, NY: David Mackay, 1973).
2. I. W. Zartman, 'Conflict Reduction: Prevention, Management, and Resolution', in F. M. Deng and I. W. Zartman (eds), *Conflict Resolution in Africa* (Washington, DC: Brookings Institution, 1991), pp. 299–319; R. Haass, *Conflicts Unending* (New Haven, CT: Yale University Press, 1990); T. Armstrong, *Breaking the Ice* (Washington, DC: United States Institute of Peace, 1993).
3. J. L. Husbands, 'Domestic Factors and De-Escalation Initiatives', in L. Kriesberg and S. J. Thorson (eds), *Timing the De-Escalation of International Conflicts* (Syracuse, NY: Syracuse University Press, 1991), pp. 97–116; J. G. Stein, 'Domestic Politics and International Conflict Management', *International Security*, 12 (1988), pp. 203–11.
4. See note 2.
5. Husbands, 'Domestic Factors'; L. Kriesberg, 'Introduction: Timing, Conditions, Strategies, and Errors', in Kriesberg and Thorson, *Timing the De-Escalation*, pp. 7–9.
6. R. D. Putnam, 'Diplomacy and Domestic Politics: Logic of Two-Level Games', *International Organization*, 42 (1988), pp. 427–60; see also P. Gourevitch, 'The Second Image Reversed: The International Sources of Domestic Politics', *International Organization*, 32 (1978), pp. 881–912.
7. Y. Bar-Siman-Tov, *Israel and the Peace Process 1977–1982: In Search of Legitimacy for Peace* (Albany, NY: State University of New York Press, 1994).
8. Y. Rabin, *The Rabin Memoirs* (Boston, MA: Little, Brown, 1979), p. 135; A. Eban, *An Autobiography* (New York, NY: Random House, 1970), pp. 435–6; M. Dayan, *The Story of My Life* (Tel-Aviv: Edanim, 1976), pp. 490–2 (in Hebrew); G. Rafael, *Destination Peace: Three Decades of Israeli Foreign Policy—A Personal Memoir* (New York, NY: Stein & Day, 1981), pp. 170–1, 177–8.
9. Y. Harkabi, *Arab Strategies and Israel's Response* (New York, NY: Free Press, 1977), pp. 70–149; B. Kimmerling, 'Exchanging Territories for Peace: A Macrosociological Approach', *Journal of Applied Behavioral Science*, 23 (1987), pp. 13–33.
10. On value complexity in peacemaking, see Y. Bar-Siman-Tov, 'Value Complexity in Shifting from War to Peace: The Israeli Peace-Making Experience with Egypt', *Political Psychology*, 16 (1995), pp. 545–95.
11. Y. Bar-Siman-Tov, *The Israeli–Egyptian War of Attrition 1969–1970: A Case Study of Limited Local War* (New York, NY: University Press, 1980), pp. 175–85; M. Brecher, *Decisions in Israel's Foreign Policy* (London: Oxford University Press, 1974), pp. 454–517; D. Margalit, *Message From the White House* (Tel-Aviv: Ot-Paz, 1971), pp. 156–83 (in Hebrew).
12. Brecher, *Decisions*, pp. 489–500, 510–15.

13. Ibid., p. 496.
14. Ibid., p. 498.
15. Ibid., pp. 498–9; Margalit, *Message*, pp. 156–83.
16. Brecher, *Decisions*, p. 511.
17. M. Dayan, *Story of My Life* (London: Weidenfeld & Nicolson, 1976), p. 567; H. Kissinger, *Years of Upheaval* (Boston, MA: Little, Brown, 1982), pp. 608, 622, 624, 790.
18. Kissinger, *Years of Upheaval*, pp. 652, 789.
19. Ibid., p. 817.
20. Ibid., p. 608.
21. *Knesset Records*, 22 January 1974, pp. 10–61.
22. M. Golan, *The Secret Conversations of Henry Kissinger* (New York, NY: Quadrangle, 1976), p. 161.
23. Ibid., pp. 185–7.
24. Ibid., pp. 187–8.
25. Kissinger, *Years of Upheaval*, p. 1,003.
26. Ibid., p. 1,106.
27. Golan, *Secret Conversations*.
28. Ibid., p. 188.
29. Ibid., p. 211.
30. *Knesset Records*, 30 May 1974, pp. 1,459–511.
31. Rabin, *Memoirs*, p. 243.
32. Y. Rabin, *Record of Service* (Tel-Aviv: Ma'ariv, 1979), p. 442 (in Hebrew).
33. Golan, *Secret Conversations*, pp. 217–18.
34. Rabin, *Memoirs*, pp. 247–9.
35. Ibid., p. 251.
36. Ibid., p. 257.
37. Ibid., p. 255.
38. Rabin, *Record of Service*, pp. 465–72.
39. Ibid., pp. 460–1.
40. *Knesset Records*, 24 March 1975, pp. 2,307–24.
41. Rabin, *Memoirs*, p. 268.
42. Rabin, *Record of Service*, pp. 491–501.
43. The two others were Mordechai Ben-Porat and Amos Hadar.
44. Zevulun Hammer and Yehuda Ben Meir voted against; Hillel Zeidel abstained.
45. *Knesset Records*, 3 September 1975, pp. 4,080–136.
46. Rabin, *Memoirs*, p. 271; Rabin, *Record of Service*, pp. 485–6; E. Sprinzak, *Political Violence in Israel* (Jerusalem: Institute for Israel Studies, 1995), p. 61 (in Hebrew).
47. E. Weizman, *The Battle for Peace* (New York, NY: Bantam Books, 1981), pp. 76, 190; A. Perlmutter, *The Life and Times of Menachem Begin* (New York, NY: Doubleday, 1987), pp. 327, 336; A. Naor, *Begin in Power: A Personal Testimony* (Tel-Aviv: Yediot Aharonot, 1993), pp. 18–19, 109–11 (in Hebrew).
48. Weizman, *Battle for Peace*, pp. 76–7; Naor, *Begin*, pp. 18–19, 109–11.
49. Bar-Siman-Tov, *Israel*, pp. 23–32.
50. W. B. Quandt, *Camp David: Peace Making and Politics* (Washington, DC: Brookings Institution, 1986).
51. Bar-Siman-Tov, *Israel*, pp. 92–5.
52. Ibid., pp. 95–7, 100–2.
53. Ibid., pp. 109–12.
54. Ibid., pp. 125–32; J. Carter, *Keeping Faith: Memoirs of a President* (New York, NY: Bantam Books, 1982), pp. 394–9; Weizman, *Battle for Peace*, p. 372; M. Dayan, *Breakthrough: A Personal Account of the Egypt–Israel Peace Negotiations* (London: Weidenfeld & Nicolson, 1981), pp. 177–9.
55. Bar-Siman-Tov, *Israel*, pp. 147–50.
56. Ibid., pp. 150–2.
57. Ibid., pp. 155–61.
58. Ibid., pp. 161–7.
59. Ibid., pp. 172–8.
60. Ibid., pp. 183–5.
61. Ibid., pp. 224–33.

62. Ibid., pp. 195–211.
63. D. Makovsky, *Making Peace With the PLO: The Rabin Government's Road to the Oslo Accord* (Boulder, CO: Westview Press, 1996), pp. 31, 34, 82–3, 114–20; S. Peres, *The New Middle East* (New York, NY: Henry Holt, 1993), pp. 9–10; S. Peres, *Battling for Peace* (London: Weidenfeld & Nicolson, 1995), pp. 320–3; Rabin, *Knesset Records*, 13 July 1993, pp. 8–12; *Ha'aretz*, 31 August 1993.
64. Makovsky, *Making Peace*, pp. 111–13.
65. Ibid., p. 62.
66. Three MKs from the Likud abstained.
67. Netanyahu, *Knesset Records*, 21 September 1993, pp. 7,685–700; *Foreign Broadcast Information Service (FBIS): Daily Report*, 15 September 1993, p. 26, 24 September 1993, p. 22, 6 May 1994, p. 44; *Knesset Records*, 5 October 1995, pp. 30–101.
68. *Jerusalem Post*, 30 August 1993; *FBIS*, 30 September 1993, p. 51; *Ha'aretz*, 27 July 1995.
69. Sprinzak, *Political Violence*, pp. 108–30; Y. Bar-Siman-Tov, *The Transition From War to Peace: The Complexity of Decisionmaking—The Israeli Case* (Tel-Aviv: Steinmetz Center for Peace Research, 1996), pp. 87–90.
70. *Yediot Aharonot*, 30 August 1993, 28 September 1995.
71. Bar-Siman-Tov, *Transition*, pp. 91–2.
72. Ibid.
73. M. Zak, *King Hussein Makes Peace* (Ramat Gan, Israel: Bar-Ilan University Press, 1996), pp. 292–9 (in Hebrew).
74. Besides the three MKs from Moledet who voted against, five MKs from the Likud and one from the National Religious Party abstained.
75. E. Yuchtman-Yaar, T. S. Hermann, and A. Nadler, *Peace Index Project: Findings and Analysis, June 1994–May 1996* (Tel-Aviv: Steinmetz Center for Peace Research, 1996) (in Hebrew).
76. *Ha'aretz*, 16 January 1997.
77. Ibid., 17 January 1997.
78. Yuchtman-Yaar, Hermann, and Nadler, *Peace Index*.

3 Voters' Attitudes on the Arab–Israeli Conflict and the 1996 Elections

ABRAHAM DISKIN

The interrelationship between voters' attitudes and politicians' attitudes is well known. In fact, this relationship forms one of the main arguments of many linkage theories. On the one hand, voters tend to be quite volatile in their stances once political leaders make significant policy changes. On the other hand, politicians tend to express popular positions and to implement popular policies in order to increase their own popularity.

Thus, for example, in past surveys of Israeli public opinion most voters expressed negative attitudes toward a full withdrawal from the Sinai Peninsula, but this changed with Anwar Sadat's visit to Jerusalem. After the peace agreement with Egypt, a vast majority supported the withdrawal. Most voters objected to negotiations with the PLO, but this changed with the disclosure of the first Oslo agreement. As for Israeli politicians, many, for example, who have supported the establishment of an independent Palestinian state, or who have believed that no real peace can be achieved with Syria, have tended to refrain from committing themselves publicly to such positions because of their apparent unpopularity.

The outcome of the latter phenomenon is that politicians often prefer individual, partisan, and short-term considerations to general, long-term considerations. In Israel, where many of the political disputes involve existential questions, such a tendency may cause irreversible damage. Nevertheless, because of changes in the 'rules of the game' (i.e., the introduction of direct election of the prime minister, the adoption of internal party primaries, and the overall

'Americanization' of the political process, especially during election campaigns), such political tendencies have only intensified in recent years.

The dramatic changes in the Middle East, including both new peace opportunities and new existential threats, underline the importance of public opinion. This chapter will analyze some major features of Israeli voters' attitudes toward the Arab–Israeli conflict. Given the interdependency of voters and politicians, the chapter concentrates on the relationship between voters' attitudes toward the Arab–Israeli conflict and voting behavior. Attitudes on these issues are also compared to attitudes on issues that are not related to the conflict. In addition, question of differences between Jewish and Arab voters is addressed. The investigation of these differences is essential when focusing on questions of peace and war between these two Middle Eastern communities.

THE DATA[1]

A few weeks before the May 1996 Knesset and prime ministerial elections, between 7 May and 17 May, the Leonard Davis Institute held a national public opinion survey.[2] The data were gathered in 28 geographical clusters and intended to represent the entire electorate, including Arabs, religious Jews, new immigrants, voters residing in rural areas, and a small number of voters residing in the occupied territories. The total number of respondents was 1,064.

A similar survey was conducted after the elections; however, the findings shown below (with the exception of Tables 3.1, 3.2, and 3.13) represent the distributions and correlations found in the first survey only. That is because the results of the postelection survey tended to be quite similar to those of the pre-election survey. The data for the second survey[3] were gathered in the same 28 neighborhoods from 14 July to 24 July 1997. Although it was not a perfect panel survey, the interviewers were instructed to interview respondents of the same households. The number of respondents in the second survey was 1,087.

The respondents of the July survey tended to adapt themselves to the results of the elections. Thus, as shown in Tables 3.1 and 3.2, the support for right-wing attitudes and for right-wing and small parties became slightly higher. Column A in Table 3.1 represents the May distribution of voting intention in the prime ministerial election. Column B represents the answers to the question: 'Which candidate did you support in the May election for prime minister?' Column C represents the actual support of the voters in July.

Table 3.1: Support for Peres and Netanyahu in the May 1996 and July 1996 Surveys

	A	B	C
Peres	43.9%	41.2%	39.8%
Netanyahu	40.1%	41.1%	40.6%
Undecided/blank ballot	7.0%	6.9%	6.6%
Refused to answer	9.0%	10.8%	13.0%
N	1,064	1,087	1,087

Hereafter, the distinction between 'right-wing' and 'left-wing' voters will be indicated by the support for Netanyahu and Peres, respectively. Other indicators of voters' identification with the 'right wing' or the 'left wing' led to conclusions similar to those presented below.

The greatest difference between the May and the July surveys related to the question for which results are shown in Table 3.2.

Table 3.2: Do You Agree With the Following Statement: 'Given the introduction of direct election of the prime minister, it is easier to support small political parties in the Knesset elections'?

	May 1996	July 1996
Absolutely agree	22.4%	26.6%
Agree	30.1%	31.4%
Maybe	21.9%	20.9%
Disagree	18.9%	16.2%
Absolutely disagree	6.6%	4.9%
N	1,040	1,059

In both surveys, respondents understood that the new system would enable voters to split their vote such that the power of the small parties would increase. This, however, became much clearer after the elections. The new constitutional framework has had a decisive impact on the Israeli political system. Nevertheless, as yet no direct correlation between its implementation and attitudes toward the Arab–Israeli conflict has yet been identified.

DECLARED REASONS FOR VOTING

The politicians' responsiveness to voters' stances on the Arab–Israeli conflict seems justified by the voters' declarations about their electoral motives.

It seems that the issues associated with foreign and defense policies, particularly with the Arab–Israeli conflict, played a major role in the elections. Thus, the respondents were asked to indicate what was the main reason for the support of a specific party in the Knesset elections. Some 47.3 per cent of the respondents asserted that voters tend to support a specific party because of its stances on foreign and defense issues. The second most important reason, cited by 20.1 per cent, was that 'people support parties that represent people like themselves'. Some 15.4 per cent said the leadership of the political parties was the main explanation for voting behavior, and the remaining 17.3 per cent mentioned other reasons. Only slight differences were found between those who intended to support Shimon Peres in the prime ministerial elections and those who intended to support Binyamin Netanyahu. The results are shown in Table 3.3.

Table 3.3: The Reasons Mentioned by Peres and Netanyahu Supporters for the Support of a Specific Political Party in the 1996 Knesset Elections

The main reason that people support a specific party	Peres supporters	Netanyahu supporters	Others	Total
Support the foreign and defense policies of the party	42.8%	53.3%	44.9%	47.3%
Support other policies of the party	9.1%	7.3%	8.3%	8.3%
Support the leadership of the party	18.2%	13.7%	11.5%	15.4%
The party represents people like themselves	20.6%	16.6%	27.6%	20.1%
Desire to prevent the success of another party	2.0%	2.4%	2.5%	2.3%
Other reasons	7.3%	6.6%	5.1%	6.7%
N	451	409	156	1,016

Table 3.4: The Reasons Mentioned by Jewish and Non-Jewish Voters for the Support of a Specific Political Party in the 1996 Knesset Elections

The main reason that people support a specific party	Jewish voters	Non-Jewish voters
Support the foreign and defense policies of the party	52.8%	21.9%
Support other policies of the party	6.1%	18.5%
Support the leadership of the party	13.9%	21.3%
The party represents people like themselves	17.5%	33.1%
Desire to prevent the success of another party	2.6%	0.6%
Other reasons	7.1%	4.5%
N	848	178

It is evident from Table 3.4 that the parties' stances concerning the Arab–Israeli conflict are far more important to Jewish voters than to non-Jewish voters. Furthermore, it seems that most of the differences between the supporters of Peres and Netanyahu stemmed from the fact that most of the non-Jewish respondents included in the survey were Peres supporters. The largest percentage of Arab voters responded that the most important reason for the support of a specific party is that the party 'represents people like themselves' (33.1 per cent). Nevertheless, even among Arab voters, the second most important reason for partisan support was the foreign and defense policies of the parties (21.9 per cent); the third most important reason was identification with the leadership of the parties (21.3 per cent).

BASIC ATTITUDES TOWARD THE PEACE PROCESS

Following the 1996 double elections, many observers suggested that the Israeli public was split on questions relating to the Arab–Israeli conflict, such that approximately half of the voters support the peace process and the territorial concessions associated with it, while the other half object to such developments.

The findings indicate that such an interpretation is misleading. It seems that most of the voters supported the idea of peace in general and the specific peace negotiations in particular; at the same time, there existed a majority who were not ready to meet some of the territorial demands made by Israel's Arab partners.

The respondents were asked to express their level of support for a long series of statements. Tables 3.5–3.7 show the distribution of the levels of support among Peres and Netanyahu supporters for statements about the peace process. From these tables it clearly emerges that, although Peres supporters do tend to be more supportive of the peace process, even among Netanyahu supporters there are more who favor the continuation of the negotiations than who oppose it. Among those who supported Peres, a majority 'absolutely agreed' that 'one should support the peace process between Israel and different Arab partners', Syria, and the Palestinians. Among Netanyahu supporters, only a minority either 'disagreed' or 'absolutely disagreed' with such policies. Supporters of Netanyahu and Peres alike seem to be less enthusiastic about the negotiations with Syria. Nevertheless, even here only a minority of Netanyahu followers 'disagree'.

Table 3.5: Do You Agree With the Statement: 'One should support the peace process between Israel and different Arab partners'?

	Peres supporters	*Netanyahu supporters*
Absolutely agree	66.9%	15.8%
Agree	29.8%	43.5%
Maybe	1.5%	23.6%
Disagree	1.3%	13.7%
Absolutely disagree	0.4%	3.3%
N	456	423

Table 3.6: Do You Agree With the Statement: 'One should support the continuation of the negotiations between Israel and Syria'?

	Peres supporters	*Netanyahu supporters*
Absolutely agree	58.5%	10.1%
Agree	32.2%	35.5%
Maybe	6.9%	17.6%
Disagree	1.9%	22.6%
Absolutely disagree	0.4%	14.1%
N	463	425

Table 3.7: Do You Agree With the Statement: 'One should support the continuation of the negotiations between Israel and the Palestinians'?

	Peres supporters	*Netanyahu supporters*
Absolutely agree	63.4%	7.8%
Agree	32.3%	34.8%
Maybe	3.0%	25.4%
Disagree	0.4%	20.2%
Absolutely disagree	0.9%	11.8%
N	465	425

Tables 3.8–3.10 represent the level of agreement of Peres and Netanyahu supporters to three possible major territorial concessions. Israel is consistently requested by its Arab partners in the negotiations to make these concessions within the framework of peace agreements with Syria and the Palestinians. It is clear from these tables that Peres supporters tended to be more dovish than Netanyahu supporters; but it is also clear that most of the supporters of Peres and Netanyahu alike prefer not to make such concessions. Some 81.7 per cent of Netanyahu followers do not agree to a full withdrawal from the Golan Heights, whereas 41.7 per cent of Peres followers either 'agree' or 'absolutely agree' to it. A lower total of Netanyahu followers, 67.1 per cent, do not agree that Israel should give up its control over the Jordan Valley; 48.6 per cent of Peres followers either 'agree' or 'absolutely agree'. A large number, 85.5 per cent, of Netanyahu followers do not agree to future partition of Jerusalem, whereas 36.4 per cent of Peres followers either 'agree' or 'absolutely agree' to it. It is also evident from these tables that concessions in Jerusalem are less popular among all voters compared with possible concessions in the Golan or the Jordan Valley. It is quite clear that all of these tendencies were well known to the campaign managers of both Likud and Labor. The two parties' campaign messages were designed on the basis of similar findings.

Table 3.8: Do You Agree With the Statement: 'Within the framework of a peace agreement with Syria, Israel should agree to full withdrawal from the Golan Heights'?

	Peres supporters	*Netanyahu supporters*
Absolutely agree	30.1%	2.8%
Agree	11.6%	0.5%
Maybe	17.0%	0.7%
Disagree	26.0%	14.3%
Absolutely disagree	15.3%	81.7%
N	465	427

Table 3.9: Do You Agree With the Statement: 'Within the framework of a peace agreement with the Palestinians, Israel should agree to give up its control over the Jordan Valley'?

	Peres supporters	*Netanyahu supporters*
Absolutely agree	25.9%	1.9%
Agree	12.7%	2.1%
Maybe	20.1%	6.4%
Disagree	28.5%	22.5%
Absolutely disagree	12.7%	67.1%
N	463	423

Table 3.10: Do You Agree With the Statement: 'Within the framework of a peace agreement with the Palestinians, Israel should agree to partition of Jerusalem'?

	Peres supporters	*Netanyahu supporters*
Absolutely agree	24.9%	2.8%
Agree	11.5%	1.4%
Maybe	15.2%	1.2%
Disagree	19.1%	9.1%
Absolutely disagree	29.3%	85.5%
N	461	427

SOCIOECONOMIC LEFT–RIGHT IDENTIFICATIONS

Although in most democracies the terms 'left' and 'right' are used to indicate stances on social and economic issues, in Israel these terms rarely have such connotations. The term 'left-winger' is usually applied to someone who holds dovish ('left-wing') positions on the Arab–Israeli conflict, and the term 'right-winger' is usually ascribed to someone who holds hawkish ('right-wing') positions. One of the questions in the Leonard Davis surveys requested the respondents to locate themselves on a five-point scale of socioeconomic left–right dimension. Table 3.11 shows the results for four groups.

Table 3.11: Self-Placement on a Socioeconomic Left–Right Dimension (1 = 'extreme right'; 5 = 'extreme left')

	1	2	3	4	5	N
Netanyahu supporters	5.3%	40.2%	43.6%	9.9%	1.0%	413
Peres supporters	0.7%	11.6%	33.8%	46.5%	7.5%	456
Jews	3.5%	29.7%	42.5%	21.0%	3.3%	856
Arabs	1.1%	9.0%	23.6%	57.3%	9.0%	178

All four of the groups show very strong centrist tendencies. The combined percentage of those designating themselves as either 'extreme right-wingers' (1) or 'extreme left-wingers' (5) is 10.1 per cent or less in all groups. The modal answer among Jewish respondents and among Netanyahu followers is 3 (center). The modal answer among Peres followers and among Arabs respondents is 4 (moderate left). It is clear, then, that the inclinations toward dovish or hawkish positions concerning the conflict are similar to those revealed by questions on social and economic affairs.

POLARIZATION

Polarization between different groups of voters was measured by the comparison of the mean answer given by respondents belonging to the relevant groups. The following values were attributed to the different possible answers: 'absolutely agree' (or 'extreme right') = 1; 'agree' (or 'moderate right') = 2; 'maybe' (or 'center') = 3; 'disagree' (or 'moderate left') = 4; 'absolutely disagree' (or 'extreme left') = 5.

The absolute value of the difference between the mean results of any two groups of respondents compared was then divided by the maximal difference possible (4), such that the measure could have reached values within the range of 0–1 only. The maximal value (1) would occur only if all of the respondents belonging to one group 'absolutely agree' with a given statement and all of the voters belonging to the second group 'absolutely disagree' with the same statement. The minimal value (0) would occur when the mean results of the two groups compared were identical.

One pair of groups measured was of Jewish and non-Jewish respondents. Another pair examined was of Jewish supporters of Netanyahu and Jewish supporters of Peres.

Thus, the mean self-placement of Netanyahu supporters according to Table 3.11 is 2.61 and the mean result for Peres supporters is 3.51. Hence, the polarization between these two groups is 0.22 ([3.51–2.61]:[5–1]). Likewise, the polarization between Jewish and Arab respondents is 0.18.

The results concerning questions related to the Arab–Israeli conflict are shown in Table 3.12. The polarization between Netanyahu followers and Peres followers seems to be quite moderate: only in two cases is the polarization measure higher than 0.3. The polarization between Jewish and Arab respondents was, in some cases, quite high. In general, the polarization between the mean position held by the Jewish voter and the mean position held by the Arab voter was greater than the polarization between the mean position held by Netanyahu supporters and that held by Peres supporters. The only exception to this tendency concerns the support for the peace negotiations between Israel and different Arab partners: here the polarization between Netanyahu and Peres supporters is approximately identical to that between Jewish and non-Jewish voters.

Table 3.12: Polarization Between Jewish and Arab Voters and Polarization Between Netanyahu and Peres Supporters on Statements Concerning the Arab–Israeli Conflict

	Polarization between:	
	Netanyahu and Peres supporters	*Jewish and Arab voters*
One should support the peace process between Israel and different Arab partners	0.24	0.23
One should support the continuation of the negotiations between Israel and Syria	0.38	0.33
One should support the continuation of the negotiations between Israel and the Palestinians	0.34	0.33
There is a good chance that in the near future a comprehensive peace in the Middle East will be reached	0.24	0.43
There is a good chance that in the near future a peace agreement with Syria will be reached	0.22	0.40
There is a good chance that in the near future a peace agreement with the Palestinians will be reached	0.29	0.38
Military experts believe that security can be guaranteed within the framework of a comprehensive peace in the Middle East	0.24	0.40
Military experts believe that security can be guaranteed within the framework of a peace agreement with Syria	0.25	0.43
Military experts believe that security can be guaranteed within the framework of a peace agreement with the Palestinians	0.27	0.43
Within the framework of a comprehensive peace agreement in the Middle East, Israel should agree to reduce the IDF	0.21	0.65
Within the framework of a comprehensive peace agreement, Israel should agree to give up its nuclear capability	0.21	0.65
Within the framework of a peace agreement with Syria, Israel should agree to full withdrawal from the Golan Heights	0.15	0.69
Within the framework of a peace agreement with the Palestinians, Israel should agree to the partition of Jerusalem	0.22	0.70
Within the framework of a peace agreement with the Palestinians, Israel should agree to give up its control of the Jordan Valley	0.25	0.66
The Arab world would have desired to destroy the state of Israel had there been a chance to do so	0.17	0.64
Syria would have desired to destroy the state of Israel had there been a chance to do so	0.16	0.65
The Palestinians would have desired to destroy the state of Israel had there been a chance to do so	0.19	0.61

The polarization measurements prove that there is a huge gap between Arab voters and Jewish voters concerning the 'image of the enemy'. Whereas most Arab respondents did not believe that Israel's neighbors are interested in the destruction of the state of Israel, Jewish voters—Peres and Netanyahu supporters alike—were very suspicious of the Syrians, the Palestinians, and the 'Arab world' in general. It is very plausible that other differences found between Jewish voters and non-Jewish voters stem mainly from the differences concerning the 'image of the enemy'. This basic difference may explain why Arab respondents were ready to make territorial concessions that are associated with the security issue. It may also explain why most non-Jewish respondents favored the notion of Israel giving up its nuclear capability and reducing its army within the framework of a comprehensive peace settlement.

The sharpest polarization between Jewish voters and Arab voters was found on the Jerusalem question. It is clear that this issue is highly symbolic and involves attitudes beyond the security issue. Even among Jewish left-wingers there was a high degree of objection to the partition of Jerusalem. This is seen, for instance, in Table 3.10. It should be noted that the group of Peres supporters in that table includes his Arab supporters.

CONCLUSION

As indicated by the findings shown in Table 3.13, most Israeli voters tended to believe, not only before the elections, but also in July, that Shimon Peres was better qualified for the position of prime minister than Binyamin Netanyahu. Nevertheless, it seems that although most voters supported the peace process, given the basic suspicion of Israel's Arab partners to the peace process and the fundamental reluctance about 'total' territorial concessions, especially in Jerusalem, many voters were torn between contradictory attitudes.

Table 3.13: Responses to the Question: 'Who is better qualified for the position of prime minister, Shimon Peres or Binyamin Netanyahu?'

	May	*July*
Shimon Peres	56.9%	55.1%
Binyamin Netanyahu	34.4%	34.3%
Other	8.6%	10.6%
N	1,064	1,087

The Labor Party focused its electoral campaign on the slogan 'Bibi is not fit [to be prime minister]'. Likud centered its campaign on the slogan 'Peres will divide Jerusalem'. Both slogans were arguably the most effective possible for the respective parties. It seems that many of the 'floating voters' were divided, up to election day, between those who believed 'Bibi is not fit but Peres will divide Jerusalem' and those who believed 'Peres may divide Jerusalem but Bibi is not fit'.

The results of the elections show that many people preferred to support a 'less qualified' politician for prime minister. This was so despite the fact that a vast majority also supported the continuation of the peace process begun by the Rabin and Peres governments.[4-6]

It should be emphasized that in many well-defined societal groups, identification with one of the candidates was very pronounced. Thus, 96 per cent of the Arab voters, 90 per cent of kibbutz members, and 79 per cent of the Druze voters supported Peres. On the other hand, 89 per cent of those living in 'religious cities' and 87 per cent of Israeli citizens living in the West Bank supported Netanyahu.

Based on the evidence presented here, and given the fact that a small majority of Israeli voters have supported parties to the right of Labor in all elections since 1977, it seems likely that the final results of the[1] elections were dictated by primary partisan and societal identifications, by deep feelings of suspicion toward the different Arab partners, and by the refusal to meet Arab territorial demands that seemed excessive to most Israeli voters.

NOTES

1. Geographical clusters for the public-opinion surveys were designed according to data supplied by the Central Bureau of Statistics, Government of Israel, Jerusalem, 1996.
2. Public-opinion survey conducted for the Leonard Davis Institute of International Relations, May 1996.
3. Public-opinion survey conducted for the Leonard Davis Institute of International Relations, July 1996.
4. A. Diskin, 'Israel', *European Journal of Political Research*, 32, 3–4 (December 1997), pp. 405–16.
5. A. Diskin and M. Hofnung, *The 1996 Knesset and Prime Ministerial Election* (Jerusalem: Nevo, 1997).
6. A. Dowty *et al.*, 'The Role of Domestic Politics in Israeli Peacemaking' (Leonard Davis Institute for International Relations, the Hebrew University of Jerusalem, and Konrad Adenauer Foundation, September 1997).

4 The Israeli Right and the Peace Process

EHUD SPRINZAK

Most observers were stunned on 30 May 1996 by Binyamin Netanyahu's victory in Israel's elections. The surprise did not simply involve the pre-election public opinion polls, most of which had consistently favored Prime Minister Shimon Peres. It also had to do with the defeat of one of Israel's most effective cabinets ever, a government responsible for the Oslo accords with the Palestinians, for the peace treaty with Jordan, and for an unprecedented improvement in Israel's international status and legitimacy. The economic fruits of the peace accords and the positive business atmosphere created in Israel between 1993 and 1996, expressed both in consistent economic growth and in a dramatic decline in unemployment, constituted another reason for the expected Labor victory. But most of all there was the Rabin assassination. The murder of Prime Minister Yitzhak Rabin on 4 November 1995 shocked the nation and the world. Since the Israeli right was held responsible for the intense anti-Rabin campaign, conducted for months before the murder, most observers believed that Netanyahu would have to pay the political price. Even the majority of Israel's ultranationalist activists did not believe that the young and inexperienced Likud leader could win.

The purpose of this chapter is to review the politics of Israel's right between 1992 and 1996 in order to shed light on two events, Rabin's assassination and Netanyahu's electoral victory. The chapter focuses on the internal dynamics of the parliamentary and extraparliamentary right, and on the interaction between the political elites of the right and the Israeli people. It will be maintained that the key factor in the radicalization of Israel's right, a process that led to Rabin's assassination, and also in creating the conditions for the Netanyahu victory, was Muslim Palestinian terrorism. Although many factors influenced the evolution of right-wing politics in Israel, Muslim Palestinian terrorism was crucial for four reasons: it dramatically reduced the government's popularity after the signing of the Oslo accords; it created enormous right-wing frustration with the two individuals held 'responsible' for the terrorism, Yitzhak Rabin and Shimon Peres; it closed the ranks among the different schools of the Israeli right, with the extremists setting the tone; and its resumption in February–March 1996 resuscitated the right and strengthened Netanyahu's position in the election campaign.

THE ISRAELI RIGHT IN 1992: AN INTERACTIVE MAP

The characteristic feature of the contemporary right, an old school in Israeli politics that was consolidated after the 1967 Six Day War, is not a conservative socioeconomic platform (which it does not possess) but instead an aggressive approach to the solution of the Arab–Israeli conflict and a maximalist view of the future borders of the state of Israel. Most Israeli right-wingers refer to their camp as the 'national camp'. They see themselves as the 'loyalists' of the Greater Land of Israel and believe that the state of Israel has both the right and the capability to retain the entire West Bank, occupied in 1967. They are also great supporters of the settlement movement in the occupied territories and regard the settlements as the most meaningful manifestation of present-day Zionism. These Eretz Israel (Land of Israel) loyalists are skeptical about the willingness of the Palestinians to live in peace with Israel and believe, in general, that 'territory equals security'. They also maintain that Israel's military and economic power provide a sound basis for an aggressive foreign policy.

As a political camp, the Israeli right is made up of several political parties—the Likud, Tzomet, Moledet, and the National Religious Party (NRP)—and two sociopolitical-religious settlement movements, Gush Emunim and Kach. Whereas the Likud and Tzomet, with few exceptions, represent the pragmatic and parliamentary politics of the Israeli right, Moledet, the NRP, and particularly the settlement movements speak on behalf of the nation's radical right. They are more militant in their pursuit of the Greater Land of Israel, more aggressive toward the Palestinians, and do not care much about the distinction between parliamentary and extraparliamentary politics. The Israeli radical right is, furthermore, less concerned about the principles of pluralist democracy, ready to turn a blind eye to extralegal acts against Arabs, and in general puts its version of Zionism above all other norms of the Jewish state. Whereas the Likud and other parties have best represented the interests of the Greater Israel principle in the Knesset and the government, the settlement movements have spearheaded the extraparliamentary activities of the right and set its ideological agenda.[1] Right-wing politics in Israel, therefore, is best regarded as an interaction of several schools and orientations that often cross party and movement lines. During the 1992–96 period, the Israeli right contained five distinct schools: the parliamentarians, the pragmatists, the extremists, the terrorists, and the moderates.

The parliamentarians focus on the Knesset and regard the parties of the right as the major carriers of the nationalist agenda. This school is characterized by a pragmatic parliamentary orientation and a belief that Israeli politics is decided by the ordinary electoral process and by what the government and the Knesset do or do not do. The elections of 1992 dealt the parliamentarians a huge blow; the Likud was relegated to opposition and Prime Minister Yitzhak Shamir had to step down. For a while it appeared that the party's days were numbered and that Likud's political hegemony of 1977–92 was gone. But the electoral debacle was deftly exploited by Binyamin Netanyahu. A former ambassador to the United Nations and deputy foreign minister, Netanyahu persuaded his Likud colleagues to follow Labor's example and select their leadership in a primary system. Buttressed by several rich American supporters and a spirit of party revitalization, Netanyahu surprised the Likud's old guard by winning the primaries with an overwhelming majority. In 1993, the young leader took over the party, started to pay its huge electoral debts, and restructured it entirely. He changed the party's constitution and made sure his loyalists were in total control of the party's Central Committee and bureaucratic machinery. Because of their minority status in the Knesset, however, during 1992–96 the parliamentarians played only a small role in Israel's right-wing politics.

The pragmatists consist of the leading groups among the religious settlers in the occupied territories, followers of the Gush Emunim philosophy and the legacy of Rabbi Kook.[2] Despite the small number of these highly motivated settlers (about 30,000), the pragmatists constitute a dynamic and influential elite group. Most of the Israeli right considers them the 'pioneering vanguard' of the entire camp and abides by their ideological leadership. Since the mid-1980s, the pragmatists have been represented in Israeli politics by the Council of the Settlers of Judea, Samaria, and Gaza (Yesha Council) and have enjoyed the unequivocal support of the NRP and Moledet.[3]

Like settler activists in general, the pragmatists have always been strong opponents of the peace process, have never had compunctions about prolonging the Israeli occupation of the West Bank and Gaza, and have repeatedly expressed 'understanding' about anti-Arab vigilante acts. But unlike other settler activists, the pragmatists have strong political instincts and understand that their antipeace struggle can only succeed if supported by a large number of ordinary Israelis who live within the Green Line. Having learned from past experiences, such as the abortive 1982 effort by settlers to stop the evacuation of northern Sinai, the pragmatists know that extremist settlers have sometimes severely damaged the cause of the Land of Israel.[4] They understand that their extremism must be cloaked in politics, businesslike rhetoric, and parliamentary decorum. Indeed, the leaders of the pragmatists are constantly seen in the Knesset, publish articles and columns in Israel's secular press, and often appear on television and radio talk shows. Although extremist in their ultimate convictions, the pragmatists have increasingly been identified as flexible and moderate, which makes them dangerous adversaries of all Labor administrations.

It should be stressed, however, that the pragmatists have never been complete cynics or hypocrites. Their idealistic vision of the Jewish state includes a great concern for the state of Israel, admiration for the army, and a desire to see the nation united. Pragmatist rabbis seriously believe in the sanctity of secular Israel, and their sons are eager to serve in the nation's best military units. All these elements make the pragmatists acceptable to a large number of Israelis who otherwise differ with their religious convictions and concrete political goals.

Since the Oslo accords were signed, the pragmatists have aimed at forging an antipeace consensus that can neutralize Labor's peace politics. This strategy is based on the conviction that the Oslo accords are disastrous and that the Israeli public should be apprised of the danger they pose. To their dismay, the pragmatists have learned that the majority of Israelis do not care about the settlements or about the Greater Israel idea. Hence they have focused their propaganda on Palestinian terrorism and contended that, contrary to Labor's promises, the Oslo process has reduced the personal safety of Israelis rather than increasing it.

The extremists also come from Gush Emunim and are inspired by the ideo-theology of Rabbi Kook. But unlike the pragmatists, they adhere to the radical legacy of the Gush, its past defiance of different Israeli governments, and its uncompromising attitude toward the Palestinians. The extremists are also preoccupied with messianic convictions.

Led by Gush Emunim legends such as Rabbi Moshe Levinger[5] and Rabbi Dov Lior, both of whom live in the high-friction area of Hebron and Kiryat Arba, the extremists do not believe in political expediency and are rarely concerned about making a negative impression on the Israeli public. In addition to rejecting the peace process, they have little trouble in challenging the government's legitimacy, in justifying the killing of innocent Arabs, and in advocating military confrontation with the Palestinians. Although bitter setbacks of the past, such as the Camp David accords, the evacuation of northern Sinai, and the Oslo agreements, have not changed their minds about the upcoming heavenly redemption, they have made them frustrated and bellicose. Moreover, since the mid-1980s the extremists have increasingly been marginalized by the pragmatists. The 1992 elections, in which Rabbi Moshe Levinger tried and failed to enter the Knesset as head of a new radical party, led to further marginalization. Indeed, Levinger and his followers were blamed for splitting the right-wing vote and helping the left return to power.

The post-Oslo strategy of the extremists focused on radicalizing the extraparliamentary struggle of the right and on making it a massive campaign of civil disobedience. Also influenced by secular activists, such as Attorney Elyakim Haetzni, former Knesset member Geula Cohen, and the illustrious military commander (res.) Shlomo Baum, some of the extremists convinced themselves that the government could be brought down in the streets.

The terrorists consist of the followers of the late Rabbi Meir Kahane (assassinated in New York in 1990), and have organized themselves into two religious protest movements, Kach and Kahane Chai. They do not constantly practice terrorism, but enthusiastically support the idea of Jewish terrorism and are mentally prepared to kill innocent Arabs. The terrorists are detached from Israel's political reality; blending messianic convictions with a catastrophic reading of history, they believe that intimidation, violence, and terrorism can help them shape a new reality in the occupied territories.[6] Before the signing of the Oslo accords, the prestige of the terrorists within the Israeli right had hit rock bottom and they had become a marginal group with only few dozen provocateurs in Judea and Samaria.

The moderates are leading activists of Gush Emunim, who since the mid-1980s have moved to the center of Israeli politics and have become increasingly critical of their radical colleagues' bellicosity toward the Arabs. The moderates have not compromised their Eretz Israel ideology, but have subjected it to moral and ethical restrictions. The moderates were deeply affected by the horrors of the Lebanon War and by the traumatic discovery in 1984 of a Gush Emunim underground that planned to blow up the Dome of the Rock (a Muslim holy site on the Temple Mount) and was responsible for anti-Arab terrorism. They responded by forming a new settler orientation that was conscientious, critical of anti-Arab atrocities, and ready to work with Labor hardliners. The leading members of the moderates are Rabbi Yehuda Amital, who even tried to place a moderate religious party in the Knesset called Meimad, and Rabbi Yoel Bin Nun, a Gush Emunim founder and longtime critic of the extreme right.[7] Following the Oslo accords, a number of moderates established Tchelet (Light Blue), a small group that offered support to the Labor government provided it would agree to maintain large settlement blocs within the future Palestinian state. The moderates failed to constitute a significant political force, but succeeded in breaking the image of a unified right-wing anti-Oslo bloc, and were ready to open a constructive dialogue with the Rabin government.

AFTER OSLO: PATTERNS OF STRUGGLE OF THE ISRAELI RIGHT

The Oslo agreements, made public in September 1993 and welcomed by the majority of the nation, stunned the Israeli right. Binyamin Netanyahu, the newly elected and inexperienced Likud leader, was disoriented. As experienced as Gush Emunim and the heads of the Yesha Council were in setbacks and political disappointments, none of them expected Yitzhak Rabin, Israel's 'Mr Security', to recognize the PLO and allow the formation of a far-reaching Palestinian autonomy. The positive response of most Israelis to the agreement and their fascination with the Rabin–Arafat handshake on the White House lawn intensified the right's shock.

The right's immediate response was a virulent demonstration against the agreement, held on 7 September in Jerusalem, with the participation of nearly 200,000 people. This impressive showing had, however, no significant, large-scale follow-up.

Unable to mount an effective struggle in the streets, the

pragmatists, under the leadership of the Yesha Council, resorted to a costly public relations campaign based on the slogan 'Yesha Ze Kan' (Yesha [Judea and Samaria] is here). In addition to the message that Yesha's security was Israel's security, the campaign appealed to the nation's brotherly sentiments: the real message, driven home to hundreds of thousands of Israelis, was 'Do not forsake us!'.

The settlers' campaign, initially sluggish, was ignited by an unwelcome but highly expected development: Islamic terrorism. Oslo's grace period, which lasted nearly two months, came to an abrupt end in late October 1993. A few squads of Palestinian Muslim terrorists—mostly associated with the Hamas and Islamic Jihad movements—killed a number of soldiers, settlers, and other Israeli civilians, triggering an immediate radicalization of the settler community. A 'Jewish intifada' ensued, a settler mini-insurrection consisting of tire burnings, roadblocks, stonings, destruction of hundreds of Arab cars and other property, and even killing. After a particularly atrocious murder by Palestinian terrorists, in which a settler named Chaim Mizrahi was burnt alive, hundreds of Jews ravaged Arab villages, destroying property and attacking civilians. A few days later, hundreds of settlers took to the roads during morning rush hour and brought all Arab traffic to a standstill. After a promise from the military commander in the area that the army would act aggressively against the terrorists, the settlers agreed to evacuate—but not before declaring their determination to repeat the action if necessary.

Members of Yesha's moderate Rabbinical Council subsequently ruled that shooting Palestinian attackers was legitimate. Religious followers of these rabbis were told that no legal barriers should stop them from doing what they felt necessary.[8]

The settler radicalization was further intensified by a new series of murders. In an Arab ambush near Hebron, Ephraim Ayubi, driver for the revered rabbinical authority Rabbi Chaim Druckman, was killed; Druckman survived the attack. The terror wave peaked in January 1994 with the murder in Kiryat Arba of Pinchas Lapid and his son Shalom. Lapid, a longtime 'refusenik' from the Soviet Union who finally came to Israel in the early 1970s, was an exemplary figure in the settlement movement. The government was virtually powerless to control the emotional eruption of the settler community, especially in Kiryat Arba and Hebron.

The most significant effect of the terror campaign on the Israeli right was the regaining of political legitimacy by the extremists and the terrorists. Long marginalized by the parliamentarians and the pragmatists because of their excessive extremism, the radicals were now allowed to join the action. The pragmatists' intensifying anger made them return to Gush Emunim's early days, in which the entire movement challenged the government in the streets. In addition to the small Kach and Kahane Chai movements, two groups gained momentum: Mateh Ma'amatz (which can be loosely rendered as Action Center) and Elyakim Haetzni's Committee to Abolish the Autonomy Plan.

The new wave of terror was especially helpful to Haetzni, a Kiryat Arba attorney long known for his vitriolic rhetoric. Haetzni's warnings about a coming disaster for the settlers, which for many years had fallen on deaf ears, became much more influential in January 1994. Frustrated settlers began to heed Haetzni's calls for massive civil disobedience to bring down the government.

> A people whose government committed an act of national treason, collaborated with a terrorist enemy to steal the heart of its homeland, gave this enemy tens of thousands of guns— aimed directly at the hearts of its sons and daughters—must be ready to fight. And in this war as in every war there are risks and casualties. If we do not fight in 1994, no miracle will occur and the year will be as cursed as the previous one.
>
> Rise up and do it! We have done nothing. Protests, demonstrations, 'tent cities', even setting roadblocks are insufficient acts against a government conducting national treason. In France, defeated in 1940, when Marshal Petain gave in to Hitler and made an alliance with him—just as Lieutenant General Rabin did by shaking Yassir Arafat's dirty hand—de Gaulle did not demonstrate in protest. Although the regime was born in a democratic way ... he deserted, rebelled against a Nazi collaborating army ...[9]

Although the more pragmatic Yesha Council did not lose its organizational hold over the settler struggle against the Oslo agreements, it was Mateh Ma'amatz and the Committee to Abolish the Autonomy Plan that began to set the rhetorical tone of the campaign. Haetzni's anti-Rabin posters, increasingly seen in right-wing demonstrations, were even more malicious than his articles in the settler journal *Nekuda*. The most nefarious of these posters depicted Rabin as an unsavory Arab, smiling at Yassir Arafat and washing his hands in blood. The poster's text associated the prime minister with

Palestinian terrorism and assigned him direct responsibility for Jews killed by Hamas violence. Yet Haetzni was not alone: a number of distinguished right-wing individuals declared their support for his organization, not least among them Colonel (res.) Baum. The Yesha Council made little effort to limit the virulence of Haetzni's propaganda material; thousands of copies of the posters were distributed to all participants in Yesha antigovernment demonstrations.

Meanwhile, the role of the parliamentarians declined. Netanyahu, troubled by intraparty conflicts, especially with former Foreign Minister David Levy, as well as by the cold shoulder many Likud veterans offered him as a newcomer who had taken over the party, failed to put his mark on the anti-Oslo campaign. His dull Knesset speeches, as well as his inability to stimulate massive resistance to the accords, left the radical right in full control of the struggle. As the radical right's anti-Oslo struggle gained momentum, Netanyahu found himself increasingly tailing the extremists. Indeed, he sometimes pleaded with the activists of the radical right to be allowed to appear in their demonstrations for photo opportunities, fearing that otherwise he would be forgotten by the Israeli public. In essence, between November 1993 and November 1995 (Rabin's assassination), the struggle against the Oslo accords was taken over and even monopolized by the extreme right, with Netanyahu and the Likud simply making no difference.

THE HEBRON MASSACRE IN PERSPECTIVE

At 5:10 on Friday morning, 25 February 1994, about 500 Muslims were kneeling in a Ramadan prayer at the Isaac Hall of the Cave of the Patriarchs in Hebron. A man dressed as a captain of the Israel Defense Forces (IDF), armed with an automatic Glilon rifle, broke into the hall and began strafing the worshippers with bullets. Twenty-nine Muslims were killed instantly, over 100 wounded, before unharmed worshippers overpowered him and beat him to death. Amid the hysteria and outrage that spread through the occupied territories, further violence took place: Palestinians and Israeli soldiers clashed all over the West Bank and Gaza, leaving nine Palestinians dead and nearly 200 wounded.

The shock of the Hebron massacre intensified when the killer's identity was discovered. He turned out to be Dr Baruch Goldstein, the emergency physician for Jewish settlers in Hebron and Kiryat

Arba, a devoutly Orthodox Jew and father of four. He had treated many Jewish victims of Palestinian terrorism, and had also cared for wounded Arabs.

Goldstein's massacre was immediately described as the unpredictable act of a lone madman. The theory of an insane individual was, not surprisingly, supported by the Yesha Council, whose leaders were quick to aver that Goldstein represented no one but himself, and that the settlers were as shocked by the massacre as anybody else. However, many of Goldstein's close friends in Kiryat Arba saw it otherwise, justifying his act as a response to Palestinian terrorism. According to these friends—members or supporters of the Kach movement—the massacre was not just a deed of political–military revenge: it was a religious act and a sacred mission.[10]

Although there is no question that Goldstein perpetrated the crime alone, it was conducted within an elaborate ideological and political framework that fully justified anti-Arab terrorism. It is clear that Goldstein planned the attack well in advance, wanted to kill as many Muslims as possible, was certain that God approved of it, and hoped and believed that it would stop the peace process.[11] If we add to these facts Goldstein's long and close association with Kach, the Hebron disaster loses its random, isolated appearance. It becomes, instead, a collective act by proxy, an outburst of political violence expressing the crisis of an entire fundamentalist milieu. The current Israeli–Palestinian peace process is enormously threatening to Zionist religious fundamentalists, and the Hebron massacre was their most extreme reaction to this threat.[12]

The Hebron massacre had a dramatic radicalizing effect on both Arab and Jewish extremists. As for the Arabs, it appears certain that the massacre triggered a massive Hamas retaliation. There are many indications that squads of Izadin al-Qassam, Hamas's military arm, as well as the Islamic Jihad, were determined to engage strategically in anti-Israeli terrorism before the Hebron tragedy. Izadin al-Qassam's mastermind, Yihye Ayyash, 'the engineer', was apparently eager to strike. But Goldstein's atrocity made counterviolence much more urgent for Hamas.[13] Two Hamas car bombs in the towns of Afula and Hadera killed and wounded a large number of Israeli civilians; there was more to come.

As for Israel's pragmatic extreme right, though shocked, they blamed the authorities for Goldstein's act. Rabin's government, not the deranged doctor, was responsible because it had recognized the PLO 'terror organization' and reduced its own antiterrorist efforts.

Blood and catastrophe were imminent and the time for moderation was gone.

THE CRISIS OF TEL RUMEIDA AND THE RABBINICAL RULING ON SOLDIER DISOBEDIENCE

The Israeli government's immediate reaction to the 28 February atrocity in Hebron was to outlaw Kach and Kahane Chai, which continued to preach anti-Arab violence and praised Goldstein as a martyr. Their offices were sealed and their propaganda literature confiscated; about ten leaders of these organizations were placed under administrative detention. Government officials were privately told by Yesha activists that the banning of the Kahanist organizations was long overdue.[14] Of much greater concern to the settler establishment was the increasing likelihood that, as a by-product of the massacre, Hebron's Jewish community would be evacuated.

Before the February massacre, there were no evacuation plans for the small Jewish community of Hebron. Although he knew that this radical enclave, consisting of 500 Jews living in the midst of 130,000 Palestinians, was the most volatile settlement in the West Bank, Prime Minister Rabin did not have contingency plans for its removal. The Oslo agreements with the PLO stipulated that settlement evacuation would be discussed only during the final stage of the negotiations and after the implementation of a Palestinian autonomy in Gaza and the West Bank. But the massacre at the Cave of the Patriarchs, which led to the indefinite suspension of the peace process, created a new reality. Israeli doves, including members of Rabin's cabinet, warned that the continued presence of Jewish provocateurs among Hebron's Palestinians was a recipe for future disasters.[15]

In mid-March, the government began to seriously consider evacuating the seven Jewish families living in Tel Rumeida. Since the mid-1980s, a small number of very radical Jewish families had lived on this small hill in central Hebron. If Jewish Hebron spelled trouble for Arab–Israeli relations, Tel Rumeida was the eye of the storm. Constantly guarded by an entire army company lest they be butchered by their neighbors, Tel Rumeida's Jewish residents kept provoking the neighboring Palestinians.

The news of a possible evacuation stunned the settler leaders. Hebron, the City of the Patriarchs, second in holiness only to Jerusalem, was the first settlement site chosen by Jews after the Six Day

War. If the Rabin–Peres government, already responsible for the Oslo 'treason', could evacuate Tel Rumeida, it might evacuate all of the settlements in Judea and Samaria.

The looming crisis at Tel Rumeida produced one of the most effective mobilization efforts in settler history. Israel's parliamentary opposition was put on alert. Contingency plans were formulated for bringing tens of thousands of ultranationalist activists to Hebron, who would block the removal by planting their own bodies on the holy ground. Heads of right-wing organizations, including many support groups formed within the Green Line, were instructed to prepare for an unprecedented ordeal. Many lobbyists pleaded with Rabin to spare Tel Rumeida and argued that the danger of another massacre was minimal.

The most dramatic response to the Tel Rumeida evacuation plan was made by four prominent rabbis, namely, Shlomo Goren, Abraham Shapiro, Shaul Yisraeli, and Moshe Tzvi Neria: they issued several Halakhic (Jewish religious law) rulings categorically prohibiting evacuation of Jewish settlements in Eretz Israel. Goren, Israel's former chief rabbi and a highly regarded Halakhic authority, was the first to rule against settlement removal; he did so in a detailed answer to a question submitted to him in November 1993 by the Council of Judea and Samaria Rabbis.[16] In an expanded version of that judgment, written in the aftermath of the Hebron massacre, he declared:

> The criminal initiative to evacuate Hebron ought to be met with *messirut hanefesh* [utmost devotion]. The ruling on such a heinous crime, as the ruling on saving life, is '*yehareg velo ya'avor'* [be killed but do not sin]. If the government succeeds in its plan, God forbid, the evacuation of Hebron must be responded to by *kria* [rending one's garment—a sign of death in the family] ... According to the Halakhah, the significance of the destruction of Hebron, God forbid ... is as the killing of people, which requires *kria* ... This is why we have to give our life in the struggle against this vicious plan of the government of Israel, which relies on the Arabs for its majority, and be ready to die rather than allow the destruction of Hebron.[17]

Although Rabbi Goren's ruling, which preceded the Tel Rumeida crisis, produced only a minor controversy, the ruling of Shapiro, Yisraeli, and Neria reverberated all over the country. These three rabbis were by far the most influential in the religious-Zionist milieu. The first two were the heads of Yeshivat Mercaz Harav, Gush

Emunim's founding yeshiva; Neria, the oldest of the three, was the founding father of all yeshivas of Bnei Akiva, the religious-Zionist youth movement. What was shockingly novel about the three rabbis' ruling was that it was addressed to all of the nation's soldiers: they were all being publicly told that evacuation orders were illegal, and that any order to evacuate Jewish settlers from Jewish land must be disobeyed.[18]

The most damaging aspect of the rabbis' ruling was not, however, the potential refusal of a few religious soldiers to participate in Tel Rumeida's evacuation, but its symbolic import: highly regarded spiritual authorities no longer respected the sanctity of the Israeli army. Long recognized as the nation's only guarantee of survival, the IDF has never been regarded as just an instrumental institution for compulsory service, but as a moral calling and a virtue. The very rabbis who now called for disobedience had themselves been part of the post-1967 religious exaltation of this norm. Almost all Israelis grasped the profound significance of the rabbinical ruling and the issue refused to leave the headlines.

Although the rabbinical ruling failed to gain endorsements from non-religious Jews, it was approved by the majority of Israel's Orthodox rabbis. Rabbi Eliezer Waldman, head of Kiryat Arba's *hesder* (combining religious studies with military service) yeshiva, saluted the ruling and promised 'to obey it. This government was born in sin. It depends on the votes of the PLO and has no right to go against any Jewish settlement.' Rabbi Dov Lior, Waldman's colleague and Kiryat Arba's chief rabbi, was even more adamant: he privately issued a special ruling that Jews should be ready to give their lives over Hebron.[19] One interpretation of Lior's judgment was that suicide was permissible in case of forced evacuation.

In the end, neither Hebron nor Tel Rumeida was evacuated. Based on evaluations that suggested a high likelihood of violent confrontation with the settlers and possible Jewish fatalities, Rabin decided to let the settlers remain.[20] A message to that effect was delivered to Israel's Council of the Chief Rabbinate on 4 April 1994 by Deputy Defense Minister Mordechai (Motta) Gur, who had close ties with the settlers. Toeing the line between their official duty as state rabbis and their respect for Shapiro, Israeli, and Neria, Israel's chief rabbis produced this announcement:

> The Council of the Chief Rabbinate has registered with great satisfaction the announcement of Deputy Defense Minister

Motta Gur that the government of Israel has no intention of evacuating either Jewish settlers or Jewish settlements ... It is therefore clear that the question of military orders to evacuate settlers or settlements—which are against the Halakhah—is not on the agenda and the army must be taken out of the political debate.[21]

However, the relief felt by the Council as well as by several other rabbinical bodies was greatly diluted by a new blow to the settlers. That April the Gaza–Jericho plan, suspended since the Hebron massacre, was finally implemented. Arafat was allowed to land in Gaza and the Palestinian autonomy became a fact. The extremist rabbinical ruling, which under other circumstances might have been reversed, remained in full force. Orthodox rabbis who until then had been hesitant were now ready to support it openly. On 3 May 1994, a large rabbinical gathering, calling itself the Eretz Israel Rabbinical Union, fully endorsed the ruling on soldier disobedience. Rabbi Nahum Rabinovitz, head of the *hesder* yeshiva of Ma'ale Adumim, called on his colleagues to take Torah scrolls into the streets of Jerusalem and stay there 'until our outcry is heard in Heaven and our message penetrates secular hearts too'. Representing over a thousand rabbis from all over the country, the new body issued an unequivocal warning to the government:

The so-called peace agreement, made by a government supported by a tiny majority with a critical Arab Knesset vote, is a complete contradiction to peace. The implementation of the agreement may lead, God forbid, to great danger to human life. This is why anyone who can stop this 'agreement' and does not do so, breaks the rule 'you shall not stand idle when there is danger to your brother'.[22]

The struggle against his government's legitimacy did not leave Rabin unaffected. A secular sabra to the bone, he had never liked the settlers and their messianic rhetoric. During his first term as prime minister, he had been the target of many Gush Emunim protests. Convinced that they would do anything to fulfill their dream of Greater Israel, he was wary and mistrustful toward them. In 1994, with the intensification of their struggle against his peace policies, Rabin lost his patience; he completely lacked sympathy or empathy with the settlers' sense of impending disaster about the possible collapse of their territorial dream. Unlike President Ezer Weizman, who had psychologically disarmed many of these angry people by paying visits to their settlements following terror attacks, Rabin remained cold and aloof. Repeatedly humiliating them with name-calling, including *kugelagers* (a mechanical part of a car's wheel that squeaks noisily) and 'propellers' (i.e., people who make noise and vent hot air), Rabin conveyed to the settlers that, regardless of their pain, he was determined to move ahead with the peace process. There was no real victor in this tragic psychological warfare—neither Rabin, the bitter and personally insecure prime minister, in front of whose house protesters screamed 'traitor' and 'assassin', nor the many settlers who felt marginalized and humiliated by their government. But increasingly, the settlers' political struggle against Rabin assumed a personal character: they hated him, he despised them.

DIN RODEF AND DIN MOSER

The rabbis' confrontation with Yitzhak Rabin reached a new height in February 1995. Following an unprecedented series of Hamas and Islamic Jihad suicide bombings inside Israel, which took the lives of 87 Israeli civilians, wounded 202, and traumatized the entire nation, the heads of Yesha's Rabbinical Council decided to consider putting the government on trial according to the laws of *din rodef* and *din moser*. *Moser* and *rodef*, according to the Halakhah, are among the worst kinds of Jew: they betray the community through acts that may cause the loss of innocent Jewish life. A *moser* provides Gentiles with information about Jews or illegally gives them Jewish property. Since the Halakhah views Eretz Israel as a sacred property of the Jewish people, Jews are obliged to execute a moser found guilty of giving away part of it. A *rodef* is a person about to commit or facilitate an act of murder; he must be killed immediately so as to save Jewish life. This rule does not apply to a murderer caught after the deed, who has to go on trial. *Din rodef* is, according to a certain interpretation, the only case where the Halakhah permits the killing of a Jew without a trial.

The fact that the escalation of Muslim terrorism was largely a response to Goldstein's massacre was hardly noticed by the ultra-nationalist rabbis or anybody else in Israel's extreme right. Instead, the radical right blamed two individuals, Yitzhak Rabin and Shimon Peres, for the terror attacks. By evacuating Israeli soldiers from Gaza and Jericho, allowing the formation of a large Palestinian police force, and relaxing the security forces' struggle against Palestinian extremism, Oslo's two architects had made it possible for Hamas and Islamic Jihad to kill Jews.

Thus, the rabbis addressed a long question about din moser and din rodef to 40 Halakhic authorities.

> What is the rule about this bad government? Can they be regarded as accomplices in acts of murder committed by terrorists, since in their plans they are responsible for the strengthening and arming of these terrorists? ... Should they be tried according to the Halakhah? And if proved guilty as accomplices in murder, what should their sentence be? If they are, indeed, ... punishable in court, is it the obligation of every individual to bring them to trial in a court of justice, or, for lack of an alternative, in an ordinary secular court? Is it not the obligation of the community's leaders to warn the head of the government and his ministers that if they keep pursuing the agreement, after the terrible experience of [Oslo 1] in all of Judea and Samaria, they will be subject ... to the Halakhic ruling of din moser, as ones who surrender the life and property of Jews to the Gentiles?
>
> ... We know that the very interest in the issue may stimulate, God forbid, an intense controversy in the nation. Aware of the actual conditions on the ground, we are worried that the situation will get worse, that these questions will be asked by the majority of the people and that many of the victims [of terrorism] may be filled with sentiments of revenge.[23]

Although the rabbis' letter was formulated as a question addressed to other, more prominent rabbis, it was itself a very incriminating document. It treated the causal relation between the government's peace process and Muslim terrorism as a given, and referred to Palestinians collectively as terrorists. No distinction was made, for example, between the peaceful PLO and the terrorists of Hamas. There was, moreover, no reference to a possible link between the Hebron massacre and the eruption of Muslim terrorism. The three rabbis who drafted the letter, Dov Lior, Eliezer Melamed, and Daniel Shilo, already seemed close to concluding that Peres and Rabin qualified for din moser and din rodef.

Especially notable, in this context, was the harsh language increasingly used against Israeli leaders by North American Orthodox

rabbis. In a stormy meeting with Shmuel Hollander, Israel's Orthodox cabinet secretary, who visited New York over the High Holy
Days, some of these rabbis compared Arafat to Hitler and told the
stunned official that his boss was both moser and rodef.[24] Rabbi
Abraham Hecht, the prominent head of New York's large Sharei Zion
synagogue, said in public what many of his colleagues had been
saying privately: 'according to Jewish Halakhah, Rabin deserves to
die. He who intentionally transfers living people, money, or property
to strangers commits, according to the Halakhah, a crime punishable
by death. Maimonides maintained that he who kills such a person is
doing the right thing.'[25] In a television interview, Hecht said that to
kill Rabin was a *mitzvah* (Jewish obligation) and he was sorry he was
personally unable to fulfill it.

Following Rabin's assassination, there were further indications
that many discussions of din moser and din rodef had preceded the
murder. The moderate Rabbi Yoel Bin Nun openly charged several
rabbis with authorizing the killing. In a meeting with Israel's chief
rabbis, he mentioned Dov Lior and Ma'ale Adumim's Nahum
Rabinovitz. Bin Nun further maintained that a young rabbi from
Gush Etzion, Shmuel Dvir, who in the past several months had made
death threats against Rabin, had told other people he knew of a rodef
ruling by seven prominent rabbis.[26] Although none of Bin Nun's
charges could be fully substantiated, and he later apologized in
public, his allegations exposed the culture of Halakhic defiance that
preceded the assassination, including the wide discussion of moser
and rodef. It is unlikely that any of the aforementioned rabbis issued
a death sentence on Rabin and Peres, but a number of them allowed
their students to believe that Rabin and Peres had more than qualified
for the infamous titles. With, perhaps, the exception of Rabbi Shlomo
Aviner, who forbade his students to use slanderous language against
the heads of state,[27] rabbis such as Lior, Rabinovitz, and so on
had increasingly joined the campaign of invective. The culture of
Halakhic character assassination was well expressed in the *haredi*
(ultra-Orthodox) journal *Hashavua*, which railed against Rabin with
such terms as 'traitor', 'madman', and 'non-Jew':

> There are, today, [settler] groups that favor violence of the first
> order. They even demand permission to assassinate the heads
> of the government, especially Prime Minister Yitzhak Rabin,
> against whom there is din rodef ... The heads of the national
> haredim maintain that an extreme line against the government—

which stands under din rodef—must be adopted. All speakers with whom we talked tried to maintain that the discussion is totally theoretical and there is no intention to kill Rabin and Peres ...

The new situation puts before the haredi public alternatives never faced before. One possibility is to forcefully challenge the group that took over the government of the state ... There is no reason that we must allow the vicious maniacs who run this government to take Jews as sheep to the slaughter. 'Rabin is a traitor,' says Rabbi Gadi Ben-Zimra, 'and I have no problem in saying this. It is clear that the government betrays all values ... and puts the state in danger.'[28]

The outlawing of Kach and Kahane Chai and the inability of their members to display their original emblems led to the rise to fame of Eyal (an acronym for Israeli Fighting Organization), a new Kahanist organization. Eyal was formed in 1993 by a Tel-Aviv University student, Avishai Raviv. Raviv, who first gained notoriety by demanding the resignation of the Arab head of Tel-Aviv University's Student Association on the ground that an Arab could not be trusted, was eventually expelled from the university. He moved to Kiryat Arba, where he and a small number of activists started to attract media attention through provocative anti-Arab rhetoric and aggressive ceremonies condemning Jewish 'traitors'. Raviv proposed contingency plans for expelling Hebron's Arabs in the event of an Israeli pullout from the city, and even staged special horror shows for Israel's television networks. Masking their faces, armed Eyal activists moved into the Arab *casbah* (central marketplace) of Hebron and performed, in front of the camera, random terrorist acts against the local population.[29] Raviv and his comrades became major promoters of the character assassination of the nation's top leaders. Responsible for the mass production of vicious anti-Rabin posters, they were also involved in disseminating a picture of Rabin in Nazi uniform.[30]

BEFORE THE ASSASSINATION: THE RABBINICAL STRUGGLE AGAINST OSLO 2, THE RISE OF ZO ARTZENU, AND THE 'PULSA DI NURA'

In the summer of 1995, the radical right felt itself more delegitimized than ever by the Rabin government. At issue was the implementation of Oslo 2, the second stage of the agreement between Israel and the PLO. Stipulating that the Palestinian autonomy should now be expanded to seven major West Bank cities and several hundred villages, Oslo 2 significantly reduced Jewish control over Judea and Samaria, and provided for the introduction of thousands of armed Palestinian policemen to the area. The Israeli right was increasingly frustrated; the Gaza–Jericho autonomy, contrary to the right's expectations, seemed to be working well and Arafat's police had not become a terrorist gang. Against this background, settler demonstrations were less and less effective; efforts by right-wing leaders, such as Knesset member Hanan Porat, to call for early elections fell on deaf ears.

Again, the spiritual authorities of the settlers launched a dramatic response. After a lengthy consultation, which included hearings of senior military officers, a distinguished rabbinical body ruled that it was illegal to evacuate military bases in Judea and Samaria and that soldiers should disobey any such orders. The ruling was an aggressive extension of the similar decree of over a year earlier. What was new was the rabbis' expansion of their judgments to purely military matters. Everyone recognized that there is a huge difference between civilian settlements and military compounds. No civilian rabbi in Israel had ever ruled, or claimed to be competent to rule, on technical matters involving the location of military bases. The rabbinical statement, which was endorsed by 15 prominent rabbis, including Rabbis Shapiro, Neria, Yaacov Ariel, and others, read:

> We hereby determine that there is a Torah prohibition on evacuating IDF bases and transfer the sites to Gentiles ... A permanent military camp is a Jewish settlement in the full sense of the term. Its uprooting and relinquishment into the hands of Gentiles falls under the same rule as the removal of an Eretz Israel settlement, which is prohibited by law. It is therefore clear that no Jew is allowed to take part in any act aiding in the evacuation of a settlement, camp, or military compound ...
>
> Never before has the army put its soldiers in a situation in which they had to act against their conscience. We call upon the government and the army to avoid putting soldiers through a decision involving a choice between the army's orders and loyalty to their ethical convictions.[31]

The new rabbinical ruling created a national commotion even stronger than the one 15 months previously. President Ezer

Weizman, who had been particularly attentive to the settlers' distress, was furious. Weizman, a respected former general, refused to admit to his residence a representative group of rabbis who came to explain; he demanded categorically that the new ruling be canceled. The attorney general declared his intention to try the rabbis for incitement. Hebrew University professor Aviezer Ravitzky, a leading Orthodox academic, asserted that the ruling implied the symbolic collapse of 'the Israeli social contract'. In *Yediot Aharonot*, Israel's largest daily, Ravitzky charged the rabbis with expressing 'an extremist political position characteristic of a minority group, not the opinion of Israel's religion'. Ravitzky doubted whether most *hesder* yeshiva soldiers would obey the ruling, but warned against the danger of insubordination.[32]

A number of army generals expressed outrage; meanwhile, some yeshiva students said they would not obey the rabbis. Rabin made it clear that soldiers who did obey the ruling would be instantly court-martialed. Infuriated, Rabin told journalists:

> It is unheard of that a democratically elected government will be forced by rabbis, using the Halakhah, to allow soldiers to disobey orders. There has never been anything like this in Israel's past history. It is one of the worst things possible that a small number of rabbis, who do not represent the majority of Israeli rabbis, can make such a decision. It is unthinkable that we turn Israel into a banana republic. The entire Knesset, not just the government, ought to reject this matter.[33]

The public uproar did not, however, move any of the main signatories to retract. Nor did it weaken the ultranationalists' determination to bring down the 'illegal' government in the streets; indeed, it led to further radicalization. The divisions among Israeli Jews in the summer of 1995 were as wide as ever.

The intensifying frustration over the inability of the rabbis or the Yesha Council to derail the peace process led to the meteoric rise of a new radical-right movement, Zo Artzenu (This Is Our Land). It was formed by two relatively unknown settlers, Moshe Feiglin and Shmuel Sackett, residents of Ginot Shomron, an affluent bedroom community close to the Green Line. They were soon joined by Rabbi Benny Elon, the young head of the Orot Yeshivah in Jerusalem. Zo Artzenu's contribution to the antipeace struggle involved new measures of aggressive civil disobedience and new campaign rhetoric. From July to October 1995, its activists engaged in illicit settlement, blocking of the nation's major highways, and aggressive protests in front of government offices. In the summer of 1995, Zo Artzenu activists set the agenda of the radical right and dictated its style of struggle.

Thus, the time was ripe for Feiglin and Sackett to test Zo Artzenu's ideas with Operation 'Doubling' II. Begun on 8 August, the operation involved the establishment of 30 new strongholds as 'twin settlements' in the West Bank. Thousands of activists were eager to launch extralegal settlements and refuse the army's evacuation orders. Hundreds were arrested and sent to prison. Settler–soldier confrontations were now heavily reported in the press and a formidable protest movement quickly developed.[34]

Boosted by their growing publicity, the heads of Zo Artzenu decided to bring their campaign across the Green Line. The intent was to start disrupting life and public order in Israel proper, signaling the government that unless it suspended the peace process, its own ability to function would be literally stopped in the streets. Operation Roadblock, conducted by several thousand Zo Artzenu volunteers, was orchestrated in almost military fashion. Spread among nearly 80 road junctions across the country and coordinated by Rabbi Benny Elon flying above in a chartered helicopter, these activists succeeded in disrupting transportation for several hours. Nearly 3,000 policemen were needed to clear the roads and highways, not before 130 activists, including Feiglin, had been arrested.

Although succeeding in gaining publicity, Zo Artzenu was unable to induce the Israeli populace to join its struggle. Most Israeli drivers did not appreciate being stuck at intersections for hours, and in fact tended to become resentful toward Zo Artzenu and its antipeace struggle. Later efforts to repeat the disruption on 13 and 29 September—the second anniversary of Oslo 1 and the signing day of Oslo 2, respectively—showed decreasing effectiveness. Another provocative venture, a spectacular plan to have hundreds of thousands of Israelis turn on their lights and appliances all over the country and flood the electric grid, failed miserably: no serious disruption was reported by the Electric Company.

The intense attention given to Zo Artzenu, as well as its increasing role in shaping the agenda of the radical right, did not result solely from its disruptive tactics. Of special attraction for the media were its new faces and voices. The most active members of Zo Artzenu were American immigrants; in media interviews, they stressed commitment to the American tradition of civil disobedience. For Israel's mainly liberal and left-wing journalists, the new images were a far cry from the conservative and messianic rhetoric of Gush Emunim.

Heavily reported in the foreign press, Zo Artzenu's rhetoric was particularly effective among American audiences: the young movement succeeded in establishing nearly 40 support groups in the United States, and received much of the funding for its large operations from US sources. Feiglin, born to Australian parents but married to an American, remarked:

> There is an American approach to freedom that does not exist in this country and I live among Americans who know the real meaning of individual freedom. Freedom does not mean that the government, which won the elections, is free to do whatever it pleases ... When a person who barely wins the majority, moves to take away the most precious objects of the Jewish majority in the country, and speaks in the name of democracy, he cannot expect his actions to go without resistance. The reason the opposition comes mostly from American immigrants is because they understand the meaning of democracy.[35]

Although Zo Artzenu failed to bring down the Israeli government in the streets, it greatly intensified the delegitimation of the government. The movement's operations served as rallying events for the entire hard core of the radical right, whose number reached into the hundreds, as well as thousands of other activists. Old and new posters and slogans, calling Rabin and Peres traitors, assassins, or collaborators with terrorism, abounded. Not a few of the activists began to speak and chant about the need to execute the 'traitors'.

On 6 October 1995, just two days after the holiday of Yom Kippur, an odd group of extremists gathered in front of the prime minister's Jerusalem residence. The purpose of the meeting, convened by former Kach activist Avigdor Eskin, was to conduct the traditional Pulsa di Nura ceremony against Rabin. Pulsa di Nura, which means 'blaze of fire' in Aramaic, is the most severe death curse that can be made against a Jewish sinner. This mystical punishment is imposed very rarely and, if at all, by Kabbalistic rabbis. To execute the curse, ten rabbis and community heads must convene in a synagogue, fast for three days, and then perform the curse at midnight. The text of the curse reads:

Angels of destruction will strike him. He is damned wherever he goes. His soul will instantly leave his body ... and he will not survive the month. Dark will be his path and God's angel will pursue him. A disaster he has never experienced will befall him and all curses known in the Torah will apply to him.[36]

It is not known whether all the formal requirements of the Pulsa di Nura were fulfilled by the group convened before Rabin's residence. The fact that Israeli citizens, although very few and very extreme, considered its invocation during Yom Kippur was, however, telling: in the autumn of 1995, the verbal violence against Rabin now included death threats. Another ominous indication occurred a week later when Rabin visited a gathering of Anglo-Saxon Israelis at Netanya's Wingate Sport Institute, and met an aggressive group of hecklers, one of whom approached him menacingly.[37] It seemed that it was all too easy to threaten the prime minister from close range.

FROM RABIN'S ASSASSINATION TO THE ELECTION CAMPAIGN

Yitzhak Rabin was pronounced dead at 11:10 p.m. on Saturday, 4 November 1995. He had been shot 80 minutes earlier, just a few minutes after delivering a rousing speech at a huge Tel-Aviv peace rally an important theme of which was nonviolence. None of the participants expected that the event would conclude with the first political murder of the Jewish nation's premier in nearly 2,000 years.

Rabin's assassination stunned the nation; it also dealt a devastating blow to the Israeli right. On 5 November 1995, no one believed that Binyamin Netanyahu had a chance to beat Rabin's successor, Shimon Peres, in the upcoming elections. Opinions about Netanyahu's responsibility for the murder varied, however. The prime minister's widow, Leah Rabin, and many left-wing activists argued that the Likud leader, who did not aggressively counter the rhetoric of the extreme right, was as responsible for the assassination as the extremists. Others rejected this claim, but maintained that Netanyahu bore indirect responsibility. Everyone on the left agreed, however, that Netanyahu's efforts to deny any responsibility and his refusal to apologize for his low profile before the assassination were reprehensible. There was a general consensus that the young Likud leader was politically dead.

The sharpest attack on the Israeli right was launched by the moderates among the settlers. As noted, Rabbi Yoel Bin Nun blamed several Gush Emunim rabbis for issuing a Halakhic death sentence on Rabin. Another moderate leader, Rabbi Yehuda Amital, maintained that the entire educational system of the religious right, which sanctified Eretz Israel at the expense of all other norms, had created the conditions for Yigal Amir's act.

Between November 1995 and February 1996, the Israeli right hit rock bottom. A national soul-searching revealed the magnitude of the government's delegitimization by leading right-wing spokespersons. The large preassassination alliance among the parliamentarians, the pragmatists, the extremists, and the terrorists collapsed, with each school trying to distance itself from the terrible act. Many activists of the extremists and the terrorists were called in for investigation and a few were even arrested. A right-wing victory in the coming elections looked more and more impossible.

The Rabin assassination had another effect on the right: a tacit acquiescence of the Oslo accords. Although the leaders did not change their opinions about the sanctity of the Land of Israel or the illegitimacy of the PLO, the traumatic murder showed them that they were left with two alternatives: to tacitly accept Oslo, or to prepare for potential civil war. Shocked by the killing, they did not hesitate to choose the former option. The choice was made easier by Oslo's main architects, Prime Minister Shimon Peres and Minister of Economics and Planning Yossi Beilin, who made it clear that they did not seek revenge and were interested, instead, in national reconciliation. Peres, Beilin, and other Labor leaders assured the settlers that they intended neither to return to the 1967 borders nor to dismantle most of the settlements; this gesture eased the settlers' de facto acceptance of Oslo. Indeed, the pragmatists were certain that Amir's act had defeated them and there was no more they could do for Eretz Israel.[38]

Israel's right was salvaged by Hamas. A series of four suicide bombings in February and March 1996 destroyed the solid lead Peres' had over Netanyahu. The bombings, which took the lives of 70 Israelis and wounded 200, created a 'countertrauma' to the trauma of Rabin's assassination. Shimon Peres, originator of the optimistic slogan 'the New Middle East', was left helpless against the reality of the old Middle East. His young rival, long known for his skepticism about the region, had nothing to do but reap the political fruits. But in this case, Netanyahu did better: instead of attacking the government, he graciously offered his support for the fight against terrorism. In any case, polls showed that though Peres still led, it was no longer by a wide margin.

The return of Netanyahu and the parliamentarians to center stage also profoundly affected the radical right. The pragmatists, their dream of Greater Israel resuscitated, set to work mobilizing thousands of young settlers and students to help Netanyahu's campaign.

From March to May 1996, Netanyahu skillfully positioned himself for the elections. He knew that to win, he had to unite the entire right behind him. Two challengers for the leadership of the right, Ariel Sharon and Rafael Eitan, had dropped out of the race, though Eitan, leader of the Tzomet faction, made Netanyahu guarantee him a prominent position in the future government. But there was still former Foreign Minister David Levy, who had left the Likud over a bitter personal feud with Netanyahu. When the latter, however, gave in to Levy's excessive demands, including the position of foreign minister in the right-wing government, Netanyahu indeed stood at the helm of a united camp. Labor's low-key campaign, based on confidence that Netanyahu was no match for Peres, played into the hands of the underdog. Winning the elections by the narrowest margin in Israeli history—29,457 votes—at the age of 47 Netanyahu became the nation's tenth prime minister.

THE SOLIDIFICATION OF ISRAEL'S 'SOFT' RIGHT AND NETANYAHU'S VICTORY

Undoubtedly, Netanyahu would never have become prime minister without the role played by Hamas and Islamic Jihad. But there was another factor in this surprising victory: Netanyahu and his Likud colleagues' success in mobilizing the strong support of Israel's religious camp. During the last two weeks of the campaign, one saw not only Likud and settler activists in the streets, but thousands of yeshiva students who had never served in the army or intended to do so. There was also a strong mobilization by supporters of Shas, a Sephardi ultra-Orthodox party. Such activists were neither members of Israel's traditional right (radical or pragmatic) nor simply activists of their own parties: they, together with other elements, constitute what I refer to as the 'soft right'.

Ever since the Likud's 1977 victory, it had been apparent that in addition to right-wing hardliners, Likud governments enjoyed the support of the nation's conservative camp, which included traditionalist Sephardim, lower- and middle-class Ashkenazim, and the ultra-Orthodox. Israel's conservatives have never fully identified with the ideological right or its dream of Greater Israel; their attitude toward the settlements has been lukewarm at best. What they always had in common was religious Orthodoxy or respect for it, lower socioeconomic status, hostility toward the burgeoning upper-middle class, disapproval of secular mores, and intense hostility toward the Arabs. The rise in the 1980s of ultraliberal civil rights, and anticlerical organizations such as Peace Now and the Meretz Party, largely oriented toward compromise with the Palestinians, further strengthened the conservatives' association with the Likud. Meretz in particular, which made an ideology of Westernization, epitomized everything they hated in Israel's secular culture.

The Labor-led government of 1992–96 was highly effective. The Rabin–Peres cabinet signed the Oslo accords with the Palestinians and the peace treaty with Jordan. It raised Israel's diplomatic and economic status to unprecedented heights, while boosting economic growth and eliminating unemployment.[39] But there was a high political price for these achievements: all of them, which also included a large investment in secular–humanistic education and generous support for ultraliberal causes, were made 'courtesy of' Meretz and Israel's Arab parties. Had the 1992–96 government brought real peace to Israel's war-weary society, these factors would probably have had only a minor alienating effect; most of Israel's conservatives have long shared the left's yearning for peace and tranquillity. Beginning as early as December 1993, however, terrorism undermined the peace process and curtailed its political benefits. Thus, the right's aggressive attacks on the government increasingly appealed to the conservatives; they came to regard the Rabin–Peres cabinet as 'Arab lovers' who cared about neither Jewish life nor Jewish values.

We shall never know how Yitzhak Rabin would have fared against Netanyahu in the 1996 elections. Some believe he would have won because of his military past and record of integrity; others argue that he would have suffered the same disabilities as Peres, and moreover that the Likud, unharmed by the Rabin-assassination effect, would have been stronger. No one believes, however, it would have been an easy victory: the Labor–Meretz–Arab coalition had done more to push the conservatives toward the Likud than the Likud itself.

A critical factor in transforming the conservative camp into the soft right was the nation's new electoral system. In 1996, Israel's traditional parliamentary system went through a dramatic change. For the first time, Israelis voted separately for the prime minister and the Knesset. Unlike the old system, in which the prime minister was elected by the Knesset, the 1996 elections offered the opportunity to choose directly between Peres and Netanyahu. The new system therefore had a polarizing effect on the final outcomes.[40]

Thus, apart from terrorism, the most significant factor in the 1996 elections was Netanyahu's success in solidifying the entire right-wing/conservative camp. Many people, particularly haredim, who would never before have voted for a secular candidate, gave their support to Netanyahu, encouraged to do so by their rabbis.

The rabbinical decision to back Netanyahu could not have been so instrumental without another important sociocultural process in Israeli society, the rise of the *haredim leumi'im* (nationalist ultra-Orthodox), a contradiction in terms just a few years earlier. The haredim, who never accepted the legitimacy of secular Zionism, were long known for their expedient attitude toward the Zionist state and lack of interest in issues of war, peace, territories, and the Palestinians. Convinced that all these minor problems would vanish once the Messiah came, the haredim focused exclusively on the survival of their community and the prosperity of their yeshivas. Their inclination to support the Likud had nothing to do with ultranationalist or territorial aspirations, and was mostly because of Likud's greater traditionalism.

In the 1970s and 1980s, however, certain *haredi* attitudes toward the Land of Israel began to change. A nationalist orientation started to creep in, and the cult of Eretz Israel became increasingly influential. One of the hasidic schools, Habad, particularly identified with the new approach. Rabbi Schneerson, the Lubavitcher Rabbi, who had never set foot in Israel, was apparently thrilled by Israel's return to Judea and Samaria in 1967, and ruled against territorial concessions. Indeed, Habad hasidics took an active role in financing and participating in the huge anti-Oslo demonstration in Jerusalem on 7 September 1993.

Two additional processes fostered the *haredi leumi* phenomenon: the increasing 'haredization' within the Gush Emunim milieu and the impact of Kahanism on marginal *haredi* students. In the 1980s, a number of Gush Emunim yeshivas underwent a process of haredization. They insisted on greater Jewish introspection and devotion to pure Halakhic studies, and even started to encourage deferment of military service for outstanding students. This led, dialectically, to an increased nationalization of certain haredi schools, which could not resist the appeal of the Eretz Israel cult.[41]

Meanwhile, *haredi* anger at Palestinian violence intensified. Although most of the haredim had always been hostile toward the 'sons of Ishmael', the increasing violence against yeshiva students in the Old City of Jerusalem, *haredi* and non*haredi* alike, raised bitter memories of Diaspora pogroms. The presence in Jerusalem of Rabbi Meir Kahane and his followers, who had long glorified violent acts of revenge against Arabs, galvanized this anti-Arab sentiment.

The *haredim leumi'im* became the winning card in Netanyahu's victory. They provided the cadres who worked day and night during the last weeks of the campaign. Having received the blessings of all haredi rabbis, who wanted to block the establishment of another Labor–Meretz government, the activists brought their message to all haredi neighborhoods. Their efforts raised the haredi vote for Netanyahu to an unprecedented 95 per cent. The extra 10 per cent of this haredi vote formed the critical mass that solidified the soft right and made the electoral difference for Netanyahu.

NOTES

1. For an overview of Israel's right up to the 1992 elections, see E. Sprinzak, 'The Israeli Right', in K. Kyle and J. Peters (eds), *Whither Israel* (London: I. B. Tauris, 1993).
2. On Gush Emunim see G. Aran, 'Jewish Zionist Fundamentalism: The Bloc of the Faithful in Israel (Gush Emunim)', in M. E. Marty and S. Appleby (eds), *Fundamentalism Observed* (Chicago: University of Chicago Press, 1993); E. Sprinzak, *The Ascendance of Israel's Radical Right* (New York, NY: Oxford University Press, 1991), Ch. 5.
3. Sprinzak, *Ascendance*, pp. 124–37.
4. Ibid., pp. 99–105.
5. On the profile and political style of Levinger, a leading extremist, see Sprinzak, *Ascendance*, pp. 139–41.
6. On the Kahanist violence, see E. Sprinzak, 'Violence and Catastrophe in the Theology of Rabbi Kahane: The Ideologization of the Mimetic Desire', *Terrorism and Political Violence*, 3, 3 (Fall 1991).
7. Sprinzak, *Ascendance*, pp. 151–60.
8. *Yesha Rabbis' Communique*, No. 9, May 1993.
9. E. Haetzni, 'Civil Disobedience Now', *Nekuda*, 1994, pp. 25–7.
10. See, for example, M. Ben-Horin (ed.), *Baruch the Man: Memorial Book for Dr Baruch Goldstein, the Saint* (Jerusalem, special edition, 1995).
11. *Report of the State Investigation Committee Studying the Massacre in Hebron's Cave of the Patriarchs* (Jerusalem: Government Printer, 1994) (in Hebrew).
12. E. Sprinzak, 'When Prophecy Fails: The Crisis of Jewish Fundamentalism in Israel', *Contention*, 4, 2 (1995).
13. This conclusion is based on circumstantial evidence and on the fact that before the Hebron massacre Hamas neither resorted to suicide terrorism within the Green Line nor threatened to use it.
14. Interview with settler leader Aharon Domb, 9 November 1994.

15. This is based on the author's conversations with Eitan Haber, Rabin's bureau chief, in March 1994.
16. N. Shragai, *Ha'aretz*, 1 December 1993 (in Hebrew).
17. Ibid., 7 March 1994.
18. S. Dror, *Ha'aretz*, 1 April 1994 (in Hebrew).
19. G. Alon, *Ha'aretz*, 1 April 1994 (in Hebrew).
20. The author was personally involved in writing one of these memorandums.
21. A. Golan, *Ha'aretz*, 5 April 1994 (in Hebrew).
22. N. Shragai, *Ha'aretz*, 5 May 1994 (in Hebrew).
23. Rabbi D. Lior, Rabbi D. Shilo, and Rabbi E. Melamed, 'What Is the Rule About This Bad Government?', in D. Arieli-Horowitz (ed.), *Religion and State in Israel, 1994–1995* (Jerusalem: Center for Jewish Pluralism, 1996), pp. 120–23 (in Hebrew).
24. S. Shiffer, *Yediot Aharonot*, 11 September 1995 (in Hebrew).
25. S. Shamir and R. Sa'ar, *Ha'aretz*, 9 November 1995 (in Hebrew).
26. N. Shragai and S. Ilan, *Ha'aretz*; Z. Zinger, *Yediot Aharonot*, 13 November 1995 (in Hebrew).
27. See comments in Rabbi S. Aviner, *The Prime Minister: Essays in Honor of the Kingdom of Israel and Eretz Israel* (Bet El: Bet El Publishing Services, 1996).
28. S. Ilan, 'Hashavua: Rabin and Peres: Israel's Evil People: Yudenrat Men and Capos', *Ha'aretz*, 12 November 1995 (in Hebrew).
29. *Ha'aretz*, 13 April 1995, 19 November 1995 (in Hebrew). It should be noted that Raviv was later identified as an informant of the General Security Services.
30. *Ha'aretz*, 20 November 1995 (in Hebrew).
31. *Yediot Aharonot*, 13 July 1995 (in Hebrew).
32. Ibid.
33. Ibid.
34. N. Shragai, *Ha'aretz*, 31 July 1995 (in Hebrew).
35. R. Naor, 'Moshe Feiglin, Zo Artzenu Chairman …', *Ma'ariv Magazine*, 18 August 1995.
36. D. Elboim, 'The Murder Curse', *Yediot Aharonot*, 13 November 1995.
37. Arieli-Horowitz, *Religion and State*, p. 287.
38. This is based on a number of conversations between the author and several radical-right rabbis after the Rabin assassination.
39. S. Weiss, *14,729 Missing Votes: An Analysis of the 1996 Elections in Israel* (Tel-Aviv: Hakibbutz Hameuchad, 1997), Ch. 4 (in Hebrew).
40. Ibid., Ch. 5.
41. E. Don-Yehiya, in M. E. Marty and R. Scott Appleby (eds), *Accounting for Fundamentalism* (Chicago, IL: University of Chicago Press, 1994).

5 The Labor Party and the Peace Process

REUVEN Y. HAZAN

Israel has no foreign policy, only domestic policy.

Henry Kissinger

Shifting from war to peace may be a particularly desirable foreign policy, but if this is an arduous and costly process, involving the highest stakes and core values of the country, party cohesion becomes crucial to its success. The Middle East peace process is certainly a very demanding one that involves core Israeli interests. As such, it sheds light on the general issue of intrapartisan politics in the foreign policymaking of democratic societies.

In Israel, the peace process was strongly associated with the Labor Party, and particularly its leaders, Yitzhak Rabin and Shimon Peres. This party returned to power in 1992, and its leaders made dramatic decisions that heralded a new phase in the stultified peace process that had begun at the Madrid Peace Conference in October 1991. It was Rabin's assassination in 1995, along with the ousting of Peres and the Labor Party from power in 1996, that crippled the peace process.

This chapter aims to assess the effects of a protracted peace process on a governing party, and, at the same time, how the internal cohesion of a party in power can affect a new, major foreign-policy strategy. This relationship, in the case of the Israeli Labor Party and the Middle East peace process, proves to be interdependent. That is, the peace process had a strong impact on the party's internal cohesion, and the inner partisan divisions influenced the peace process.

The chapter examines whether party cohesion is necessary for successfully 'selling' a peace process to the voters or, conversely, whether internal divisions can hamper a party's ability to do so. Specifically, the chapter investigates whether the Labor Party leaders took into consideration the reactions they would face within their party; assesses whether the general public's reaction to the peace process influenced the internal relationship between the party and its leaders; and posits that these two relationships—between the leaders and the party, between the party and the people—are connected in the process of foreign policymaking. Therefore, the relationship among leaders, party, and voters on the one hand, and the relevance of this relationship to foreign policymaking on the other, form the focus of this chapter.

THE RELATIONSHIP BETWEEN DOMESTIC POLITICS AND FOREIGN POLICY

The linkage between domestic politics and foreign policy is often discussed in the international-relations literature. The cumulative conclusion is that these two domains of policymaking are indeed related to each other. However, we do not have much theoretical or empirical knowledge about how and when domestic politics and foreign policy are linked, or under what conditions they influence each other. Much of the existing literature neglects the interaction between these two arenas, and focuses instead on the impact of the one on the other. Yet, while we do have some knowledge about the interactions between domestic and international conflicts (Blainey, 1973; Wilkenfeld, 1973), we know very little about the relationship between domestic politics and peacemaking (Stein, 1988; Husbands, 1991). Moreover, while we do not know much about why, how, and when the interactions between international and domestic politics influence peacemaking, we know next to nothing about how internal party conflicts affect foreign policy. That is, although the literature has addressed how the relations *between* parties influence peacemaking (for an analysis of the Israeli case, see Bar-Siman-Tov, Chapter 2), it has basically ignored how the divisions *within* parties can affect this process as well.

If, in democratic systems, foreign policy is influenced by domestic politics, then it is important to know which domestic actors can exert this influence. The literature has correctly assumed that both domestic political actors and domestic political factors must be taken into account. However, the list of actors and factors (in the political arena alone) is limited to governments, parties, voters, pressure groups, public opinion, mass media, and others. Nowhere have the relations within a governing party received attention in this context. Although studies have dealt with the influence of coalition politics on foreign policy, there has been no study of how the politics within the dominant party in a coalition affect foreign policymaking.

As Putnam (1988) suggests, bargaining between two enemies that is aimed at reaching a peace agreement may foster a second level of bargaining within the domestic political arena—the debate over whether or not to support the agreement, the attempt to build a coalition in order to ratify the agreement, and so on. However, there exists yet a third level, namely, within each party, and particularly within the dominant party. Yet scholars have not paid attention to the need to assess partisan unity before embarking on a peacemaking agenda, nor to the need to maintain partisan cohesion when peacemaking becomes a prolonged policy.

The way in which a government disseminates information on foreign policy to the public is part of its attempt to structure and control the public's reaction and elicit its support. In a case where a populace is strongly polarized and, moreover, a shift in foreign policy requires an attitudinal change on an issue of national consensus, a government may try to circumvent the public and implement a one-shot, dramatic, strategic shift. However, if the protracted nature of the policy shift makes this impossible, the government will need public support in order to remain in office and successfully implement its new strategy.

The Middle East peace process between Israel and both the Palestinians and Syria became a protracted phase of negotiations.[1] In the case of the former, this is because of the numerous stages stipulated by the Declaration of Principles (DOP), signed in September 1993. In the case of the latter, it is the result of an ongoing cycle of bargaining and stalemates. Both tracks, therefore, were subsumed into the public sphere and, with the passing of time, also came to possess electoral ramifications, thereby generating partisan politics.

Moreover, in the case of the Middle East peace process, foreign policy dominates domestic politics in Israel. Foreign policy was the single most important and decisive issue in the 1996 elections, the prime ministerial contest between Shimon Peres and Binyamin Netanyahu revolving around it. Foreign policy was found to be the main determinant for an overwhelming majority of Israeli voters (Arian and Shamir, 1999).

The comparative-politics literature has already recognized the need to examine the relations within parties in order to correctly assess government stability and policymaking. King (1976), and a series of articles that utilized his models of legislative–executive relations, have shown that the relations between ministers and backbenchers within each of the governing parties—rather than the relations between parties or between the government and the opposition—are the most vital determinant of a government's survival. These findings need to be extended into international-relations research on the domestic influences on foreign policy.

Can intraparty factors encourage or deter a governing party from initiating a peace process? Can peacemaking produce intraparty divisions that will endanger or even derail a peace process? As we shall see, a government's ability to implement its foreign policy and to elicit popular legitimacy is indeed influenced by the extent of partisan cohesion within the dominant party. We shall also see that intrapartisan politics is an important factor that needs to be integrated into the research on domestic influences on foreign policy; without this element, even an intermediate-range theory on this relationship would be, at best, ambitious if not inadequate.

THE DOMESTIC CONTEXT OF ISRAELI PEACEMAKING

The leadership of the Labor Party knew that when they made their attitudinal shift concerning the Palestinians—by recognizing the Palestine Liberation Organization (PLO) and negotiating directly with Yassir Arafat—they would encounter strong opposition in Israel. However, they thought this opposition would be limited to the hard-core right wing. If the PLO was willing to end the state of war, renounce its aim of eliminating Israel, and suppress terrorism by other Palestinian groups, both Prime Minister Rabin and Foreign Minister Peres thought that the public at large would support the peace process.

The Labor leaders also knew that territorial concessions to Syria would encounter domestic opposition. Yet if the entire Sinai Peninsula (three times the size of Israel) had been returned to Egypt in exchange for peace, with limited domestic difficulties, why could this not be repeated in the case of Syria, where a much smaller relinquishment of territory was involved? In return for removing the most salient threat to Israel's survival, and completing the process of making comprehensive peace with the Arab world, both Rabin and Peres hoped that the Israeli populace would once again accept territorial concessions.

However, acts and gestures by both the Palestinian and Syrian leadership failed to impress the people of Israel enough to rally behind their government and its policies. The Labor Party leaders thus failed to anticipate the extent and intensity of the opposition to the peace process. The inability to effectively control the risks emanating from the peace process, and the resulting public perception of the cost–benefit ratio of this policy, culminated in a failure to create the required attitudinal change and fostered quite the opposite reaction—it galvanized the opposition. Thus, the peace process never received the necessary wide legitimacy that its architects expected. Coping with opposition to this policy became increasingly difficult as time went on.

The political developments in Israel during Labor's tenure in government have been discussed elsewhere, particularly in the many analyses of the party's electoral defeat. The relations between the Israeli government and both the Palestinians and the Syrians have also received due attention. However, the internal developments within the Labor Party and their impact on the peace process have yet to be addressed.

The next section describes in this context the major, relevant events from Labor's accession to power in 1992 to its electoral defeat in 1996. The situation within the Labor Party before the decision to recognize the PLO and sign the Oslo agreement is then analyzed. Did the decision create a rift in the party, or unite it? Was the party ripe for such a move, or did Rabin and Peres force it down this road? Special attention is paid to the period leading up to Rabin's assassination. The months preceding that event were a most difficult time for the party in general and its leader in particular, with the polls showing the public losing faith in the peace process and curtailing its support for the government. Did the public pressure induce a change of heart about the peace process at either the party or the leadership level in the Labor Party? The period between Rabin's murder in November 1995 and Peres's defeat in the May 1996 elections is then examined, particularly the situation in the party leading up to the elections. The chapter concludes by offering a policymaking model in relation to Labor's electoral defeat, with implications for the influence of partisan politics on foreign policymaking in democratic societies in general.

THE PARTY AND THE PROCESS:
INTERDEPENDENT DEVELOPMENTS

The purpose here is not to offer a comprehensive description of the peace process, nor to outline all of the partisan developments. Only instances of the interaction between these two domains are relevant to our concerns.

Although the first part of this section focuses primarily on the Palestinian track of the peace process, this is not meant to suggest that the Syrian track was irrelevant at the time. On the contrary, in the latter half of 1992, there seemed to be some initial progress on this front. However, as soon as the negotiations with Syria became substantial, they came to a standstill. Despite recurrent attempts to revive the Syrian track in 1993 and 1994, there was too little progress to elicit a debate within the Labor Party. In contrast, the negotiations with the Palestinians became a crucial issue for the Labor Party after one year in office, and continued to dominate the party's time and energy in regard to defense, foreign, and at times even economic policy. Moreover, as the former director-general of the Prime Minister's Office observed, 'The explosive potential was in the Palestinian context; if we could disarm this, it could lead to achievements on other fronts as well. The Syrian front, on the other hand, was neither as volatile nor as potentially beneficial.'[2] In the second half of the Labor Party's tenure, discussed in the latter part of this section, the Syrian track was reinvigorated and a clear relationship between partisan politics and peacemaking emerged in this context.

In 1992, the primary event was the Labor Party's decisive victory in the June elections. Without Labor, no coalition could be formed either to its right or its left. Labor had regained its dominant position in Israeli politics for the first time since losing the 1977 elections. A Labor-led coalition government was formed, based on only three parties: Labor, with 44 seats, was clearly the dominant partner; Meretz, a pro-peace party with 12 seats, was the secondary party; Shas, an ultra-Orthodox religious party with six seats, was the junior member. Despite its being a closed, minimum-winning coalition—which, according to coalition theory, should produce a stable government—its majority of only 62 of the 120 seats of the Knesset would plague it throughout its tenure.

Another important event was that Yitzhak Rabin became prime minister. Rabin, as chief of staff, had led the Israeli army to victory in the Six Day War of 1967. As defense minister in the National Unity coalitions from 1984 to 1990, he was also associated with the harsh reaction to the Palestinian intifada. Now, as prime minister, he once again became identified with a focus on Israel's security, in light of three actions he took during his first year in office. In mid-December 1992, he ordered the deportation of 415 Hamas terrorists to Lebanon. In late March 1993, he imposed a closure on the territories after a wave of fatal stabbings by Palestinians. In late June, he launched a week-long massive bombardment of southern Lebanon, known as Operation Accountability. These events had entirely negative repercussions for Israel in the international media and in the global diplomatic arena, yet had positive consequences for Rabin in terms of strengthening his hardline, security-driven image in the eyes of the Israeli public. When the time came to promote the peace process, it was this hardline perception of Rabin that gave him domestic credibility and made him the right person in the Labor Party to sell the agreement to the Israeli public. As his top aide put it, 'If you want to make drastic concessions for peace, you must first show the public that you took drastic measures for security.'[3]

During the election campaign, Rabin repeatedly stated that a peace agreement was possible 'within six to nine months'. As 1992 came to a close, the first six months of his tenure showed little progress on the peace process. In the first half of 1993, little occurred to improve this situation. On the contrary, there was a focus on internal politics in this period.

In April 1993, the issue of a national health insurance bill began to be debated in Labor, and showed its potential for generating conflict. The health minister, Haim Ramon, one of Labor's younger and more charismatic leaders, firmly endorsed this bill, whereas many other ministers opposed it. In July, the bill was brought to the Knesset for its first reading. Although it passed, 13 Labor MKs voted against it. Ramon threatened to resign if the party did not back the bill and push it through the legislative process. This issue continued to plague the Labor Party throughout its tenure in government, creating a split that would undermine its entire infrastructure.

The latter half of 1993 saw a shift back to the peace process, with the most significant of events since Anwar Sadat's decision to visit Israel in 1977. In mid-September, the world watched as Yitzhak Rabin and Yassir Arafat shook hands on the White House lawn, and Peres and Mahmoud Abbas (Abu Mazen) signed the DOP (Oslo 1), ushering in a new era of relations in the Middle East.

However, as Rabin flew to Washington for the main global media event of the year, his coalition began to unravel at home. Two of the

Shas MKs faced criminal prosecution. The Israeli Supreme Court ruled that these two could not remain in office while their criminal cases were pending. This prompted Shas's departure from the coalition and the establishment of a minority government, formally comprising only 56 of the 120 Knesset seats. Because of the outside support of the two Arab parties, accounting for five seats, Shas's departure did not cause the government's fall. With Shas outside the coalition, however, the government lost the support of a Jewish majority in the Knesset, placing it in a precarious situation with respect to the peace process and highlighting the need for cohesion and discipline within the two parties that formed the minority government, particularly within the dominant Labor Party.

Domestic politics remained salient in 1994, as the Labor Party was besieged from within. The controversy over the national health insurance bill, which had festered in the party for almost a year, led to Ramon's resignation. He soon thereafter created a new party to run in the elections for the Histadrut labor federation. This new list was made up of Labor members who opposed the old Labor leadership in the Histadrut that had controlled it since its inception, along with members of the Meretz and Shas parties. The makeup of this list (which reflected the governing coalition originally formed by Rabin) together with the decision to run against Labor in its core organization, constituted a most serious challenge to the party.

While Labor was dealing with internal rivalry and with the Histadrut elections, acts of violence began to undermine the fragile peace process. In late February, 35 Palestinians died in a massacre by a Jewish settler in Hebron. In early April, two buses were blown up by Palestinian suicide bombers in Afula and Hadera, taking the lives of 13 Israelis. Despite the violence, Rabin and Arafat signed the Cairo agreement in late April, and their economic representatives signed a cooperation agreement in Paris, demonstrating that the peace process pushed forward despite terrorism.

The Cairo agreement, however, did not help Labor. The party was defeated in the Histadrut elections and lost its majority that had prevailed for 45 years. Ramon's breakaway list won the largest percentage of votes and took control of the Histadrut. Labor's public image was damaged, and the party entered a crisis period.

In mid-1994, with the domestic political arena in turmoil, the peace process again moved ahead. In July, Rabin flew to Washington for another groundbreaking ceremony, this time with King Hussein of Jordan. But a temporary rise in the polls during early October 1994, in response to the signing of the peace treaty with Jordan, did little to help the government—especially since later that month terrorism struck again, this time in Jerusalem. Immediately after that attack, an Israeli soldier was kidnapped by Palestinians. The entire country was gripped by the unfolding drama; an army raid on the house where he was being held resulted in the soldier's death. Within days, a Palestinian suicide terrorist blew up a crowded bus in Tel-Aviv, killing 22 Israelis and wounding 50. With further attacks in Gaza in November and again in Jerusalem the following month, terrorism had become a grave problem. Rabin was concerned about the decline in public support both for the peace process and for the Labor Party. Domestic and partisan problems plagued the government as well.

The Labor Party's main traditional bases had been lost or weakened, from the Histadrut to the kibbutz movement (which was in financial disarray). Inflation was on the rise; labor relations were troubled; a new tax on the stock market was fiercely resented. Moreover, while in 1993 the opposition had been constrained by internal rivalries, by 1994 it had rallied behind Netanyahu's leadership, and at times he led Rabin in the polls. The Labor ministers, beginning to fear an electoral defeat, no longer solidly supported the government, its policies, or its leader.

This was not just a mid-term crisis, but a much more profound instability. At the same time that Labor's infrastructure was being undermined, the new electoral system had made the undecided or 'floating' voters the pivotal group. With the direct popular election of the prime minister to be implemented for the first time in the 1996 elections, the entire political arena was in a state of flux. The next elections would be won by a person, not a party, and victory would be based on which way the floating voters turned in the prime ministerial race, regardless of the number of Knesset seats that parties won. In other words, the Rabin government's chances would affect, for better or worse, Rabin's chances in the prime ministerial contest. Yet by late 1994, the party leader had been abandoned by his team and left to fend for himself.

Polls showing a movement of voters from the peace camp to the undecided category induced exasperation in the Labor Party. By December 1994, Rabin appeared to be stretched to the limit. He openly attacked anyone who criticized his policies, berated his fellow ministers, and even threatened to settle accounts with some of the Labor MKs when the next elections came. Several of Labor's young leaders called an emergency meeting to 'save the party', a gathering that was perceived as anti-Rabin.

On the eve of Rabin's trip to Oslo to accept the Nobel Peace Prize, he and several Labor MKs exchanged sharp accusations. One MK called out to him, at a party meeting before his departure, 'Yitzhak, the house is burning. Stay home and help put out the fire ... We are committing political suicide.'[4] As 1994 came to a close, the party appeared fractured. Less than two years before the next elections, Rabin was perceived as a leader who had resorted to settling partisan accounts; the ministers fought among themselves, fearful of being ousted; the old bastions of Labor's power and funds were imploding.

The Labor-led government, halfway through its term in office, was explicitly associated with the peace process. Yet, over a year after its surprising and euphoric beginning, the process had failed to attract massive support. In a poll on the eve of the Nobel Peace Prize ceremony, only one-third thought Rabin and Peres should go to the ceremony; a majority favoring delaying the prizes until 'real peace' was achieved.[5]

Partisan troubles continued in early 1995, now coupled with a stalemate in the peace process. A terrorist attack on a soldiers' hitch-hiking station in January killed 21 and wounded over 60. The subsequent antigovernment protests were massive and angry. Polls continued to show declining support for Labor. *Time* magazine published a poll that not only put Rabin well behind Netanyahu, but indicated that Labor would win only 27 seats in the Knesset—a decrease of 40 per cent, and Labor's worst showing ever.

As relations within the government deteriorated and Labor institutions crumbled, even the party's Knesset faction began to disintegrate. Rabin had not made clear whether he would run again in 1996, and the constant speculations only weakened his position. Although Ramon stated that he would not run against Rabin, Peres did not formally bow out, and other ministers openly declared their intentions to challenge Rabin for the party leadership. With the Histadrut out of the party's hands, the infrastructure that it could lean on in times of trouble was gone. Moreover, Ramon ousted hundreds of loyal Labor activists from key positions, further aggravating the discord. Partisan cohesion was at such a low ebb that even the chairman of the coalition voted against the 1995 budget, tantamount to a vote of no-confidence. Rabin, in speaking of the party, began to use the term 'anarchy' frequently.

On the peace front, there seemed to have been little headway. The negotiations were hampered by terrorism, and the Israeli public did not feel that the process had enhanced individual security. In April, an attack in Gaza killed eight people. In July, a bus bombing in Tel-Aviv killed six and wounded over 30. The next month two buses were blown up in Jerusalem, killing four and wounding over 100. After each attack there were street demonstrations against terrorism and the Labor government. A vicious cycle emerged: the lack of progress in the peace process caused problems in the Labor Party, which generated further difficulties in the peace process.

Most problematic was the escalation of a rift within Labor that would eventually become a split. There were several 'hawks' in the party who had backed Rabin as long as the party and the peace process were doing well. However, when both seemed to break down, they began to voice their concerns. Particularly in regard to sensitive issues, such as a withdrawal from the Golan Heights, this group became a vocal opposition within the party.

Early in 1995, there appeared to be renewed progress on the Syrian front. In February, the Israeli and Syrian chiefs of staff met in Washington. The next month saw an agreement on a working program toward the formulation of a military annex to a future peace treaty. However, as in the past, progress quickly succumbed to Syrian backtracking. Nevertheless, whatever progress was made on the Syrian front raised fears among some in Labor of a repeat of what had happened with the PLO—that is, secret negotiations leading to an agreement. They worried that such a development would be presented as a fait accompli and would involve a withdrawal from the Golan.

By this time, several Labor MKs had formed a group known as the Golan lobby or the Third Way. Initially this group attracted much support in the party, and included government ministers and several of Rabin's close allies. However, when some members began to contemplate breaking away from the party, many key figures departed. The remaining core consisted of five Labor backbenchers, all identified with the party's hawkish pole and supportive of the Histadrut old guard.

This group of MKs opposed withdrawal from the Golan even if there was a possibility of peace with Syria. They proposed a bill that, if passed, would require a majority of 70 of the 120 MKs, or of at least 50 per cent of the registered voters in a national referendum, to ratify any peace treaty that would include a withdrawal from the Golan. Passage of this bill would indeed have blocked any possible peace treaty with Syria. When the defiant MKs decided to press ahead with their bill, the Labor Party found itself facing unattractive alternatives: if the MKs were allowed to raise their bill, it would probably pass with the help of the opposition; if they were not allowed to raise it, they would gain much publicity, while forcing the party to take a clear stand on the Golan and face the wrath of the populace, which largely opposed a withdrawal; if the party deflected the bill altogether, peace negotiations with Syria would be stalled. After several contentious meetings, all of the other Labor MKs, including the prime minister, voted to prohibit the five rebellious members from raising the bill. The eventual result was the Third Way's departure from the party, but the divorce process was very drawn out.

With the party split over the issue of a future peace treaty with Syria, the domestic arena again exploded. In March, allegations of financial misconduct in the Histadrut, and the illegal use of its facilities during the 1992 Labor primaries, filled the headlines. Labor could not reverse its tailspin in the polls, and several of its MKs began openly calling for Rabin's resignation. Although Ramon had been evicted from Labor when he ran against it in the Histadrut elections, the party, almost as a sign of desperation and an admission of defeat, now voted to readmit him.

As the party organs decayed, the split within Labor widened. In May, the Third Way began to debate whether it would run as a party in the next elections. In mid-June, the organization called for the dissolution of the Knesset and new elections, and continued to move toward a split from Labor.

When the Golan bill came to a vote, three Labor MKs voted with the opposition, but the result was a 59:59 draw and the bill was dropped.[6] However, the signal to Syria was that Rabin did not have a majority in the Knesset to ratify a peace treaty involving territorial concessions. The fissure within Labor thus made progress on the Syrian track virtually impossible.

Moreover, after the Knesset reconvened from its holiday recess, the three Labor MKs informed Rabin that they would not support the Interim Agreement with the Palestinians (Oslo 2) when it came up for a vote. The party's internal discord was about to jeopardize the entire peace process. Indeed, when the Interim Agreement was finalized and brought before the Knesset for ratification in early October 1995, two of the Labor MKs who had founded the Third Way voted with the opposition against the agreement. The agreement, however, passed by a margin of 61:59. Had the remaining Third Way member also voted against it, the entire peace process as well as the government might have collapsed. Later that month, the Third Way split from Labor, officially became a party, and declared that it would run in the Knesset elections one year away.

The following month, on 4 November 1995, a huge pro-peace rally was held in Tel-Aviv, the largest of its kind so far. The event was so important that both Rabin and Peres came to speak to the crowd, something they had avoided on past occasions. Rabin's impromptu speech clearly expressed his commitment to the peace process. But as the rally came to an end, three shots were fired that changed Israel, Israeli politics, the Labor Party, and the peace process forever.

In summary, the Labor Party and the peace process had a quasi-systemic relationship at least during 1993–95. That is, the partisan and peace developments were generally interrelated, events in one arena affecting the other. For example, unity within the party facilitated progress in the peace process, which in turn created a political dynamic that affected the entire political system in general, and solidified the relationship between the Labor Party and its leaders in particular. However, the fracturing of the party and difficulties in the peace process had reciprocal effects as well.

The six-month period between the assassination and the elections saw a significant change both in Labor's internal mechanics and in the peace process. Hence this period is discussed separately, later in the chapter. Attention is now focused on the situation within Labor during two particularly critical periods, the one leading up to the first Oslo agreement and the one preceding Rabin's assassination.

THE PARTY AND THE PLO: PRESSURE FROM ABOVE OR FROM BELOW?

The most important event for the Labor Party during its tenure of 1992–96 was the decision, in mid-1993, to recognize the PLO and begin negotiating a withdrawal from the territories captured in the 1967 Six Day War. During its campaign, Labor had not expressed any willingness to move in this direction and in fact had opposed it. The new decision was made by its leadership, particularly Rabin and Peres, without recourse to internal discussion or debate on the topic. The question is whether in this case the party leadership moved dangerously ahead of its parliamentary representatives or rode a wave of party support.

This decision, not surprisingly, was greeted with shock and horror

by the opposition and large segments of the public, which was unpre-
pared for the new initiative. Since the decision, there has been rather
stable support for the process by about 50 per cent of the public,
including the period since mid-1996 when Labor fell from power.
However, those favoring the agreement have never formed more
than a bare majority, and the division of the country into two equal-
sized and polarized groups endures.

Was the reaction within the Labor Party similar to that of the
public at large? Did the lack of intraparty discussions before this
decision reflect a strategic move by the leadership to create a fait
accompli, motivated by the lack of progress on any other front in the
peace process during the previous year? Was this an attempt at
political 'shock treatment', aimed at dislodging the party from its age-
old position on the Palestinian–Israeli conflict? Or, conversely, had
Labor already moved significantly in this direction, so that its
leadership's decision was a culmination of trends in the party?

Based on the available empirical data, the answers to these
questions point toward party cohesion behind the leadership. Labor
had sufficiently transformed its position on the Palestinian issue that
when the Oslo negotiations were made public, the shift encountered
little or no opposition within the party. Indeed, even those who were
expected to reject the shift failed to do so, and Labor as a whole fell
in line behind the new policy and supported its leadership.

Before the 1992 elections, when Labor formulated its platform, it
had already removed an article opposing the establishment of a
Palestinian state. Six months after assuming power, before there were
any indications of possible negotiations with Arafat—as opposed to
the ongoing talks with the Palestinian delegation in Washington,
following the Madrid formula—polls showed that Labor no longer
opposed direct negotiations with the PLO. In late December 1992,
Israel Radio surveyed the 44 Labor MKs on their position toward the
PLO. An overwhelming majority of 30 said they would support
negotiations with it.[7] Some of those opposed were clearly not part of
the anti-PLO group, but chose not to take such a public position at
that time. For example, Foreign Minister Peres was one of the 14 who
replied negatively. The results of this poll prompted several Labor
MKs to request a special party meeting that would take a decision
calling on the government to begin direct talks with the PLO; this
initiative stalled on a technicality.

The opposition's response to this poll showed just how significant
the shift in the Labor Party was. The chairman of the Likud Party

asserted that the poll showed that Labor had lied to the Israeli public during the election campaign when it opposed negotiations with the PLO. He declared, moreover, that if such a clear majority within Labor supported direct talks with the PLO, this constituted a vote of no-confidence in the prime minister, who still opposed such a move.

As rumors of the secret talks in Oslo between Israeli and PLO officials started to appear in the Israeli media, the Labor Party began to debate the issue. By July, when the issue was raised before the party Knesset caucus, the party showed even more cohesive support for negotiations, with only one MK objecting. There were disagreements on how and when to open such a channel, but even the party hawks no longer opposed such a policy in principle. Rabin now knew that if the secret talks with the PLO bore fruit, the party would not rebel. In other words, partisan politics helped open the door to a new departure in foreign policymaking.

If we ask what explains such partisan cohesion, despite the dramatic policy shift and the expected public opposition, the answer lies in the internal composition and evolution of the Labor Party. Rabin and Peres had each headed a 'camp' within the party since the mid-1970s. The Peres camp had been, and remained, the stronger. Rabin, traditionally more hawkish, never enjoyed massive support within the party. Even after his victory over Peres in the 1992 leadership contest, which largely reflected electoral considerations (Peres had failed four times to lead the party to electoral victory), the party organs—and particularly the central committee—were still controlled by Peres supporters. Rabin was cognizant of this, and often mentioned his lack of support in the party organs when addressing the central committee.

Although in the 1990s the Rabin camp was also known as the hawkish camp, its hawkish positions were not as strong as they appeared. Most of the Labor hawks were motivated by pragmatic considerations, not by principle. There was a hard core of true hawks, but they made up a small group that was very loyal to Rabin. Aside from this nucleus, there were powerful political figures who were perceived as hawkish because of their backing of Rabin in the party leadership contest. In reality, this group had supported Rabin because they thought he was the only person who could lead the party back to power, and their true positions were the opposite of hawkish.

The internal division within Labor was, therefore, between the larger Peres camp and the smaller Rabin camp. The Peres camp was particularly dovish, and supportive of any progress in the peace talks.

The Rabin camp, though relatively hawkish, did not in principle oppose concessions that would advance the peace process. Therefore, as soon as Peres and Rabin agreed that the time had come to recognize the PLO and negotiate directly with Arafat, the party coalesced behind the unified leadership. 'Everything we did together was accepted,' said Peres, 'this was the source of our authority.'[8] This sentiment was echoed by the director-general of Rabin's Office, who declared that 'Rabin and Peres knew that if they worked together, the party would fall in line.'[9] The Peres camp had already adopted dovish positions; the Rabin camp, despite its wavering, posed no objection once it became clear that Rabin supported the shift.

In summary, the Labor Party had begun to change its outlook toward the PLO before winning the 1992 elections, a trend that was only strengthened during its first year in office. Thus, the leadership's decision to recognize the PLO did not cause division in the party. On the contrary, the party gave its leaders a base of support that encouraged them to make such a decision. Since the hawkish group was not as strong or as principled as the media suggested, most of the party was happy to see Peres convert Rabin to a more dovish stand. Thus the party united behind the leadership's decision to begin direct talks with the PLO, without the need for a debate on the issue.[10] Such comprehensive partisan unity enabled the leadership to break with a decades-old foreign policy principle and embark on a strategic shift that had little public support before its implementation.

THE PARTY AND THE POLLS: UNWAVERING SUPPORT OR SECOND THOUGHTS?

Slightly over a year after the Oslo agreement was signed, after a euphoric period of accomplishments and progress, the drawbacks of the agreement started to become apparent, and the party grew concerned about the electoral ramifications.

In mid-1994, terrorism reappeared, and on a much larger scale than previously known. As the year drew to a close, the period of euphoria seemed to be in the distant past. By early 1995, after additional terrorist attacks, the lines had been drawn: the opposition took an extreme position; the public lost its sense of security and blamed the peace process; Rabin was personally attacked at every appearance he made; problems within Labor became serious; and even the president (a largely ceremonial position) asked that the peace process be reconsidered. Reports appeared in the media claiming that the turn of events had brought on second thoughts, that Rabin no longer supported the peace process with the Palestinians, that the government had worked itself into a difficult situation with no easy way out, and that with the national elections only a year away, all of this was generating partisan infighting.

By mid-1995, with the polls showing constantly declining support for Labor, party unity began to unravel. It was the opposition's propaganda, rather than the government's policies, that was winning the hearts and minds of the Israeli public, particularly now that the Likud infighting had been set aside and the entire right wing had united against the government's policies. Thus, the media now reported that Rabin had reached the conclusion that neither the public nor parts of his own party were willing to take the risks that the party leadership was willing to take.

Yet, despite a united opposition gaining public support, an indecisive and divided government, and all of the apparent military and electoral drawbacks of continuing the peace process, Rabin's support for it did not waver. It was his decision to move ahead despite the mounting terrorism that brought the groundswell of personal attacks. With Labor's fortunes declining, Rabin was deserted by many of his colleagues and left to fight alone.

Although subsequently Rabin did begin to have second thoughts, they were at the tactical rather than strategic level. He did not regret coming to terms with the PLO, but realized that the rise in terrorism was a problem he had failed to take into account. When the situation within his party became problematic, he allowed the peace process to slow down. In the hope that Arafat would be able to rein in the terrorists, he allowed phases stipulated in the DOP to be greatly extended and segments of the agreement to be reopened for debate.[11] Most of his meetings with Arafat at that time were devoted to the issue of restraining terrorism.

It was at the height of this period, when partisan conflicts seemed to be taking a toll on peacemaking, that Rabin was assassinated.

THE PARTY UNDER PERES:
THE RISE AND FALL OF THE PEACE PROCESS

Shortly after Rabin's funeral, Labor chose Peres as his successor, and Peres immediately formed a government. The partisan composition was similar to that of the outgoing one. This was the first minority government ever to be sworn in by the Knesset. The new prime minister had to make a primary decision about the timing of elections. He could call for new elections, or he could continue to govern for almost a full year, until the next elections were due. Peres chose the latter. In light of this, and because of the government's precarious nature, there was a proximate decision that had to be made as well: should the government move ahead decisively on the peace process, or should it slow down the negotiations so as to solidify its position? Peres decided to move full speed ahead. Indeed, the new Labor-led government pushed forward on both tracks: the redeployment in the territories stipulated by the Interim Agreement with the Palestinians was carried out, and the negotiations with the Syrians were accelerated. Peres was eager to show that Rabin's assassination had not stalled the peace process, particularly on the Palestinian track.[12]

The Syrian front, however, showed the greatest initial progress when direct Israeli–Syrian negotiations began at the Wye Plantation in Maryland. Yet the familiar Syrian tactic of creating progress and then quickly backtracking was repeated once again.[13]

By February 1996, Peres knew that he had done all he could. The Interim Agreement had been implemented as much as possible. The redeployment in Hebron, he believed, would inflame the country and dominate the election campaigns, putting Labor in a defensive position. Further movement on the Palestinian track would thus lead to the undermining of partisan unity and would have to wait until after the elections. The Syrian track had moved quickly, then stalled. There was not enough time to wait for Syria to come around and negotiate a full agreement before the next elections. Hence, Peres decided to call for early elections in May.

During his five months as prime minister, Peres had the loyal support of the entire Labor Party, now that the Third Way faction had split away. Ramon had returned and was made interior minister; Ehud Barak, the popular former chief of staff, was promoted to foreign minister; and the party closed ranks behind its leader. The Knesset, however, was difficult to deal with, since after the Third Way's departure the minority government and its outside supporters no longer commanded a majority. Although the coalition itself was stable, and the opposition had lost both public support and much of its fervor in the wake of the assassination, the domestic political forces needed for substantial progress with the Palestinians and the Syrians were lacking.

In other words, although the partisan arena did not present

obstacles to peacemaking, at that time the domestic political arena did. It was only at this point that interparty politics together with public opinion began to constrain foreign policy. Until then, despite the significant impediments posed by the domestic political arena, peacemaking had moved ahead at a brisk pace. During the Rabin period, from mid-1992 to late 1995, it was intraparty political dynamics that explained both the extent and the pace of peace-making better than the more general, domestic political arena.

Peres's decision not to hold elections immediately after the assassination and to keep the peace process moving was largely because of his perception of renewed partisan unity. However, a series of events exogenous to partisan politics—particularly involving the domestic political arena and terrorism—caused the Peres government to lose control of the peace process, despite Labor's renewed cohesiveness and the opposition's temporary retreat. The Israeli case, therefore, provides evidence that beyond the inter-national arena of peacemaking, if one wants to correctly assess the influence of domestic politics on foreign policymaking, one must take at least two levels of domestic politics into account—i.e., both interparty and intraparty.

CONCLUSION: THE PARTY AND THE PUBLIC

Numerous postmortems have sought to assess why Shimon Peres and the Labor Party lost the 1996 elections. The common thread of these analyses is the lack of contact between Labor and the public. Therefore, if we place the relationship between the Labor Party and the peace process in an analytical framework, the loss of the elections indicates the importance of a third factor, namely, the public. It is here that dynamic opinion representation can provide an interpretive model for our context, and help explain the impact of partisan politics on foreign policymaking in democratic societies.

Ideas about 'influence from below' play a large part in many studies of representative democracy. The relationship between public opinion and policymaking is presumed to be unidirectional, involv-ing public opinion's effect on policymakers. To most scholars, responsiveness—essentially, influence from below—is what democ-racy is all about. Public opinion is exogenous and omnipresent, and politicians must follow it, especially with daily polls providing continual plebiscites. Normative theory and empirical reality have thus converged to create a model in which pressure is exerted on politicians to conform with the 'known' and documented preferences of the public. Political leaders thus become delegates rather than trustees (or representatives).

Yet this literature reflects a preponderantly American focus. European scholars, on the other hand, acknowledge the possibility of opinion molding from above. Instead of being impelled by the public, elites can influence it by trying to sell it the policies they want to initiate. Instead of representative democracy being based on policies arising from the people, it can be based on accountability through elections, with specific policies working their way down from the elites.

In fact, despite the simplicity and applicability of dichotomous models in general, public policy is never either entirely mass-driven or elite-driven. Consequently, the interesting question for our context is one of degree. It is clear that the Labor leadership's decision to recognize the PLO took the country by surprise. Did this top-down model achieve its goal, then, in terms of opinion formation? That is, notwithstanding the progress in the peace process, was public opinion converted to the cause that Labor had initiated?

Regardless of extenuating events, the answer lies in the interaction between the party leadership and the mass electorate. Although representation from below might be more consonant with the original notion of direct democracy, representation from above should not be suspect in a country where existential decisions have to be made. Elite-driven opinion formation does not constitute a sinister model of representation: on the contrary, it has always been the prevalent mode of the cohesive, ideological, and disciplined Israeli political parties and their leadership. Moreover, in their efforts to devise policy initiatives, these parties have acted as the main intermediaries between politics and society, at times almost dominating this interaction.

The relationship between the voters and their elected officials after the Oslo agreement was, to say the least, static. Moreover, measures aimed at altering public opinion were few and far between. In terms of elite-driven opinion formation, there was virtually no dynamic interaction between Labor and the public. This lack of dialogue not only explains the electoral defeat, but may reflect an inherent defect of Israeli democracy.

Whether it is elite-driven or mass-driven, opinion convergence between policymakers and the public should, over time, be the way in which normative democracy works. Interaction should foster convergence. Such interaction can, indeed, mobilize the public to support the government's policy initiatives. Because of the lack of interaction between Labor and the public, the undecided were never mobilized behind the Rabin and Peres governments, resulting in a lack of legitimization among slightly more than half of a polarized polity.

In summary, partisan disintegration during the vital phases of the peace process harmed the political cohesion of the Labor Party, reduced the party's ability to interact with the people, and prevented a convergence of opinion on the peace process. Thus, partisan politics within Labor hampered the party's ability to sell the peace process to the people. Moreover, since only 14,729 additional votes—less than 0.5 per cent in an electorate of over three million—would have won the 1996 elections for Peres, one may assert that in the case of the Labor Party and the peace process, partisan politics played a paramount role. The result of this particular domestic factor was not just the defeat of Peres and Labor, but also a major setback in the peace process.

REFERENCES

Arian, A. and Michal, S. (eds), *The Elections in Israel 1996* (Albany, NY: State University of New York Press, 1999).

Blainey, G., *The Causes of War* (New York, NY: Free Press, 1973).

Husbands, J. L., 'Domestic Factors and De-Escalation Initiatives', in L. Kriesberg and S. J. Thorson (eds), *Timing the De-Escalation of International Conflicts* (Syracuse, NY: Syracuse University Press, 1991), pp. 97–116.

Inbar, E., *War and Peace in Israeli Politics: Labor Party Positions on National Security* (Boulder, CO: Lynne Rienner, 1991).

King, A., 'Modes of Executive–Legislative Relations: Great Britain, France, and West Germany', *Legislative Studies Quarterly*, 1 (1976).

Putnam, R. D., 'Diplomacy and Domestic Politics: Logic of Two-Level Games', *International Organization*, 42 (1988), pp. 427–60.

Stein, J. G., 'Domestic Politics and International Conflict Management', *International Security*, 12 (1988), pp. 203–11.

Tachau, F., 'The Knesset and the Peace Process', *Israel Affairs*, 2 (1995), pp. 142–55.

Wilkenfeld, J. (ed.), *Conflict Behavior and Linkage Politics* (New York, NY: David Mackay, 1973).

Acknowledgment

I am grateful to Shimon Peres, former prime minister and foreign minister of Israel; to Shimon Sheves, director-general of Prime Minister Rabin's Office; to Eitan Haber, head of Prime Minister Rabin's Bureau; and to Zeev Kirtchuk, parliamentary assistant to Prime Minister Rabin, for their time and cooperation. Support for this research was provided by the Leonard Davis Institute for International Relations of the Hebrew University of Jerusalem and by the Konrad Adenauer Foundation.

NOTES

1. This article does not deal with the Israeli–Jordanian peace process, largely because of its uniqueness in the overall Middle East peace process. That is, the negotiating phase was fairly brief and the peace treaty involved minimal territorial concessions by Israel.
2. Interview with Shimon Sheves, 10 August 1997.
3. Interview with Eitan Haber, 16 June 1997.
4. *Yediot Aharonot*, 6 December 1994.
5. Ma'ariv, 9 December 1994.
6. Likud and Labor each removed one MK from the vote, because of the hospitalization of one of the Likud MKs.
7. Kol Yisrael, 26 December 1992. For more data from surveys of the Knesset members on issues relating to the peace process, see Tachau (1995).
8. Interview with Shimon Peres, 24 July 1997.
9. Interview with Shimon Sheves, 10 August 1997.
10. For a similar movement toward the left by the Labor Party in the 1980s, and an in-depth analysis of party doves vs. hawks, see Inbar (1991).
11. Interview with Eitan Haber, 16 June 1997.
12. Interview with Shimon Peres, 24 July 1997.
13. According to Peres, 'That stupid, stupid man Assad, he moved too slow. He told me that he wanted to finalize the agreement before the elections. I replied that I was ready to do so, but that we had to raise the level of the negotiations to our rank. Assad said that he was willing to meet with me, but continuously refused to set a date. That was typical.' Interview with Shimon Peres, 24 July 1997.

6 The Israeli Arabs and Israeli Foreign Policy: Minority Participation in Ethnonational Politics

HILLEL FRISCH

According to at least one prominent scholar, the Arabs in Israel suffer from double peripheralization or marginalization: they are marginal both in Israeli public affairs and in Palestinian politics.[1] Consider, then, the following examples where Israeli Palestinians played an important role in Israeli foreign policy.

In April 1996, Prime Minister Shimon Peres called off the Grapes of Wrath operation in Lebanon. Twenty-four hours earlier, Arab Member of Knesset Abdul al-Wahhab Darawshe, leader of the Arab Democratic Party (ADP), had called on Arab citizens of Israel to 'turn in a blank ballot' in the upcoming prime ministerial election between Peres and Binyamin Netanyahu if the military campaign continued. The loss of the Israeli Arab vote, accounting for 18 per cent of Israel's population (a lower percentage of the potential electorate), would have ruined Peres' five chances in the May elections. It later turned out that more than 94 per cent of the Israeli Arab vote proved insufficient to ensure Peres's victory.[2]

In the 1992 elections, the United Arab List (headed by Darawshe and the ADP) and the Democratic Front for Peace and Equality (DFPE) were able to secure only five seats in the Knesset. Although, out of a 120-seat parliament, this is not very many, the situation of coalition politics made the Arab parties an important part of any blocking majority. Because of this blocking majority, Labor failed to pass a bill restricting PLO activities in Jerusalem.[3]

In 1994, Israeli Arab leaders acted as unofficial envoys for the government. Darawshe led the first Israeli delegation ever to Syria, officially to extend his condolences to President Hafez Assad on his son's recent death, but mainly to revive the dying peace talks. The visit was approved by both Prime Minister Rabin and the Interior Ministry. A senior official in the Prime Minister's Office cautiously supported the visit, saying that it had 'something in it that's encouraging'.[4] Although Darawshe was castigated for the trip by Israeli hardliners, he could point to the fact that he concurred with the prime minister's position on the Golan Heights.[5]

These examples seem to contradict the conventional wisdom about the Israeli Arabs' status in Israeli society. How can a minority that identifies itself as both Arab and Palestinian, that is, as being of the same nationality and culture as a national movement and a wider pan-Arab nation that are actually or potentially hostile to the Jewish state, and that holds positions almost diametrically opposed to the Jewish majority, exert such influence? In attempting to explain this riddle, this chapter considers the literature on the influence of ethnic and diaspora groups on foreign policy. It then describes the special situation of the Israeli Arabs; compares Arab and Jewish perceptions of the Grapes and Wrath operation; and points to some key similarities between the strategies employed by African Americans and by the Israeli Arabs in exerting influence over foreign policy.

ETHNIC GROUPS AND FOREIGN POLICY

Broadly speaking, there are two categories of ethnic involvement in the foreign policy of states: where ethnic groups, typically diaspora groups, exert a benign influence on the state's foreign policy; and where ethnic groups are potentially secessionist or are linked to potentially or actually irredentist states, which only intensifies opposition to the secessionist movement and its external supporters.

Diaspora Groups

A review of the literature on the relationship between modern diaspora groups—defined as 'ethnic minority groups of migrant origins residing and acting in host countries but maintaining strong sentimental and material links with their countries of origin—their homelands'[6]—and foreign policy reveals the following characteristics.

Diaspora groups are most effective in democracies.[7] To grasp the technical means by which diasporas in democracies influence foreign policy, one need look no further than the example of the pro-Israel lobby of American Jews.[8] The Israel lobby is widely regarded as the most effective and influential diaspora lobby in the United States. There are three main means by which Jewish Americans and other diaspora groups exert foreign policy influence. The first is by presenting one's case in terms of the state's national interests and/or principles. Jewish Americans lobby for military, economic, and diplomatic support for Israel on the basis that Israel is an important and loyal strategic ally, is the only democracy in the Middle East, and has been a refuge for Holocaust survivors. The second is by dint of voting power—which for Jewish Americans is far greater than their percentage of the general population. Jewish Americans have an average turnout of 90 per cent in presidential elections, well above the paltry 50 per cent for the general American electorate. Jewish Americans also are concentrated in large urban areas and large states. The third means is financial support for preferred candidates. Jewish Americans earn much more on average than the general American population, and have effective Political Action Committees. Usually, however, resourcefulness and dedication can compensate for lack of financial strength.[9] Thus, advocacy, electoral significance, and political donations or activism form the basis for effective lobbying by diaspora groups.

Most diasporas maintain an affinity for their homeland even if removed by several generations.[10] 'There are copious examples of this, including Greek, Jewish, African, Polish, Armenian, and Serbian American diasporas.'[11] This, of course, depends on what stage of assimilation the diaspora is in. Peleg suggests that diasporas become less cohesive as they gain upward socioeconomic mobility.[12] Such assimilation lowers both the commitment to the country of origin and the ethnic community's ability to mobilize as it becomes less cohesive. Coufoudakis, in his study of the Greek American lobby, suggests a linear relationship between influence and cohesion.[13]

In aid of their homeland, diasporas will, if necessary, mobilize in defiance of their government's view of the national interest. However, most ethnic-group lobbies will present their case in terms of their own interpretation of national interests and/or principles. In 1974, Greek American lobbying efforts managed to compel Congress to impose an arms embargo on Turkey to punish it for its invasion of Cyprus. The embargo damaged relations with an important strategic ally, while causing no change in its actions. The embargo clearly ran counter to America's national interests, but the Greek lobby argued that Turkey's aggression violated the national principles of the rule of law and of using force only as a last resort.[14]

Diasporas that concur with the government's view of national interests are influential regardless of societal status. An example is the Cuban American lobby. Although Cuban Americans have not attained an income or professional level anywhere near that of the white majority, they nevertheless exert significant electoral influence because they support the US national interest of undermining Fidel Castro.[15] However, the autonomy of the foreign-policy establishment is also an important variable. Greek Australians, for example, have a greater impact on their host country's foreign policy than do Greek Americans on theirs, in part because the Australian foreign-policy establishment is more autonomous—not only professionally, but also in terms of commitment to policy goals regarded as vital to the national interest.[16]

Diasporas often exert influence in foreign policy as both a means and an end.[17] According to Shain, 'many ethnic elites have discovered that by focusing on political causes in their homelands they are better positioned to mobilize their community for domestic empowerment'.[18]

Even ethnic groups previously excluded from affecting foreign policy can rapidly gain influence by presenting their case in terms of the national interest.[19] As will be discussed in greater detail later in this chapter, African Americans are a good example. During the 1960s, when Black Power separatists called Christianity a slave religion and advocated radical Third World ideologies contrary to national interests, they were ignored. However, beginning in the 1970s, the National Association for the Advancement of Colored People denounced Black Power and embarked on a more moderate course. Since the mid-1980s, African Americans 'have emerged as one of the strongest voices on US policy toward Africa and the Caribbean'.[20] In 1986, the efforts of TransAfrica, a moderate black lobby organization, were critical in Congress's passing of the Comprehensive Anti-Apartheid Act, despite the objections of President Reagan. Most recently, TransAfrica's lobbying may have been decisive in President Clinton's decision to invade Haiti in 1994.[21] An ethnic group's influence is highest when its involvement in foreign policy is considered to some extent legitimate by the public at large because the ethnic group is perceived as exporting the country's ideals.[22]

Diasporas support their homelands against historical enemies; if there is no imminent external threat, they will act to oppose oppressive regimes in their homelands. So long as the white-supremacist Rhodesian and South African governments were in power, African American leaders largely ignored the excesses of African dictatorships. In 1977, black Congressman Charles Diggs opposed any discussion of Ugandan dictator Idi Amin's brutal regime on the House floor because it might 'divert public attention from human rights conditions in South Africa'.[23] Kilson concludes that for the African American intelligentsia, 'the fact of black rule always preempted the quality of black rule'. The statement applies to other ethnic groups as well—that is, so long as there are external threats.

Secessionist or Irredentist Tendencies

In contrast to diasporas, ethnic minorities linked to potentially or actually irredentist or secessionist states are likely to have a negative impact on the state's foreign policy. Hungarians in Romania and Slovakia, by their very existence, aggravate rather than attenuate interstate frictions. The same can be said of Russian groups in the former Soviet republics.

Since secessionist ethnic groups seek exclusion from the current state, they do not participate in a benign manner in their host state's politics. Instead, they seek ways to damage or even destroy their current state by poisoning its relations with its neighbors and accepting aid from its antagonists. Turkey's Kurds, for example, benefited from conflict between Turkey and other states. In 1925, Sheikh Said's Kurdish rebel movement profited from Turkish tensions with Britain and accepted aid from the latter. The Kurdish movement, however, faltered when Turkey and Iran cooperated in combating the rebels in 1930.[24] More recently, the Kurdish Workers Party (PKK) accepted aid from Turkey's traditional regional competitors, Syria, Iran, Iraq, and Armenia, and especially lucrative assistance from Greece.[25]

The PKK, through its rhetoric and resort to violence, has harmed Turkey in ways that a benign ethnic lobby would regard as irrational. According to Olson, the Kurds have disrupted Turkish efforts to join the European Union.[26] This would seem illogical, even from the PKK's standpoint, since membership in the EU would make Turkey more vulnerable to European demands for increased civil rights and equality. The Kurds have also exacerbated internal Turkish divisions between Sunnis and Alevis, hindering processes of democratization and economic liberalization.[27] Normally, a disenfranchised ethnic minority would enthusiastically accept greater opportunities for political and economic empowerment. But Turkey's Kurds are a hostile secessionist minority, seeking independence by undermining the state that controls their homeland.

THE ISRAELI ARABS AND THE DIASPORA MODEL

The Israeli Arabs do not exhibit the behavioral traits of the Kurds or of any other secessionist ethnic group. The Israeli Arabs do not try to push Israel into war with its neighbors. On the contrary, the Arab political parties consistently call for withdrawal from Lebanon and peaceful relations with Syria (though it may be argued that that is because Israel would defeat Syria in a full-scale conventional war). The Arab parties also are ardent supporters of the peace process; and a successful arrangement with the Palestinians would mean fewer Israeli soldiers engaged in low-intensity conflict. With enhanced economic liberalization and free trade with Arab states, the Israeli Arabs would of course be better off materially. The most glaring difference between the Kurds and the Israeli Arabs is the relative lack of violence among the latter, such violence being typical of secessionist minorities.

Yet the relationship between the Israeli Arabs and the state of Israel hardly conforms to the diaspora model, for at least two reasons: the Israeli Arabs do not identify with the state; and the state as a Jewish state is hardly neutral to ethnicity, as the following analysis of the identity of the Arab population and the ethnorepublican nature of the state suggests.

The Nature of the Israeli Arab Community

In a 1974/75 survey of Israeli Arabs, only 14 per cent agreed that it was suitable for them to call themselves 'Israelis'.[28] In a 1980 survey, only 16.2 per cent of Israeli Jews believed that the Israeli Arabs were loyal to Israel, whereas 47 per cent of Israeli Arabs believed this. A 1984 survey found that an overwhelming 75 per cent of Israeli Arabs identified themselves as 'Palestinian Arab', 'Palestinian', or 'Arab' and only 24 per cent as 'Israeli Arab' or 'Israeli Palestinian'.[29]

In 1995, the author of a study consisting of an opinion survey of Israeli Arabs' self-identity drew some alarming conclusions:

[the] dominant factor in Israeli Arabs' identity is nationalism ... Whenever they cross into Jewish territory they imagine that they will be caught up in a humiliating situation. After leaving Jewish territory with its connotations of alienation and prejudice, their return to Israeli-Arab territory inspires them with calm and 'at homeness', all of which awakens a sense of territoriality.[30]

These findings suggest that the Israeli Arabs would not tend to exert a benign influence over Israeli foreign policy.

Indeed, their views on foreign policy diverge widely from those of the Jewish majority. In a poll on foreign policy conducted just before the May 1996 elections, 92 per cent of Israeli Arabs responded affirmatively, and only 2 per cent negatively, to the question whether 'for a peace agreement with the Palestinians is it worthwhile to give up settlements'; by contrast, 50 per cent of Jews responded negatively and 31 per cent affirmatively. The two groups were even more polarized regarding withdrawal from all of the Golan Heights: 85 per cent of Israeli Arabs were in favor compared with only 11 per cent of Jews.[31] One would expect intuitively, then, that as both Arabs and Palestinians, the Israeli Arabs would be unable to influence policy in the Jewish state.

Minority Influence in an Ethnorepublic

The second problem lies in the inherent institutional differences between pluralistic democracies such as the United States on the one hand and Israel's ethnorepublicanism on the other. Peled argues that Israel is a republic in which there are two types of citizenship: republican citizenship, enjoyed by Jewish citizens who belong to the moral community that the state must promote, and liberal-civic citizenship, enjoyed by all citizens, including Arabs, and entailing full human and civil rights.[32]

Peled claims that this reality, in which Jews advance the goals of the moral collective and Arabs advance their welfare as individuals, is acceptable to the liberal ethos—particularly with the growing salience of communitarianism over the past 20 years. He concedes, however, that most communitarians will place the public good before civil rights only where belonging to the community is voluntary in the first place. Communitarians debate libertarians over the right to curtail civil rights in order to promote the goals of the moral community. Israel, therefore, is not a republican state but an ethno-republican one.

Peled's article implies that foreign policy in an ethnorepublic (and perhaps even in liberal-democratic states) is not subsumed under civil or human rights. Therefore, the foreign-policy establishment is under little constraint to take into consideration citizens' views in proportion to their numbers or by any other criterion of equality. Empirically and contextually, foreign policy in the Israeli ethno-republic is regarded by the dominant Jewish community as republican. This attitude is strengthened by the fact that the minority community views foreign policy in ethnorepublican terms that are congruent with the standpoint of the 'enemy side'; the obvious conclusion is that so long as Israel is an ethnorepublican state, the Israeli Arabs will be marginal to foreign policy and the peace process. In other words, Israel might be a democracy, but its ethnorepublican nature prevents the Israeli Arabs from exerting an influence over its foreign policy. Thus, the mystery of their influence remains.

The differences in attitudes between Arab and Jewish citizens of Israel regarding foreign-policy issues are strikingly demonstrated by the divergent press analyses of Israel's Grapes of Wrath offensive of April 1996, particularly after the bombing of Kafar Kanna. The operation began on 10 April in response to escalating Hizbollah rocket attacks on northern Israel, and involved increasing Israeli troop levels in its occupied security zone in southern Lebanon, as well as heavy retaliatory bombardment of Hizbollah. The Israeli army had the capability to rapidly return accurate fire against areas from which Hizbollah had launched rockets. Using this to its advantage, Hizbollah launched rockets from the vicinity of the United Nations refugee camp in Kafar Kanna. The Israeli army returned fire and its artillery shells killed over 100 Lebanese civilians, mostly women and children.[33] The result was international and domestic outrage, ultimately leading to the cessation of the Grapes of Wrath operation.

Newspaper reactions from Israel's Arabic and Hebrew press, respectively, will now be compared. Newspapers work according to commercial considerations, and therefore more accurately express the real attitudes of the respective groups than do leaders playing the game of politics. A content analysis of the Hebrew newspaper *Ha'aretz*, and of the most widely read Arabic newspaper, the biweekly *Al-Sinara*, was conducted. The actual behavior of the Israeli Arab establishment and general population is also referred to.

ARAB AND JEWISH PERCEPTIONS AND THE GRAPES OF WRATH
OPERATION

Arab Perceptions

Up to the incident at Kafar Kanna, there was a pronounced difference between the political behavior of the Arab elite and the thrust of coverage in the Israeli Arab press. At first, the intervention in Lebanon did not precipitate either massive or violent protest. On the contrary, in a meeting with Peres on 15 April, the Monitoring Committee of Arab Affairs, the Israeli Arab sector's highest body, had agreed to end the protest campaign it had called for two days earlier.[34]

However, the tone set by the Israeli Arab press was more virulent, and the headlines of *Al-Ittihad*, the official newspaper of the New Communist List, were the most so. On 17 April, two days before the Kafar Kanna incident, its front-page headline read: 'Protest Demonstration in Condemnation of the Aggression on Lebanon and the Blockade on Palestine Will Take Place in Nazareth Today', with a subhead—'The Delegation of the Monitoring Committee is Stopping its Protest Activities!'—that castigated the placatory stance taken by that body. Another subhead castigating Ibrahim Nimr Husayn, the veteran mayor of Shfaram, head of the Committee, and most noted pro-Labor public figure in the Arab sector, suggested that the Committee's stance was due in no small measure to electoral politics. The tragedy, once it had occurred, was described as 'the Peres massacres in Lebanon'.

Although the headlines in the more commercial and popular *Al-Sinara* were more subdued, the tone of the columnists was no less vitriolic than the headlines of the Communist newspaper. In a column called 'Grapes of Wrath: Goals and Lessons', Dr Adnan Bakariyya wrote:

> The devastating war that the Labor government is waging against the Lebanese people has removed the last disguise from the face of the aggressive rulers of Israel and exposed the intentions of the Labor government, which has attempted through the shedding of blood and the lopping off of parts of Lebanon to increase its chances in the parliamentary elections by demonstrating its boldness and military capability to the Israeli right.

What concerns us as members of mankind and citizens of the state of Israel is the perceived need to bring an end to bloodshed both of Lebanese and Israelis. We cry out to the Israeli government and to its leader Shimon Peres to stop the massacre ... We have to translate the destructive 'Grapes of Wrath' on the heads of the innocent Lebanese and Palestinians into blank ballots in Shimon Peres's voting booth. The nations of the world, which stood up to the Iraqi occupation of Kuwait, must apply the same criteria of international justice, stand up to the Israeli invasion of Lebanon and force the Israeli war machine to withdraw from southern Lebanon ... for that is the only thing that can ensure the return of stability and security to the area ...

It is our right to ask the Arab states why they do not have the courage to call for a conference to condemn Israeli terrorism against the Lebanese and Palestinian peoples.

We have already warned of exploiting the recent international conference on fighting terrorism to help achieve American–Israeli regional gains, to accord the government of Israel the green light to engage in an operation to contain the Syrian regime, to show the latter to be incapable in time of war as well as in more settled times and thus force Syria to bow before the Israeli understanding of peace.[35]

It is clear that the writer does not distance himself from mainstream Arab positions. His reference to Israeli citizenship is not neutral, but must be perceived as a weapon to achieve goals that are common in the Arab world. Although he writes of stopping Israeli as well as Lebanese bloodshed, he makes no attempt to accept even a dovish Israeli position that would equate the Syrian presence in Lebanon with the Israeli presence there.

Another article by Walid al-Amary entitled 'Let Shimon Schwartzkopf Fall' is no less radical:

Shimon Schwartzkopf is identical with Shimon Peres, the Israeli prime minister and defense minister, who appeared in the first day of the Grapes of Wrath war shining amid his generals as they explained to him how their smart bombs wipe out Lebanese citizens—the situation of these Lebanese citizens being the same as all the rest of the Arab citizens wherever they may be. They are guinea pigs on which the smart-bomb arsenal is tested in the world. This was the very same role as that played by the Iraqis before them. If he who fires off a bomb that emanates from technological leftovers from the Second World War on a country that occupies his own is described as a terrorist then how should one describe someone who fires rockets and cluster bombs on the people he occupies, drives them away and destroys their homes and infrastructure in their own land?...

He ends with a call not to vote for Peres:

If Peres for two percent of the undecided in Israel is willing to strike at eighteen percent of the potential votes—the percentage of Arab citizens in the state—then we must respond by saying that if to placate two percent of the Jewish swing vote, he placed a siege on the Palestinian people in its land and waged a mad war against Lebanon, why should we remain complacent in the face of this hatred toward us and our role, which they intentionally disregard not merely after the elections but this time around with unadulterated cruelty even before them.

The third columnist to appear in the newspaper that day, Sahir Abu 'Aqsa, identified most with Syria, Israel's major antagonist. In an article called 'Nighttime in Beirut', she leaves no doubt as to who is responsible for the suffering in that city:

The blackout will last for a long time in Beirut after the Israeli rocket attack on the central electric grid ... until the grid is replaced there will be a long blackout ... A second dark night will follow in which Lebanon will be involved in a political plot whose aim is to lead Syria and Lebanon into the hopeless Oslo accords ...

But [Peres] and others like him should know that what was imposed by force and by military stealth will not prevail ... The situation in which states in the area must live under America's and Israel's wing will not last, because the world order in which America acts alone and does as it likes, without opposition, will not continue ... revolutionary movements and other forces will reappear, will be born and multiply ... they will change the balance of forces, at which time Israel will not be able to impose its night on Beirut or on anyone else.

Sahir Abu 'Aqsa expresses the radical millennial outlook that characterized the Palestinian left in the late 1960s and early 1970s. The passage could have been written in Beirut, Damascus, or Baghdad. None of the three writers quoted, from the Israeli perspective at least, attempted to assess the tragic episode in light of the larger regional context or the factors that precipitated the campaign in the first place.

After the Kafar Kanna incident the difference between the tone of the press and the passive political behavior of Israeli Arabs during the first ten days of the campaign vanished. On the day following the incident eight Arabs were detained for throwing rocks at policemen in Nazareth, demonstrations and rallies took place in dozens of Arab villages, and the Monitoring Committee succeeded in imposing a general strike after it had declared two days of public mourning.[36] Member of Knesset Darawshe, the head of the Arab Democratic Party, issued an ultimatum to Peres that he would call on the Arab electorate to cast blank ballots in the coming elections unless Peres stopped the campaign within 24 hours.[37]

Jewish Perceptions

The difference between these commentaries on the Kafar Kanna incident and those in the Hebrew press is striking. In contrast to the ethnically and emotionally charged criticism of the Arab press, Zeev Schiff's article 'Israel is Losing Time' is a technocratic cost–benefit analysis of the Lebanese incursion:

> the government does not have unlimited time to continue the operation. Once again it is proved that the time allotted to war is severely limited, especially regarding small countries. The surprise came in the form of two massive attacks on civilians. The operational explanation is that Hizbollah men fired mortar shells and Katyusha rockets ... This is what happened in Nabatiyya.
>
> The possible answer is ostensibly that this was a quick re-action to the sources of fire—but from a humanitarian and political standpoint there is sure to be damage to Israel. This is happening to a certain degree because Hizbollah fires intentionally from populated areas and from positions close to UN positions, but the damage to Israel's image—especially in the Arab world—is unavoidable ... The area of Kafar Kanna has long been 'contaminated' ...

Even when opprobrium is expressed it is still embedded in raison d'etat, as in Aluf Ben's 'Peres is Placing His Hopes on the Americans':

The incident in Kanna will be registered as a historical signpost in the Arab–Israeli conflict along with Dir Yassin, Kafr Qassim, and Sabra and Shatilla. The incident lead to the breaking of the blockade around Iran and now the ministers of France and Italy have gone to meet with Iranian representatives.[38]

Israeli Jewish commentators took for granted the preeminence of Israel's national security interests and weighed the pros and cons of Israeli intervention in that light, even in the most compromising moral situations. They considered foreign policy to be republican beyond any shadow of a doubt. The Palestinians do as well, except that it is a republican devotion to the other side. The Palestinian commentators are similar to the Jewish commentators in placing politics before moral anguish (though the former no doubt felt and expressed it to a greater degree), but the Palestinians did so in defending the Arab vision of a regional order in which Arabs are basically victims of American–Israeli hegemony. One should note that the Arab and Jewish newspapers in which these articles appeared are regarded as moderate relative to other newspapers. This is particularly so of *Ha'aretz*, which is considered distinctly dovish.

It is clear, then, that regarding the Grapes of Wrath campaign at least, Israeli Arabs did not attempt to make Arabs over the borders more understanding or sensitive toward Israeli perceptions or justifications for the campaign. It seems that Israeli Arabs identified not only with the victims but with the political goals of Syria and Syrian-dominated Lebanon. There certainly is no evidence, then, of the 'reverse influence' characteristic of diaspora groups. On the contrary, there is more identification with the enemy states than with the civic state in which they are citizens. This identification is on the level of ideas rather than of political behavior, and thus characterizes journalists rather than Palestinian politicians operating in the Israeli political arena.

COMPARISON OF AFRICAN AMERICANS WITH ISRAELI ARABS

Because of both the position of the Israeli Arab minority in the context of the wider conflict and the nature of the Jewish state, the literature on diaspora-group influence on foreign policy can be of little help in unraveling the mystery of Israeli Arab influence on Israeli foreign policy. There is, however, one useful point of comparison: the behavior of African Americans and of Israeli Arabs. After all, there are many similarities. African Americans constitute 12 per cent of the US population; Israeli Arabs, 18 per cent of the Israeli population. African Americans (as opposed to Greek, Jewish, Armenian Americans, etc.) attribute their historical hardships to the behavior of the majority population in the host state. Thus, African Americans often cite slavery and subsequent civil rights restrictions; Israeli Arabs cite the destruction of at least 300 Arab villages in 1948 and the Jewish military rule until 1966.[39] Both groups currently cite economic inequalities vis-à-vis their respective majority populations. Like African Americans, Israeli Arabs have achieved greater social mobility and a higher standard of living over the past several decades.[40]

The history of the African American foreign policy lobby is one where an ethnic/racial minority changed from powerless outsiders to influential insiders. After the American Civil War, the African American intelligentsia looked to American Jews as an example of strength in the face of overt discrimination. They looked, moreover, to Africa as the Jews looked to Palestine for a possible haven and for cultural, ideological, and emotional support for their identity as African Americans. Still experiencing racial repression, during the 1920s and 1930s black leaders advocated a more separatist approach, as attested by the popularity of the Garvey movement to resettle blacks in Africa.[41]

In the immediate post-World War II era, black leaders increasingly radicalized. After having loyally served America in the war, blacks expected desegregation and enhanced guarantees of civil rights. When this was not forthcoming, black leaders took an increasingly confrontational approach in both the domestic and foreign realms. Malcolm X founded the Nation of Islam, called on blacks to 'look to Africa' rather than America, and harshly criticized the colonialism of America's closest allies.[42] His views were roundly rejected by the foreign-policy establishment, both because of his malevolent attitude toward America and because he supported Communist revolutionary groups in Africa. During this period even the more moderate black leaders radicalized. In the 1930s, W. E. B. DuBois and Adam Clayton Powell founded the Council on African Affairs. But as Cold War tensions mounted in the 1950s, the Council, with its leftist messages, came to an abrupt end. Thus, black leaders remained outside of the foreign-policy establishment and had little influence.[43]

After the turmoil of the 1960s civil rights movement, black leaders began to work within the system and moderate their rhetoric. In 1974, Martin Weil best articulated this new strategy when he declared that:

> to be successful, a black movement for reform of American policy toward Africa must be perceived as a vehicle for exporting *American* ideals ... Blacks as blacks may identify with Africa, but it is only as Americans that they can change United States policy in Africa. If Afro-Americans ever gain leverage in foreign policy, it will be those black politicians who are most successful *within* the system who will do so—those who can command the respect of their black constituents and reassure white America at the same time.[44]

As a result of this strategy, African American influence within the system increased dramatically. During the 1970s, 15 African American congressmen were elected, and Representative Diggs became chairman of the House Subcommittee on African Affairs.[45] African Americans were appointed to diplomatic posts, including the ambassadorships to Senegal, Uganda, and Ghana.[46] In 1978, the TransAfrica organization was founded, and in its first year it successfully lobbied to maintain sanctions against South Africa. By the 1980s, an African American foreign-policy elite of government officials, lobbyists, financial professionals, and academics was solidifying.[47]

African American lobbyists have achieved their greatest successes during the 1980s and 1990s.[48] In 1986, as noted earlier, TransAfrica successfully campaigned for sanctions on South Africa against the views of President Reagan, and it did so by arguing its case in terms of American ideals;[49] in 1994, TransAfrica was probably instrumental in Clinton's decision to invade Haiti. Further, as black rule triumphed in South Africa, TransAfrica turned its focus to the brutality of Nigeria's military dictatorship.[50]

In keeping with the above-noted fifth characteristic of the relationships between diaspora groups and foreign policy, for African Americans foreign policy was both a means and an end. In 1991, African American leaders met with representatives of African states to discuss joint economic ventures and increased African American investment.[51] According to Shain, the African American lobby's new status has 'strengthened the bond between mainstream blacks and whites'.[52]

Thus, the experience of African American political groups suggests that to successfully influence Israeli foreign policy, Israeli Arab political leaders would benefit from following the African American model of moderation in the presentation of policy goals. The question is whether Israeli Arab politicians, in contrast to Israeli Arab journalists, have changed not so much their foreign policy goals as much as the way they are presented.

ISRAELI ARAB POLITICAL LEADERS ADDRESS THE ISRAELI NATIONAL INTEREST

An analysis of remarks made by the leaders of the two Arab parties, Abdul al-Wahhab Darawshe of the DAP and Hashem Mahamid of the DFPE, suggests that this is indeed what happened, again in sharp contrast to Israeli Arab journalists.

On 7 February 1991, Mahamid, along with other prominent leftists, Arab and Jewish, presented a petition on the Gulf War at a Jerusalem press conference. Although the petition criticized the US-led coalition's offensive against Iraq, it also resolutely condemned the Iraqi missile attacks on Israel. Indeed, Saddam Hussein found no support among Israeli Arabs.[53]

On 5 May 1992, Darawshe described Israel's current ground offensive in southern Lebanon as a 'dismal failure'—not because the attack was imperialist or Zionist, but because it failed to stop Hizbollah's Katyusha rocket attacks. Darawshe also expressed concern about the number of IDF casualties.[54]

On 8 May 1992, Darawshe led a DAP delegation to meet senior Egyptian officials with the aim of obtaining Egypt's aid in ending the Arab economic boycott of Israel. Foreign Minister Peres gave the trip de facto legitimacy by asking Darawshe to convey a message to the Egyptians.

On 4 August 1992, Darawshe met with PLO leader Yassir Arafat (whom the Israeli government then still regarded as a terrorist), in clear defiance of the government's view of the national interest. However, he explained that by 'meeting with the PLO leaders, I served the interests of both peoples—Israeli and Palestinian'.[55]

On 16 October 1992, in what may seem today a visionary move, Darawshe and four other DAP officials met with Arafat in Tunis, despite the Israeli ban on such meetings. Although he violated Israeli law, Darawshe's remarks before the meeting were presented from an Israeli point of view:

I believe a visit to [the PLO headquarters in] Tunis by Israeli MKs gives legitimization to Israel in the Arab world, and hopefully might legitimize the PLO in the eyes of Israelis ... [O]ur visit is intended to strengthen and support the moderate mainstream in the PLO, led by chairman Arafat, which is facing opposition from the rejectionists ... We firmly believe in the peace process and in achieving solutions through negotiation, and that meetings between Israelis and the Palestinian leadership can help support the moderates.[56]

In March–April 1993, in response to a wave of murders and violence in the West Bank and Gaza, Darawshe pleaded for calm, and offered a cease-fire plan with the announced intention of facilitating the peace process. His tone was conciliatory:

I believe leaders on both sides are looking for an opening that will help promote the peace process ... A continuation of the present situation will only breed more hatred and violence and serve to strengthen the extremists on both sides. This initiative contains both achievements and concessions for Israel and the Palestinians and I'm hopeful it will be accepted.[57]

On 11 August 1993, in a meeting with Israeli President Ezer Weizman, Darawshe told him: 'You are our president too. We hope you will help to achieve peace and also represent our interests.'[58]

On 24 November 1993, Darawshe demanded a ministership in Rabin's government: 'The [Israeli] Arab public is fed up with not having a say in the decision-making process. We cannot continue being disdained and regarded as only good enough to support the government from the outside.'[59]

On 28 November 1993, when it appeared that Rabin was not going to include Darawshe in his cabinet, Darawshe did not react vengefully. Labor and its left-wing partner Meretz only had 56 of the 120 Knesset seats; the two Arab parties accounted for the critical five seats that Rabin needed to sustain his government. Darawshe said he would not act to bring down Rabin's government and 'endanger the peace process'.[60]

In August 1994, when Darawshe traveled in a peace delegation to Iraq, he again explained his actions in terms of national interests, despite the enmity between Israel and Iraq: 'Iraq has a very important position as a strong country in the area ... so I believe Israel must find ways to talk with Iraq. And I think it's an Israeli interest, an Iraqi interest, and an interest for any peace lovers.'[61]

In October 1994, Mahamid denounced the recent bus bombing in Tel-Aviv. 'This act cannot be forgiven', he said, but expressed hope that the peace process would not be disrupted because that would serve the interests of the terrorists.[62]

In January 1995, Mahamid angrily denied that the PLO was influencing the Israeli Arab electorate. He said that he agreed with the PLO's goal of Palestinian self-determination, but that 'Even if the PLO were to make such a request [to vote for a particular party], I don't believe it would be answered automatically. Not every demand of the PLO is holy in our eyes. We decide in accordance with our own interests as Israeli citizens.'[63]

In May 1995, Darawshe was incredulous in responding to allegations that Arafat's pressure would persuade him to cancel the DAP's no-confidence motion against the Rabin government. He asserted that the decision on whether or not to cancel the motion would be 'based on Israeli interests and not Arafat's say'.[64]

ISRAELI ARABS' PARTICIPATION IN THE SYSTEM

Israeli Arab leaders have participated in Israel's political system and have managed to gain a role in influencing Israeli foreign policy. There are many examples in addition to the three mentioned at the beginning of this chapter. Israeli Arabs have maintained pressure on Israeli security forces in the territories to respect Palestinian civil and human rights. This includes ending the practice of torture of Palestinian suspects.[65] Darawshe opened a dialogue to encourage investment in the territories by the United States, the European Union, and the Gulf states.[66] In general, the small Israeli Arab delegation to the Knesset is disproportionately powerful. The Likud Party has been frustrated by this power; as Likud MK Uzi Landau complained: 'The Prime Minister's dilemma is to choose between Jerusalem and the struggle for it and the support of [DAP] MKs Tamar Gozansky and Abdul Wahad Darawshe. He chose Gozansky and Darawshe.'[67] In 1995, Prime Minister Rabin appointed the first Israeli Arab ever to an ambassadorship: Ali Adeeb Yihiyia became ambassador to Finland.[68] In a situation of ongoing contacts between Israeli Arabs and Palestinians in the territories, the Palestinian Authority promised Israeli Arab businessmen fewer restrictions and less red tape if they would invest in Gaza.[69] As with diaspora groups, influence in foreign policy is both a means and an end: by aiding the Palestinian cause from within the Israeli system, Israeli Arabs have gained special economic opportunities.

Like the African Americans, Israeli Arab leaders became more moderate and began to work from within the system in order to acquire greater influence. Both groups, lacking financial resources for political donations, relied heavily on electoral significance. Israeli Arab electoral strength brought an end to the Grapes of Wrath operation; overall, the Israeli Arab influence is remarkably high and the model would predict that it will continue to increase substantially.

It was during the 1991 Gulf War that Israeli Arabs began to behave similarly to the African American model. They, unlike the Palestinians, criticized Saddam Hussein—perhaps a watershed event. As early as 1993, Alexander Bligh, former Arab affairs adviser to Rabin and Shamir, declared that 'Israeli Arabs are power brokers and masters of their own fate as never before'.[70] Cooperating with the government only helped to facilitate the rise of Israeli Arab influence. According to Rekhess, Darawshe found the right balance. He never severed his ties to the Jewish establishment. He never dissociated himself from Labor, or even Likud. He hinted all along that he was intending to fight for equality from within the system.'[71] This mirrors Weil's suggestions regarding the African Americans' strategy.

CONCLUSION

Israeli Arabs can hardly be categorized as a modern diaspora similar to ethnic groups in the United States, not least because the Israeli Arabs are citizens of the very state that controls their homeland. The empirical evidence shows clearly that Israeli Arabs identify more with Israel's antagonists than with the state of Israel. However, by stating their views in terms of the national interest and utilizing their electoral significance, the Israeli Arabs have gained influence, in a manner similar to the African Americans before them. The Israeli Arab leaders have helped the emerging Palestinian Authority, worked for better relations with Arab states, and were able to stop the Grapes of Wrath operation.

It is clear, then, that even a minority in an ethnorepublic can achieve influence in foreign policy, even if that minority maintains only an instrumental link to the state, provided its political leaders work skillfully within the system, moderate their tone, and are backed up by electoral significance.

NOTES

1. M. Al-Haj, 'The Socio-Political Structure of Arabs in Israel: External vs. Internal Orientation', in J. Hofman (ed.), *Arab–Jewish Relations in Israel* (Bristol, IN: Wyndham Hall Press, 1988), pp. 92–122.
2. *Jerusalem Post*, 19 April 1996.
3. *Jerusalem Post*, 22 December 1994.
4. *Jerusalem Post*, 18 February 1994.
5. *Jerusalem Post*, 8 May 1994.
6. G. Sheffer, 'A New Field of Study: Modern Diasporas in International Politics', in G. Sheffer (ed.), *Modern Diasporas in International Politics* (London: Croom Helm, 1986), p. 3.
7. Sheffer, *Modern Diasporas*.
8. E. Tivnan, *The Lobby* (New York, NY: Simon & Schuster, 1987), pp. 54–5, 61.
9. G. Sheffer, 'Ethno-National Diasporas and Security', *Survival*, 36, 1 (1994), pp. 60–79.
10. Ibid., p. 61.
11. Sheffer, 'New Field', p. 9; L. Halley, *Ancient Affections* (Eastbourne, UK: Praeger, 1985), p. 85.
12. I. Peleg and S. Peleg, 'Toward a Theory of Ethnicity and Foreign Policy: The United States and Other Societies', *International Problems: Society and Politics*, 32, 1–2 (1993), pp. 25–38.
13. V. Coufoudakis, 'The Greek-American Lobby and Its Influence on Greek Foreign Policy, 1974–1989', *Mediterranean Quarterly*, 2, 4 (1991), pp. 70–82.
14. Halley, *Ancient Affections*, p. 95.
15. Y. Shain, 'Multicultural Foreign Policy', *Foreign Policy*, 100 (1995), pp. 69–87.
16. M. S. Michael, 'The Role of the Greek Community in the Determination of Australia's Attitude to the Cyprus Problem', *Australian Journal of International Affairs*, 45, 1 (1991), pp. 98–108.
17. M. Kilson, 'African Americans and Africa: A Critical Nexus', *Dissent*, 39, 3 (1992), pp. 361–9.
18. Shain, 'Multicultural Foreign Policy', p. 71.
19. Sheffer, 'New Field', p. 8.
20. Shain, 'Multicultural Foreign Policy', p. 74.
21. Ibid., p. 72.
22. Y. Shain, 'Ethnic Diasporas and US Foreign Policy', *Political Science Quarterly*, 109, 5 (1994/95), pp. 811–41; Kilson, 'African Americans'.
23. Quoted in Kilson, 'African Americans', p. 368.
24. M. M. Gunter, 'The Kurdish Factor in Turkish Foreign Policy', *Journal of Third World Studies*, 11, 2 (1994), pp. 440–72.
25. Ibid., pp. 443, 461.
26. R. Olson, 'The Kurdish Question and Turkey's Foreign Policy, 1991–1995: From the Gulf War to the Incursion into Iraq', *Journal of South Asian and Middle Eastern Studies*, 19, 1 (1995), pp. 1–30.
27. Ibid., p.30
28. N. Rouhana, 'The Civic and National Subidentities of the Arabs in Israel: A Psycho-Political Approach', in J. Hofman (ed.), *Arab–Jewish Relations in Israel* (Bristol, IN: Wyndham Hall Press, 1988), pp. 123–53.
29. Ibid., p. 129.
30. I. Schnell, *Perception of Israeli Arabs: Territoriality and Identity* (Aldershot: Avesbury, 1995), p. 111.
31. A. Diskin and M. Hofnung, 'The Elections to the Knesset and to the Government', in

The 1996 Knesset and Prime Ministerial Elections: Readings and Cases, Jerusalem, *Nevo,* 1997, p. 166 (in Hebrew).
32. Y. Peled, 'Strangers in Utopia: Ethno-Republican Citizenship and Israel's Arab Citizens', *American Political Science Review*, 86, 2 (1992), pp. 432–43.
33. J. Matar, 'A Diplomatic Babel', *Jerusalem Report*, 15 May 1997, p. 26.
34. *Ha'aretz*, 17 April 1996.
35. *Al-Sinara*, 19 April 1996.
36. *Ha'aretz*, 21 April 1996.
37. *Ha'aretz*, 19 April 1996.
38. Ibid.
39. Al-Haj, 'Socio-Political Structure', p. 102.
40. Ibid., p. 100.
41. Kilson, 'African Americans', p. 361.
42. Ibid., p. 362.
43. Ibid., p. 363.
44. Weil, quoted in Shain, 'Multicultural Foreign Policy', p. 80.
45. Kilson, 'African Americans', p. 365.
46. Ibid., p. 364.
47. Ibid., p. 366.
48. Shain, 'Multicultural Foreign Policy', p. 78.
49. Ibid., p. 72.
50. Ibid., p. 85.
51. Kilson, 'African Americans', p. 367.
52. Shain, 'Multicultural Foreign Policy', p. 74.
53. *Jerusalem Post*, 7 February 1991.
54. *Jerusalem Post*, 5 May 1992.
55. *Jerusalem Post*, 4 August 1992.
56. *Jerusalem Post*, 16 October 1992.
57. *Jerusalem Post*, 1 April 1993.
58. *Jerusalem Post*, 11 August 1993.
59. *Jerusalem Post*, 24 November 1993.
60. *Jerusalem Post*, 28 November 1993.
61. *Jerusalem Post*, 25 August 1994.
62. *Jerusalem Post*, 20 October 1994.
63. *Jerusalem Post*, 9 January 1995.
64. *Jerusalem Post*, 22 May 1995.
65. *Jerusalem Post*, 6 June 1993.
66. *Jerusalem Post*, 3 May 1993.
67. *Jerusalem Post*, 22 May 1996.
68. *Jerusalem Post*, 14 September 1995.
69. *Jerusalem Post*, 15 November 1994.
70. *Jerusalem Post*, 25 August 1993.
71. E. Rekhess, 'New Approach, New Power', *Jerusalem Post Magazine*, 12 February 1993, p. 10.

7 Regional Conflict, Country Risk, and Foreign Direct Investment in the Middle East

VICTOR LAVY

Since the late 1980s, Israel's economy has grown at a fast pace. From 1986 to 1989, the growth rate of gross domestic product was 3.7 per cent. From 1992 to 1995, the growth rate averaged an impressive 6.0 per cent (Bank of Israel, 1997, p. 3). Two main factors were responsible for this renewed growth: the wave of immigration from the former Soviet Union and the peace process (Bank of Israel, 1996, pp. 1–3). Since 1990, 700,000 new immigrants have arrived in Israel, a change that affected both the aggregate supply and aggregate demand in the economy. The immigration wave resulted in a 12 per cent increase in the population and a larger increase in the workforce, especially in its skilled component. The relatively quick absorption of the immigrants in the economy, and the negative pressure it exerted on wages, led to an expansion in aggregate supply that was reflected in a growth rate that was faster than that of the economies of other developed countries, without causing significant inflationary pressures (Bank of Israel, 1996, p. 2). Aggregate demand increased as well because of a significant increase in consumption. For example, the housing demand of the new immigrants led to an expansion in the construction industry, which was the initial engine of the renewed growth process.

The peace process began in 1991 with the Madrid Conference, continued with the Oslo agreement, and has, to date, concluded with the signing of the peace agreement between Israel and Jordan in October 1994. These political developments contributed to the growth process in several ways. First, they led to the development of economic ties with neighboring countries, though in modest dimensions. The much larger size of the Israeli economy and its higher level of development are often cited as the reasons for the modest scope of possibilities for trade between Israel and its neighbors (Kleiman, 1994, pp. 33–4). However, the removal of the secondary Arab boycott and the establishment of diplomatic ties with many nations had positive effects on the economy. Many Asian nations began to trade with Israel, which is particularly important since the Israeli economy is open and foreign-trade-oriented. In addition, the removal of the tertiary Arab boycott means that many multinational corporations (MNCs), which were reluctant to do business either in or with Israel because of fear that they would lose Arab business, are taking an interest in the opportunities available to them in Israel (Bank of Israel, 1996, p. 44).

The peace process made it easier for the US government to approve the loan guarantees amounting to US$10 billion over a five-year period. These guarantees gave Israel the breathing space to make the necessary investments to improve the national infra-structure and to implement many vital policy reforms, such as privatization of public companies, trade policy reforms, reduction in trade barriers, and the signing of free trade agreements with the European Union and others.

However, the most important contribution of the peace process to the Israeli economy was its effect on improving the business atmos-phere within the country, and its perception by the international business community. For example, as early as 1993 Standard and Poor, an important international financial company, announced an improvement in Israel's country risk rating, arguing that it reflected the strengthening of Israel's standing in the region in light of the peace agreements with Jordan and the Palestinians. At the end of 1995, Standard and Poor raised Israel's credit rating from BBB to A, before the issuance of Israeli government bonds in New York. Standard and Poor explained that, in addition to the improvement in Israel's geopolitical situation, there were also signs that there would be reductions in the deficit, inflation, and foreign debt (Kedar and Meltz, 1995, p. C1). *The Economist*, in a 1994 report, noted a number of positive indicators, including the privatization initiative, an increase in the level of human capital due to the immigration wave, and a decrease in foreign debt. The report argued that the improvement in Israel's country risk rating was a result of the peace process and of Israel's long-term economic prospects. Similar arguments were made in reports by other large investment banking firms, such as Salomon Brothers, Goldman Sachs, and UCS. This attitude can be summarized by the Salomon Brothers report's assertion that Israel should not be regarded as a developing country, but as a developed country like Ireland or New Zealand (Bank Leumi Le-Israel, 1994, pp. 14–17).

Israel's improved ranking in the international business community since the inception of the peace process was accompanied by a new trend in foreign direct investment in the country. Since 1992, there has been an increase in foreign capital inflow to Israel; 1995 was a record year with over US$2 billion in foreign investment, of which over US$1 billion was foreign direct investment (Bank of Israel, 1996b, p. 5). Foreign investors directed their money to a large range of sectors and industries, among them the food, automobile, and chemical industries. The most significant change, however, is in the telecommunication and high-tech sectors. For example, large multinationals, such as Bell South, Northern Telecom, and Cable & Wireless, have invested impressive amounts of capital in Israel in recent years (see Appendix B for more details).

The purpose of this chapter is to determine whether the joint occurrence of improvement in Israel's country risk rating, and of the increased level of foreign direct investment that was witnessed in recent years, reflects a causal relationship between these two variables. More precisely, the chapter will aim to determine whether the Israeli economy's improved international rating, as a result of the peace process, has led to some of the increased level of foreign direct investment in the economy. Since the peace process constitutes a regional change, the analysis embed is in a regional context and extends the questions to Israel's neighbors as well. In particular, the trends and patterns of change will be examined in country risk and foreign direct investment in Egypt, Jordan, and Syria and the dynamics of intraregional correlation in these variables among the countries in the region, before and after the initiation of the peace process in 1991. The evidence derived from the countries that are directly involved in the Arab–Israeli conflict will be compared to similar evidence derived from a sample of other Mediterranean countries (Algeria, Morocco, Portugal, Tunisia, and Turkey).

The next section briefly presents theories of the relationship between country risk and foreign direct investment, after which the changes in risk measures and foreign direct investment from 1982 to 1995 are described. The statistical methodology and the data are then presented, followed by a final section summarizing the empirical evidence on the causal relationship between country risk measures and foreign direct investment.

THEORIES OF COUNTRY RISK AND FOREIGN INVESTMENT

According to the neoclassical model, investment spending depends on the user cost of capital and is geared to maintaining the optimal capital stock and an associated level of output. Motivated by the poor empirical performance of the neoclassical theory, and also, later, of Tobin's Q-theory, recent work on investment broadly falls into two categories: studies in the 'investment, irreversibility, and uncertainty' tradition, and work that has attempted to relate investment to measures of political and country risk. The latter branch of the literature is especially relevant to the determinants of investment in developing countries, since it tends to emphasize those macro-economic or institutional features that are specific to developing countries such as vulnerability to external shocks, large external debt positions, credit rationing, complementarities between public and private investment, and shifts in income distribution.

Investment, Irreversibility, and Uncertainty

In contrast to earlier theories that assume perfect markets for capital goods, the new approach emphasizes that investment decisions are inherently irreversible, that agents typically have some discretion over the timing of investments, and that investment returns are uncertain. The emphasis on uncertainty about values or returns as a determinant of investment flows helps to explain some past anomalies. It indicates why investment may not be directly responsive to changes in interest rates or to policies that change the relative prices of capital and consumption goods, since investment is shown to depend more on the variability of prices and interest rates than on their absolute values. Since the theory does not predict the exact relationship between investment and uncertainty, this relationship becomes an empirical issue. Very little evidence is available on this subject.

Investment and Country Risk

In addition to the revision of the microeconomic foundations of investment theory summarized above, recent research has also addressed how investment behavior in the aggregate depends on measures of country risk. One approach is simply to add a country-risk premium to the global real interest rate to capture how local risk factors influence the cost of investment capital to a particular country. The risk premium may be a function of the external debt-to-GDP ratio and other creditworthiness variables. Other approaches develop hypotheses about country risk and investment within simple models of macroeconomic equilibrium. Another hypothesis is that openness to trade, through the discipline of the international market, is a way of improving the credibility of government policies. This, in turn, lowers country risk and increases sociopolitical instability. The latter, by creating uncertainty in the politico-economic environment, reduces investments.

Political risk has recently become the subject of increased interest, particularly in the context of foreign direct investment. Political risk is defined as the possibility that political decisions, events, or conditions in a specific country will affect the business climate such that investors will lose money or their profits will be reduced (Howell and Chaddick, 1994, p. 71). This definition is very broad and includes a variety of variables such as the possibility of war, of coup d'état, the kind of government and its stability, the possibility of a country nationalizing foreign investments, and the country's macroeconomic performance (Agmon, 1985, pp. 2–3). Political risk can be rated by assessing each variable and their total effect on the economy.

The development of political risk as an area for research, among both the academic and business communities, began after the Second World War. This period, which began with the GATT accord and Bretton-Woods, is characterized by a large increase in international trade and foreign investment by companies that have become international in their scope (multinational corporations). The 1960s saw the beginnings of new phenomena, including nationalization and trade boycotts. These phenomena were prevalent in developing countries, which used these practices as a way of increasing their limited capital (Howell and Chaddick, 1994, p. 72). The need for accurate estimates of political risk grew in the late 1970s and early 1980s. The two seminal events in this period were the fall of the Shah in Iran and the Latin-American debt crisis. In addition, China's new openness to foreign companies was an unexpected positive development during the period (Blank, 1980, p. 1).

These events forced businesses to understand the degree of uncertainty of the political situation in countries around the world and the influence of sudden changes on their profits. Thus, the assessment of political risk gained importance, although there has been debate as to its efficacy. There are two schools of thought in the assessment of political risk, namely, the qualitative and the quantitative.

The qualitative approach is generally used when concentrating on one country and usually for a specific project. Experts who have experience in the country in question and in the specific project are asked to assess the political risk accompanying the project. These experts are expected to use historical and cultural information, along with other macro-economic indicators, to assess the risk (Raddock, 1986, pp. 149–52).

The quantitative approach uses specific, predetermined variables to measure country risk. The obvious advantage of this approach is that it allows an easy cross-country comparison of risk (Raddock, 1986, pp. 149–52). The disadvantage is that it often affords only a cursory analysis of the actual risk in a given country. The risk indices do not generally differentiate between different industries and between different sorts of economic activities. In addition, quantitative risk analysis focuses on the risk and not on the potential for gain that always accompanies risk. Finally, even quantitative analyses are ultimately based on a subjective rating of each parameter and on how much each parameter contributes to the total country risk (Haendel, 1979).

Despite the disadvantages of the qualitative approach, it does allow firms to select certain countries that they may then choose to analyze in greater detail. More important, the country-risk ratings are often used in negotiations with the country in order to obtain better treatment from the host country, such as a lower tax rate or larger grants (Howell and Chaddick, 1994, p. 72). Another important use of the country-risk rating is in determining the rate of interest that a given country can obtain on loans in the international market. The lower the rating, the more difficult it becomes for a country or a firm based in that country to obtain credit and the credit it obtains will be loaned at a higher interest rate (Bank of Israel, 1993, p. 83).

In order to meet the demand for political-risk ratings, several companies began to supply country-risk indices. The best services are those that use the qualitative approach, but also provide a written report for each country explaining how the rating was obtained.

Although it seems clear that country risk determines, at least to a degree, the flow of foreign investment, theories of foreign investment do not deal with country risk as a factor in the foreign-investment decision. This omission can be explained in several ways. Perhaps the most important reason for ignoring country risk is that in the 1980s only 19 per cent of foreign direct investment was invested in less developed countries. Seventy per cent of all the foreign direct investment flows were directed to Japan, Germany, France, the United States, and the United Kingdom (Graham and Krugman, 1993, p. 14). Since these countries do not experience significant political unrest or dramatic changes in their economies, at least in comparison to less developed countries, firms can be expected to be less concerned with country risk when making their foreign-investment decisions.

The only references to country risk in these theories concern exchange rate and tax rate fluctuations. Unfortunately, trends in foreign investment cannot be explained by exchange rate fluctuations, for several reasons. Firms that are interested in investing abroad are generally interested in a long-term investment and, therefore, are less likely to be concerned with the exchange rate. Wide swings in exchange rates, which have been the norm since the collapse of the Bretton-Woods arrangements, make foreign operations more significant, as the ability to move production to a different location to take advantage of a favorable exchange rate becomes more important. Thus, it may not be the specific exchange rate but rather the exchange rate's volatility that makes foreign investment attractive (McCulloch, 1993, p. 42). Tax rates in all likelihood do play a role in determining the level and the direction of foreign direct investment, but since international corporate tax law is so complex, little work has been done in this area (Graham and Krugman, 1993, p. 28).

Generally, theories of foreign investment concentrate on theories of the firm. Firm-level theories tend to ignore country risk. The models assume that a market for a given product exists abroad and the firm must decide whether or not it is profitable to invest in the foreign market or to try to sell to that market from its domestic operation. Thus, country risk is not emphasized.

Some empirical work (Healy and Palepu, 1993, p. 247) suggests that GDP growth is positively correlated with direct investment. As the target country's economy grows, it becomes more attractive to foreign investors. Some risk indices, such as the *Euromoney* risk index, do take economic performance into account when creating their ranking. The aforementioned study, however, only deals with a few of the most developed countries; hence, it is not clear if this result would apply to less developed countries.

There have not been many attempts to test theories of political risk. An article by Goldsmith tested several hypotheses about a country's stability and economic growth. Goldsmith attempted to test the theory that democratic regimes are more likely to experience higher economic growth than nondemocratic regimes. He used data from developing countries, and tried to use the level of freedom in a country, as indexed by an American research organization, as a predictor for five measures of economic growth: the Country Risk Index of the *Institutional Investor*, the BERI (Business Environment Risk Intelligence) political-risk index, changes in government consumption, the domestic savings rate, and the export ratio. If democratic economies are more likely to grow, then as the amount of freedom in a country increases all of the measures of economic growth should improve. With the exception of the export ratio, none of the indicators moved in a positive direction as freedom increased. None of the results, however, were statistically significant. Therefore, Goldsmith concludes that while democratic regimes may not cause increased economic growth, they do not hinder economic growth (Goldsmith, 1994, p. 115).

RISK MEASURES AND FOREIGN DIRECT INVESTMENT

Measuring Country Risk

A basic issue is the choice of an appropriate definition of country risk. Narrowly defined, country risk arises in the context of the credit assessment of sovereign loans. An important consideration in measuring sovereign risk is assessing transfer risk. Transfer risk is the risk of potential restrictions on the ability to remit funds across national borders. For sovereign loans, this amounts to whether or not a debtor government is willing and able to service its hard-currency loan commitments. Transfer risk largely depends on macrocosmic policies including debt management, economic growth, and the composition and volatility of a country's balance of payments.

More broadly defined, country risk comprises exchange risk and political risk in addition to transfer risk. Exchange risk arises when investments are denominated in local currency and the investor is interested in remittance in a different currency. Political risk is the risk that asset values decline as a result of revolution, war, or any significant politically motivated change in economic policies. The broader measure of country risk applies when the investment universe is expanded to include loans and investment in the private sectors of host countries as well as loans of sovereign borrowers.

There are three well-known, publicly available indices of country risk: the *Institutional Investor* (II) index, the *Euromoney* (EM) index, and the *Economist* Intelligence Unit (EIU) index. These indices tend to capture the narrow transfer-risk dimension of country risk, as well as some dimension of political risk, such as incidence of social unrest and quality of legal regulatory institutions. The II index rates country credit on a scale from 0 to 100, with a higher number indicating a better rating. II scores are computed by polling 75–100 leading international banks for their overall country rankings. The EM and EIU indices are based on smaller surveys of expert opinion. The variation in these indices more closely follows movements in a common set of underlying economic indicators. The II index is the least variable of the three, but all three are highly correlated— not surprising, perhaps, since they are each designed to measure a country's capacity to service external obligations and political risk factors. Unfortunately, definitions and measures of political risk are problematic by nature. Political variables tend to be relatively subjective quantities that are not easily observable. Political situations are also complex balances of many competing interests. Moreover, the strategic or gaming dimension of politics tends to make political outcomes inherently unstable and subject, on occasion, to rapid shifts.

Nevertheless, recent research has attempted to apply a systematic, quantitative approach to measures of political risk. Political risk or instability measures may focus on either the government or the population at large. In the former approach, political risk is measured by incidence of phenomena of social unrest, such as demonstrations, riots, revolts, assassinations, and warfare. It is not generally clear which approach is preferable for measuring the impact of political risk on investment behavior. Indeed, the relative importance of the two sets of factors is likely to depend on the particular country, sector, investor, the time frame, and contractual terms, among other things.

In this analysis use is made of the II and EM indices because they are available since 1980 for all the countries included in this study. The II index includes only the final rank of the country. The EM index includes the nine categories that contribute to the final score. The components are: economic performance (25 per cent), political risk (25 per cent) (political risk refers to the odds of a country defaulting on its loans), indices of foreign debt (10 per cent), debt in default or rescheduled (10 per cent), credit ratings (10 per cent), access to bank lending (5 per cent), access to short-term finance (5 per cent), access to capital markets (5 per cent), and discount on forfeiting (5 per cent).

Dynamics of Country Risk Indices

Figures 1 and 2 present the *Institutional Investor* index (II) and the *Euromoney* index (EMI), respectively, for five Middle Eastern countries, Egypt, Israel, Jordan, Lebanon, and Syria, for the years 1982–95. The II reveals much smoother changes than the EMI, which shows sharp annual fluctuations for every country in the sample. Surprisingly, both risk indicators reveal that Israel's risk rating is the only one to have registered a dramatic improvement over the period. This improvement appears in both risk indices, but is much more dramatic in the EMI.

Figure 1: Institutional Investor Risk Index, 1982–1995

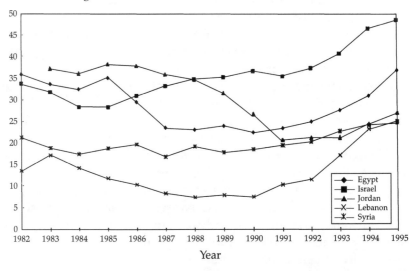

In 1982, Israel's EMI rating was about 26, climbing to 72 in 1988, before declining again to just over 50 in 1990. However, following the initiation of the peace process and the opening of the Madrid Conference, Israel's EMI reached almost 80 in 1993, settling at around 75 in 1994/95. This is more than a 250 per cent improvement since 1982. The improvement in the II rating over the same period is only by 40 per cent. The difference can probably be explained by the way each index is compiled. The II is compiled by surveying banks; thus, each bank's appraisal may be based on a variety of different factors, including 'gut feelings'. In contrast, the EMI uses a specific formula

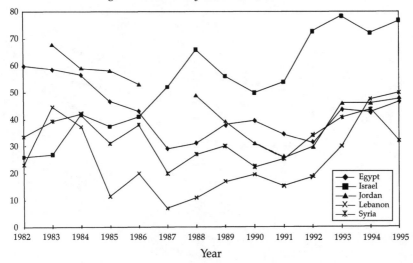

Figure 2: *Euromoney* Risk Index, 1982–1995

that includes economic performance. This can be seen in Figure 2, where Israel's risk rating improves slowly until 1985/86, and then registers a dramatic improvement until 1988. This reflects the economic stabilization program implemented in July 1985. The rating then declines from 1988 to 1990, which reflects the high unemployment caused by the influx of immigrants from the former Soviet Union. Finally, with the beginning of the peace process in 1991 and the improvement in the Israeli economy, in large part due to the successful absorption of the immigrants into the economy, the risk rating improves again.

As seen in Figure 1, Israel's neighbors' risk ratings were relatively stable from 1982 to 1995. The II rating for Egypt was 36 in 1982 and 37 in 1995; similarly, Syria improved from 21 to 25. Jordan did register a steep decline in its rating, from 37 to 27. As already noted, the outstanding feature of the figure, however, is Israel's steady improvement from a low of 28 in 1984 to 49 at the end of the period. Figure 2, which shows the EM country-risk ratings for the region from 1982 to 1994, is more erratic, but interesting trends emerge here as well. First, aside from Israel, all of the countries in the region converge to the same risk rating at the end of the period, between 42 and 46. This represents a considerable decline, or worsening, of Egypt and Jordan's risk levels since the beginning of the period, whereas Syria increased its rating from 34 to 44. Israel's risk rating, however, is the only one to have improved significantly over the period.

Figure 3: *Institutional Investor* Risk Index: Mediterranean, 1982–1995

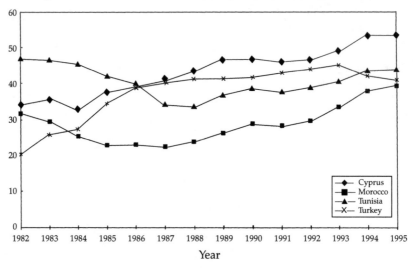

Figure 4: *Euromoney* Risk Index: Mediterranean, 1982–1995

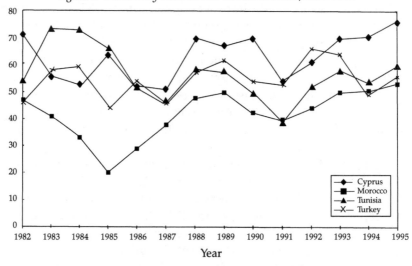

A similar pattern is apparent among the peripheral states of the Middle East (Cyprus, Morocco, Tunisia, Turkey). Figures 3 and 4 plot the country risk of states in the Mediterranean. Turkey and Cyprus both register improvements in their risk ratings over the period, but they are much smaller than Israel's improvement. Morocco improves slightly, while Tunisia declines slightly. The EMI is more volatile, but there is almost no change between the risk ratings at the beginning and end of the period, despite swings in the middle of the period. The Gulf States' risk indices (Bahrain, Kuwait, Saudi Arabia, UAE) are also stable over the period (Figures 5 and 6), although the UAE's risk ratings fell over the period and Bahrain's improved. Kuwait, despite a dip during the Gulf War, did not finish the period much below where it started. The Gulf States' indices, both the EMI and the II, converge at the end of the period.

Figure 5: Institutional Investor Risk Index: Gulf States, 1982–1995

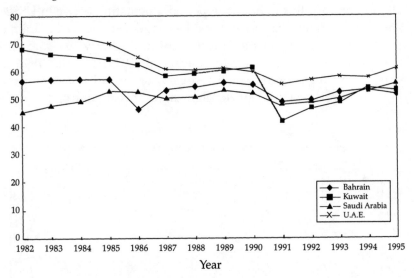

Figure 6: Euromoney Risk Index: Gulf States, 1982–1995

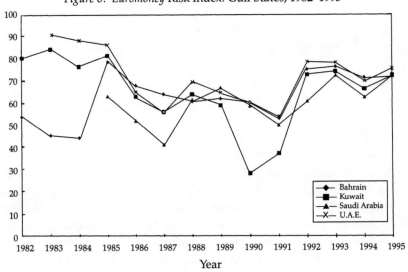

Country Risk and Foreign Direct Investment: The Simple Association

Figure 7 shows the level of foreign direct investment in millions of dollars in Egypt, Israel, and Jordan. From 1982 to 1990, foreign direct investment in Israel remained stagnant between US$50 and US$230 million dollars per annum with a peak in 1987/88. After 1990, investment began to increase steeply, reaching half a billion dollars in 1993 and a billion dollars in 1995. Investment in Jordan remained almost constant throughout the period, fluctuating between US$28 and US$43 million. Egypt, on the other hand, experienced a dramatic increase in foreign direct investment in the early 1980s accompanied by an equally dramatic decline in 1990/91. From 1992 to date, Egypt registered a small recovery, but it did not regain the high level of US$1.2 billion foreign direct investment of the mid-1980s.

Figure 7: Foreign Direct Investment, 1982–1995 (in 1990 US$)

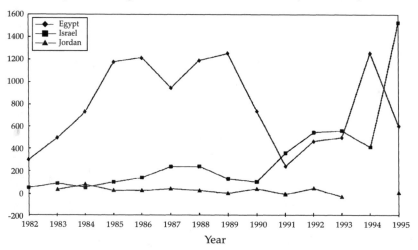

Figure 8 presents the level of foreign direct investment in the Mediterranean sample. All four countries (Cyprus, Morocco, Tunisia, and Turkey) had low and stable foreign direct investment from 1982 until 1988. From 1989, all four countries witnessed a trend of increasing foreign direct investment. The most dramatic change is the increase of foreign direct investment to Turkey, from about US$150 million in 1988 to over US$800 million in 1992. Morocco's change is

Figure 8: Foreign Direct Investment: Mediterranean, 1982–1995
(in 1990 US$)

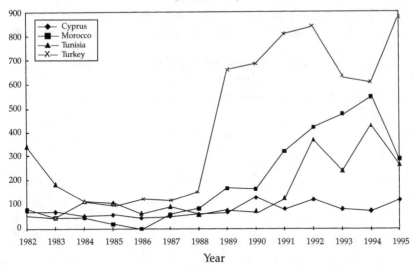

Figure 9: Foreign Direct Investment and *Institutional Investor*
Risk Index: Israel, 1982–1994

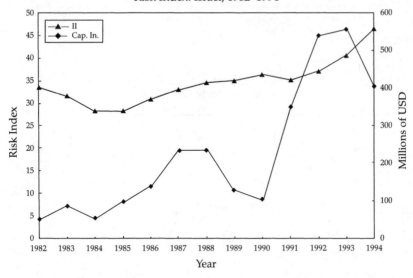

also impressive, from less than US$100 million in 1988 to almost half a billion dollars in 1993.

Figures 9–14 present the level of foreign direct investment against the two risk indices for Israel, Egypt, and Jordan. As can be seen in Figures 9–12, in the case of Israel and Egypt, the risk indices are generally correlated with investment. In Figures 9 and 10, the II shows much more stability than investment, and the EMI is almost perfectly correlated with the Israeli investment trend. In Figures 11 and 12, at least from 1985, investment patterns are correlated with

Figure 10: Foreign Direct Investment and *Euromoney* Risk Index: Israel, 1982–1995

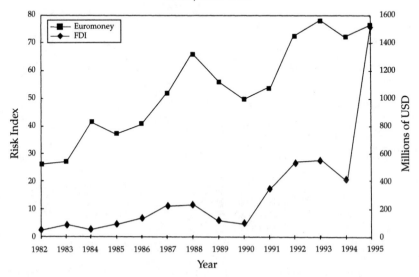

Figure 11: Foreign Direct Investment and the *Institutional Investor* Risk Index: Egypt, 1982–1995

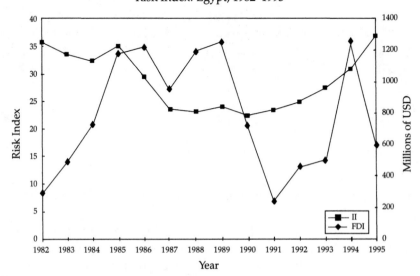

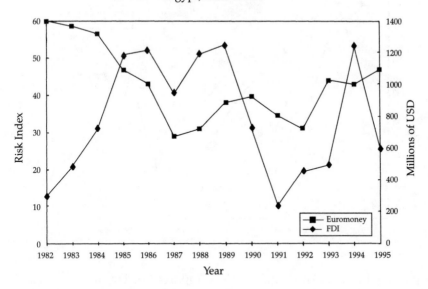

Figure 12: Foreign Direct Investment and
the *Euromoney* Risk Index:
Egypt, 1982–1995

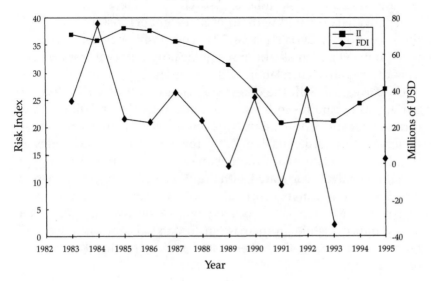

Figure 13: Foreign Direct Investment and
the *Institutional Investor* Risk Index:
Jordan, 1982–1995

Figure 14: Foreign Direct Investment and the *Euromoney* Risk Index:
Jordan, 1982–1995

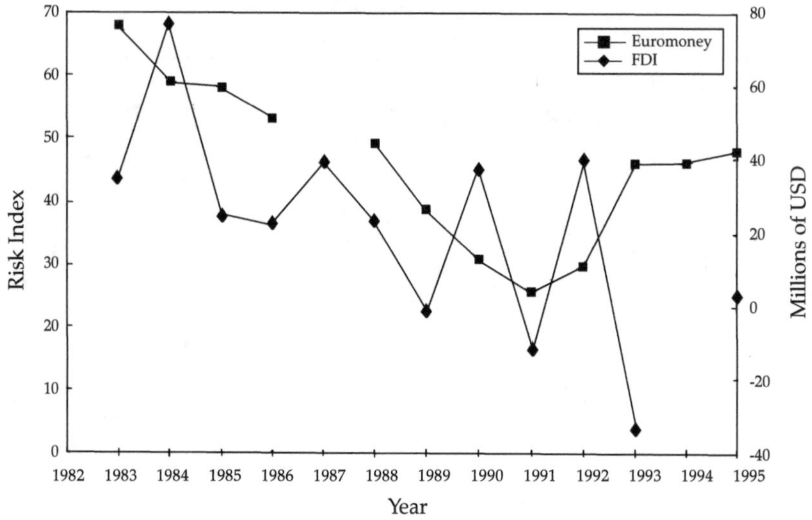

the risk indices. Although it is less apparent in Figures 13 and 14, which plot Jordan's country risk and foreign direct investment, Jordan's country risk is also correlated with its investment level.

Country Risk: Intraregional Correlations

Tables 7.1 and 7.2 present the cross-country correlations of the EM and II country-risk indices, respectively. Israel's EM risk index is negatively correlated with all of its neighbors' risk indices, with the exception of Syria's (Table 7.1). The positive correlation with Syria, however, is small and not significantly different from zero— as is the negative correlation with Lebanon. Egypt's index is positively correlated with the other Arab states' indices, as are Jordan, Syria, and Lebanon's indices. The II intraregion correlations replicate the negative correlations between Israel's risk index and those of Egypt and Jordan (Table 7.2). However, Israel's EM index is positively correlated with the Lebanese and Syrian indices. Egypt remains positively correlated with the other Arab states, but Lebanon and Syria are negatively correlated with Jordan. Thus, an increase in Israel's EM index is associated with a decrease in the other states' indices, while an increase in Jordan's II index is associated with a reduction in the other states' indices (with the exception of Egypt).

Table 7.1: Simple Correlation of Country Risk Indices: The *Euromoney* Index

	Egypt	Israel	Jordan	Lebanon	Syria
Egypt	1	–0.678	0.763	0.629	0.601
Israel	–0.678	1	–0.571	–0.037	0.041
Jordan	0.763	–0.571	1	0.437	0.571
Lebanon	0.629	–0.037	0.437	1	0.823
Syria	0.601	0.041	0.571	0.823	1

Table 7.2: Simple Correlation of Country Risk Indices:
The *Institutional Investor* Index

	Egypt	Israel	Jordan	Lebanon	Syria
Egypt	1	–0.291	0.511	0.599	0.257
Israel	–0.291	1	–0.737	0.486	0.767
Jordan	0.511	–0.737	1	–0.199	–0.491
Lebanon	0.599	0.486	–0.199	1	0.724
Syria	0.257	0.767	–0.491	0.724	1

Foreign Direct Investment: Intraregion Correlation

Table 7.3 presents the correlation of foreign direct investment between the countries in the region. The correlation coefficients in the table indicate that foreign direct investment in Israel is negatively correlated with foreign direct investment in other states in the region, with the exception of Lebanon. These negative correlations are in a way consistent with the negative correlations between the country-specific risk measures. This consistency could reflect correlation in behavior, but most likely it mainly reflects the correlation in time trends. All the other states in the region are negatively correlated with Lebanon and Israel and positively correlated among themselves—an interesting phenomenon that is not readily explained.

Table 7.3: Simple Correlation of Foreign Direct Investment

	Egypt	Israel	Jordan	Lebanon	Syria
Egypt	1	–0.435	0.071	–0.561	0.782
Israel	–0.435	1	–0.614	0.722	–0.628
Jordan	0.071	–0.614	1	–0.252	0.389
Lebanon	–0.561	0.722	–0.252	1	–0.874
Syria	0.782	–0.628	0.389	–0.874	1

EMPIRICAL ANALYSIS

Statistical Methodology

A simple statistical model that has been used in numerous econometric studies (see, for example, Ashenfelter, 1978; Ashenfelter and Card, 1985) uses the assumption that any differences between countries in the sample are fixed over time. In this case, repeated observations of the same countries can be used to make the countries comparable. Let X_{it} denote the risk measures and let Y_{it} denote the potential foreign direct investment of any country i in year t. The formal statistical model states that in the absence of any country risk or any other effects, the potential FDI of country i at time t can be written as:

$$Y_{it} = V_i + \delta_t + \varepsilon_{it} \tag{1}$$

V_i is a country-specific intercept, δ_t is a period effect common to all countries, and ε_{it} is an independent identically distributed (i.i.d.) error term. The effect of country risk on FDI is $X_{it}\beta$. Adding this term to equation (1) we get:

$$Y_{it} = X_{it}\beta + V_i + \delta_t + \varepsilon_{it} \tag{2}$$

where ε_{it} is assumed to be uncorrelated with X_{it}. The idea behind this model is that differences between countries in FDI, except those induced by $X_{it}\beta$, are not temporary: instead, they are due to differences in characteristics that can be viewed as permanent. In this model, simple differences in FDI do not estimate the causal effect of the differences in country risk because the time-covariant characteristics of countries differ. On the other hand, the assumptions of this model imply that the changes in FDI correspond across countries to the changes in country risk. Let $t = a$, denoting the postpeace-process level of FDI and let $t = b$, denoting the prepeace-process level of FDI. Thus we have:

$$E(Y_{ia} - Y_{ib}) = X_{it}\beta \tag{3}$$

The sample analog of equation (3) is called a differences-in-differences estimate of the change in risk effect because it contrasts the change in FDI between groups of countries that experienced different magnitudes of country risk.

The analysis of the risk effects begins with the simple differences-in-differences estimator (3). However, the assumption that X_{it} is independent of Y_{it} may not be realistic. A situation can easily be imagined where higher foreign direct investment leads to an improvement in country-risk ratings. Regression methods can be used to estimate the effect of an endogenous explanatory variable. To identify the effect of X_{it} on Y_{it}, it is proposed that an instrumental variable regression technique is used, using lagged values of the risk measure as instruments. To overcome the problem that arises from autocorrelation in the risk measure, four- and five-period lagged values are used as instruments. Two versions of equation (2) are used. The first is a simple one-period first difference of equation (2):

$$(Y_{it} - Y_{it-1}) = (X_{it} - X_{it-1})\beta + \varepsilon_{it} - \varepsilon_{it-1} \tag{4}$$

The country- and year-specific effects are differenced out in equation (4). $(X_{it} - X_{it-1})$ is then instrumented with $(X_{it} - X_{t-1})_{t-4}$. The second version estimated is the following 22 model:

$$(Y_{it} - \bar{Y}1) = (X_{it} - \bar{X})\beta + \varepsilon_{it} - \bar{\varepsilon} \tag{5}$$

where $(X_{it} - \bar{X})_{t-4}$ is used as an instrument to identify $(X_{it} - \bar{X})_t$. The advantage of equation (4) over equation (5) is that if ε_{it} is auto-correlated, the differencing procedure helps to eliminate it, especially if it is a first-order autocorrelation with $\varphi = 1$.

Data

The data used in this chapter were collected from three sources. All economic data were obtained from the International Financial Statistics prepared by the Bureau of Statistics of the International Monetary Fund. Specifically, data was obtained on gross domestic product (GDP), foreign direct investment (FDI), average exchange rate, population, and the US CPI for the years 1982–94. The FDI data were denominated in millions of US dollars; GDP was denominated in millions of the local currency. Real FDI per capita was then calculated by dividing FDI by the US CPI and the total population. Real GDP per capita was computed by dividing GDP by the average exchange rate, the US CPI, and the local population. For a few countries in the sample, observations on the population and GDP were missing for a few years, so the panel data are not balanced. In cases where IMF data on FDI were missing, information from UNCTAD's *World*

Investment Report for the years 1988–94 was used. It should be noted that comparing the two sources of information for FDI showed that they were almost perfectly correlated for the countries and years for which information was available from both sources.

Data on country risk were obtained directly from *Euromoney* and the *Institutional Investor*, which publish their country risk indices as indicated above. Table 7.4 provides descriptive statistics for Israel and two samples of countries: the Middle Eastern sample, which includes Israel, Egypt, Jordan, Syria, and Lebanon, and the Mediterranean sample, which includes Algeria, Morocco, Portugal, Tunisia, and Turkey. These constitute the sample used for the correlation reported above and the regressions reported below.

Table 7.4: Descriptive Statistics

	Sample					
	Israel		Middle East		Mediterranean	
	Mean	SD	Mean	SD	Mean	SD
Variables	(1)	(2)	(3)	(4)	(5)	(6)
Euromoney Risk Index	51.80	17.02	39.50	15.89	54.86	14.38
Institutional Investor Risk Index	34.71	4.92	25.12	9.51	40.90	11.88
Foreign Direct Investment	230.27	156.63	276.64	401.57	377.34	587.65
GDP	44,188.55	11,447.16	33,196.06	22,729.26	46,539.95	39,879.56
Foreign Direct Investment (per capita)	46.37	29.19	18.91	22.73	31.70	60.25
GDP (per capita)	9,658.31	1,700.08	3,613.60	3,619.94	2,333.60	1,546.65

Notes: Mediterranean sample includes: Algeria, Morocco, Portugal, Tunisia, Turkey. Sample is for 1982–94.
Foreign direct investment is measured in millions of US Dollars and has been divided by the US CPI.
GDP is measured in millions of the local currency and has been converted to US Dollars and then divided by the US CPI.

As can be seen from Table 7.4, Israel's mean risk ratings for the period 1982–94 are higher than the mean average risk ratings for the Middle East, but its mean risk ratings are lower than the mean average risk ratings of the group of Mediterranean countries. Also, Israel's mean per capita FDI is lower than both the Middle Eastern and Mediterranean averages during the period, despite the fact that its mean per capita GDP is significantly greater than both the mean for the Middle East and that for the Mediterranean sample.

RESULTS

Differences of Differences

The analysis is begun by examining the averages of and differences of foreign direct investment and country risk, between two three-year periods, as shown in Table 7.5. The first period, 1989–91, precedes the 1992 Madrid Conference and the second, 1993–95, follows it. The variables analyzed in the table are foreign direct investment and the two risk measures. The first row presents the data for Israel and the second row the data for other Middle Eastern countries. Average FDI in Israel in the second period (US$39 million) is almost four times larger than the FDI average for the first period (US$135 million). Similarly, the EMI risk rating for Israel improved from an average of 53.2 in the first period to 75.6 in the second period. A similar direction of change is observed for the II risk measure. On the other hand, Israel's neighbors' FDI did not change at all between the two periods, although they experienced some improvement in their average risk ratings. The (column) differences between Israel and its neighbors are presented in the third row of the table.

The lower part of Table 7.5 contrasts the Middle Eastern and the Mediterranean samples. Between the two periods, the Middle Eastern countries experienced, on average, a large increase in their FDI and risk measures. No similar changes are observed for the Mediterranean sample. Actually, the Mediterranean countries experienced a decline in FDI from period to period and their risk ratings barely changed. As a result the gap in FDI between the two groups of countries was reduced from an average of US$40 in the first period to zero in the second period. The gap in the risk ratings was also eliminated, from about 20 to 5–7. Note, however, that these changes are entirely due to the inclusion of Israel in the sample, but that the decline in the Mediterranean FDI is still greater than the negligible decline in FDI experienced by the Middle Eastern countries excluding Israel.

If the Mediterranean sample is perceived as an appropriate comparison group, then the difference in the level of FDI in the second period can be causally linked to the improvement in the risk ratings of the Middle Eastern countries. Of course, the assumption that all the differences between the two sets of countries are eliminated by differencing across the two periods is too simplistic and probably not realistic. However, this comparison does suggest a plausible direction of change.

Table 7.5: Level, Differences, and Differences-in-Differences of Foreign Direct Investment and Country Risk Measures

	Foreign Direct Investment			Euromoney Risk Index			Institutional Investor Risk Index		
	1989–91	1993–95	Difference (periods)	1989–91	1993–95	Difference (periods)	1989–91	1993–95	Difference (periods)
	(1)	(2)	(3)	(4)	(5)	(6)	(7)	(8)	(9)
Israel	39.4 (24.7)	135.4 (87.9)	96.0	53.2 (3.1)	75.6 (3.1)	22.4	35.5 (0.8)	45.0 (3.9)	9.5
Middle East (excluding Israel)	5.9 (7.6)	5.1 (7.8)	–0.8	28.1 (8.6)	43.2 (6.1)	15.1	19.1 (7.4)	25.0 (4.2)	5.9
Difference (countries)	33.5	130.3	96.8	25.1	32.4	7.3	16.4	20.0	3.6
Middle East (including Israel)	12.6 (18.0)	40.6 (72.8)	28.0	33.1 (12.9)	49.6 (14.5)	16.5	22.4 (9.5)	29.0 (9.2)	6.6
Mediterranean	52.3 (92.4)	38.7 (39.9)	–13.6	53.6 (14.8)	57.4 (15.6)	1.6	41.4 (12.0)	42.8 (14.3)	1.4
Difference (countries)	–39.7	1.9	41.6	–20.5	–7.8	14.9	–19.0	–13.8	5.2

Notes: Standard errors are in parentheses.
Middle East sample includes Israel, Egypt, Jordan, Lebanon, and Syria. Mediterranean sample includes Algeria, Morocco, Portugal, Tunisia, and Turkey.
Foreign Direct Investment is reported per-capita.

OLS, Fixed Effects, and First Differences Regressions

Table 7.7 presents the results of a variety of ordinary least squares (OLS) regressions used to estimate the effect of the risk indices on foreign direct investment. The table reports results for the two samples of countries, the Middle Eastern and the Mediterranean. The estimations are repeated for each of the two risk indices.

The OLS estimates presented in the first column show a significant positive association between FDI and both the EMI and II risk indices. This result is replicated for both samples, the Middle Eastern and the Mediterranean countries. The second row in the table presents the results of adding to the equation fixed effects for time and countries. This approach of adding to the model with dummy variables to control for year and country effects shows very similar results. In fact, the OLS estimate for the EMI in the Middle East does not change when fixed effect estimation is employed. Estimates using first differences also return a significant positive effect on FDI,[1] but the size of the effect is considerably smaller and the effect is much less precisely estimated.

IV, IV Fixed Effect, and IV First Differences Estimates

Instrumental variable (IV) estimation using a lag of four and five years as an instrument also yields a significant positive effect on FDI. The first-stage regressions are shown in Table 7.6. The IV estimates are larger than the OLS estimates. IV estimation combined with fixed effect estimation also shows a positive effect of the risk indices on FDI, but this effect is significantly different from zero only in columns (1) and (4) of Table 7.7. Neither the effect of the EMI among the Mediterranean group of countries, nor that of the II in the Middle Eastern sample is significant.

Finally, using IV estimation combined with first differences shows a significant positive effect of the EMI on FDI, whereas the positive effect is not significant for the II. This estimation method with the Mediterranean sample did not yield a significant result, although the effects were positive.

Summary of Results

The *Euromoney* risk index explicitly includes elements of political risk and therefore is more likely to be affected by the peace process. This

Table 7.6: First-stage Regression Estimates

	Country Risk Measure			
	Euromoney		Institutional Investor	
	Risk Index	Foreign Direct Investment	Risk Index	Foreign Direct Investment
Regression type	(1)	(2)	(3)	(4)
IV	0.4959	0.0059	0.7244	0.0105
	(0.1385)	(0.0025)	(0.0975)	(0.0041)
IV fixed effects	0.3022	0.0095	0.1019	0.0353
	(0.1391)	(0.0021)	(0.2894)	(0.0077)
IV first differences				
Risk at t-4	0.2740	0.0052	0.1355	0.0177
	(0.1484)	(0.0025)	(0.2106)	(0.0105)
Risk at t-5	0.1815	0.0018	–	–
	(0.1526)	(0.0026)		

Note: Standard errors are in parentheses.

Table 7.7: Regression Estimates, Foreign Direct Investment, and Country Risk Indices[a]

	Country Risk Index			
	Euromoney		Institutional Investor	
	Middle East	Mediterranean	Middle East	Mediterranean
Regression type	(1)	(2)	(3)	(4)
OLS	0.0088	0.0248	0.0137	0.0305
	(0.0017)	(0.0041)	(0.0055)	(0.0049)
Time and country fixed effects	0.0088	0.0195	0.0190	0.0289
	(0.0019)	(0.0063)	(0.0055)	(0.0086)
First differences	0.0023	0.0029	0.0056	0.0128
	(0.0024)	(0.0030)	(0.0076)	(0.0055)
IV	0.0120	0.0379	0.0145	0.0359
	(0.0036)	(0.0088)	(0.0049)	(0.0085)
IV fixed effects	0.0313	0.0544	0.3461	0.1206
	(0.0136)	(0.0478)	(0.9617)	(0.0483)
IV first differences	0.0167	0.0127	0.1303	0.0504
	(0.0098)	(0.0645)	(0.2088)	(0.0637)
N	49	61	49	61

Notes: Standard errors are in parentheses.
Mediterranean sample includes: Algeria, Portugal, Morocco, Tunisia, Turkey.
N is the number of observations used for the OLS estimates.

can explain why the most consistent results are obtained using this index. Column (1) in Table 7.7 presents a very diverse set of estimates of the effect of country risk on FDI. The preferred estimate is the IV first difference, the bottom row of Table 7.7, which is believed to be a consistent and credible estimate, since it corrects for the endogeneity of the risk measure, accounts for any country- and year-specific effect, and rids the error term of first-order autocorrelation if the autocorrelation coefficient is near 1.

The IV first differences estimate is twice as large as the OLS estimate, 0.0167 vs. 0.0088. Does it reflect a large effect? Calculating the foreign capital inflow elasticity with respect to the EMI at the Israeli means of the data yields an elasticity of 0.85. This means that a 10 per cent improvement in the Israeli risk rating leads to an 8.5 per cent increase in direct foreign investment, a significant effect. During the post-Madrid Conference years (1993–95), the *Euromoney* risk rating of Israel improved by 22.4 per cent. This improvement should have led, given the above-estimated elasticity, to about a 40 per cent increase in foreign direct investment in Israel. The actual increase in FDI during this period was about 96 per cent. The difference between this actual change and the change accounted for by the improved risk rating is due to other economic factors, such as faster growth of the economy.

Acknowledgment

Special gratitude is extended to my hard-working research assistant, Josiah Rotenberg.

APPENDIX A: SURVEY OF STUDIES ON THE EFFECT OF POLITICAL RISK ON FOREIGN DIRECT INVESTMENT

Early survey analyses[2] of the influences of foreign direct investment led to the belief that political risk[3] ranked very high among the matters taken into consideration by transnational corporations in determining the location of overseas operations. In contrast, the earlier statistical studies that included political environment indicators tended to find them insignificant.

Thus, Bennet and Green (1972) found political stability in 46 host countries to be insignificantly related to US foreign direct investment, for both developed country and developing country subsamples.

However, since the dependent variable was US foreign direct investment stock in 1965 and the political instability measure covered either
the previous eight or 16 years, the test may be considered rather
insensitive.[4] A similar study by Green and Cunningham (1975)
covered only 25 countries, but a wider range of independent variables, among which political stability again proved insignificant.
Using a dependent variable comprising the number of new manufacturing subsidiaries established in 11 developed countries and
48 developing countries from 1964 to 1967 by the 187 US firms in
the Harvard database on transnational corporations, Kobrin (1979)
applied factor analysis to 33 environmental (political, social, economic) variables. The factor analysis produced six clusters of variables for which three (labeled by Kobrin 'rebellion',[5] 'government
instability',[6] and 'subversion'[7]) were politically oriented. In a range of
multiple regression tests, for both all countries and developing
countries, Kobrin (1978) defined three types of 'political violence'. Of
these, only 'conspiracy' (assassinations, coups, revolutions, general
strikes) was significantly negatively related to foreign direct investment.[8] This result also held strongest where it was most likely to result
in a response inimical to the interests of foreign direct investment
(i.e., at relatively high levels of socioeconomic development and
relatively efficient bureaucracy).

Discriminant analysis was applied by Root and Ahmed (1979)
to a sample of 58 developing countries, which were classified as
'unattractive', 'moderately attractive', or 'highly attractive' for foreign
direct investment from 1966 to 1970. Of 38 economic, social, and
political variables, only six emerged as significant discriminators (at
5 per cent) between the groups. Of these, only 'the number of regular
(constitutional) changes in government leadership between 1957 and
1967' was a political variable. Although both 'number of armed
attacks by internal groups (1956 to 1967)' and 'role of Government in
the economy' were significant (negatively and positively, respectively, at 10 per cent),[9] the 'degree of nationalism' was insignificant at
that level. Furthermore, Agodo (1978) found 'political stability' to
have a positive and significant effect on foreign direct investment in
an analysis of 33 US firms that had 46 manufacturing investments in
20 African countries.

In an analysis of the determinants of annual average inflows of
foreign direct investment in 25 developing countries, Levis (1979)
used two perceptions of political stability. The first was the more
common view of political stability, which equates it with the 'absence

of domestic civil conflict and violent behavior'. The measure used was that of Feierabend and Feierabend, who identified political instability with aggressive behavior and defined it (quoted in Levis, 1979, p. 61) as the 'degree or the amount of aggression directed by individuals or groups within the political system against other groups or against the complex of officeholders and individual groups associated with them'.[10] In Levis's stepwise regression tests, this variable was third most important (of seven) and significant as a determinant of foreign direct investment for the period 1962–64, but seventh and insignificant for the lagged period (independent variable unchanged) 1965–67. The second indicator of political instability was based on the legitimacy of the regime, 'that is, the extent to which the political system and its outputs are accepted as right and proper by the population' (Levis, 1979, p. 62). The indicator[11] used for this ranked sixth and insignificant for the unlagged period (1962–64), but fifth and significant in the lagged period (1965–67). Schneider and Frey (1983) covered 54 developing countries in tests for 1976, 1979, and 1980, which included both economic and political variables. These tests found political instability to be persistently and significantly negatively related to foreign direct investment in regressions (either with GNP per capita as the sole control variable, or with a wider selection of independent variables). Although 'government ideology' was never significantly related to foreign direct investment, the proportion of a country's foreign aid coming from developed market economies was found to be a significantly positive determinant and that from socialist countries significantly negative; the amount of multilateral aid was also significantly positive.[12]

Nigh's (1985) analysis broadened the study in two useful ways. First, by pooling time-series data on US manufacturing foreign direct investment in 24 countries for 21 years (1954–75), the possibility of systematic investigation of lags was opened up. Second, four separate dimensions of political events were distinguished, by taking account of both conflictive and cooperative events, occurring both within host countries (intranation events) and between countries (internation events). 'Conflictive internation' events are unfriendly acts directed by the host country at the United States, 'cooperative internation' events are friendly acts directed by the host country at the US, 'conflictive intranation' events are associated with a deteriorating environment in a host country,[13] and 'cooperative intranation' events are associated with an improved environment in a host country.[14] For developing countries, Nigh (1985) found both conflictive and cooperative internation events and conflictive intranation political events to be significant determinants of foreign direct investment (signs as predicted) at 1 per cent when lagged by one year. When unlagged data were used for developing countries, both types of internation event were insignificant, but both types of intranation political event were found to be significant.[15] For developed countries, both types of internation political event were significant (signs as predicted) at 1 per cent when lagged by one year, with the same result for unlagged data.[16]

In a separate analysis, Nigh (1986) applied the same approach to eight Latin American countries for the same period. Here, both types of internation political event were significant for a one-year lag, but insignificant when unlagged; both types of intranation political event were significant when unlagged, but insignificant with a one-year lag. Thus, Nigh's results suggest, first, that the differentiation of political event variables, to incorporate both internation and intranation events and both conflictive and cooperative events, imparts an extra dimension of subtlety to the results; second, that part of this subtlety is reflected in differences between developed and developing countries[17] (with only internation events relevant to the former); and third, that the ability to analyze lags is valuable since (where relevant, i.e., for the developing country host) the response of investors to intranation events seems more prompt than to internation events.[18]

APPENDIX B: EXAMPLES OF RECENT FOREIGN DIRECT INVESTMENT IN ISRAEL

Since 1992, there has been an increase in foreign investment in Israel, 1995 being a record year with over US$2 billion in foreign investment, of which over US$1 billion was foreign direct investment (*Ha'aretz*, 8 April 1996, p. C2). Foreign investors directed their investments to a large range of sectors and industries. One of the new and important areas in which foreigners are investing is the food industry. A wave of foreign chains, including McDonald's, Pizza Hut, Burger King, and others entered the Israeli market, indicating the market's consumption potential. In addition, several strategic investments have been made in the Israeli market, which is seen as a bridge to other markets. The most obvious example is Nestlé, which established a partnership with Osem. Strauss and Unilever, and Vita and Rich, are other examples of Israeli companies partnering with larger foreign companies (Nachshon, 1995, p. 16).

The automobile industry has also seen several large foreign direct investments. Volvo is working with Merkavim, and Volkswagen is investing US$300 million to develop a magnesium plant in partnership with the Dead Sea Works (Yellnick, 1995, p. 9).

Another area receiving attention from foreign investors is the chemical industry. The Israel Corporation, which despite its name is a foreign investor in Israel, controlled by the Eisenberg family, recently bought Israel Chemicals and Deshanim. In addition, pharmaceutical companies and beauty product manufacturers, such as Johnson & Johnson, Henckel, and others, have opened operations in Israel (Yellnick, 1995, p. 9).

Despite all these investments, the most significant developments have taken place in the telecommunications and high-tech sectors. Bell South and Northern Telecom have both invested in Israel. Cable & Wireless bought 10 per cent of Bezeq, and Madge bought Lannet. Finally, Intel will open a new plant in Kiryat Gat (Yellnick, 1995, p. 9). These are just a few examples of large investments in this area.

It should be noted that some of these investments have been heavily criticized—for example, Shamrock's investment in Coors, where it was argued that the investment was made with Israeli capital. The large government assistance that will be extended to Intel was also criticized as unnecessary. However, this does not alter the fact that foreign companies have become interested in Israel and see it as a potential market and as a place in which they should have operations. In addition, it should be noted that in successful developing countries the level of foreign investment is approximately 3 per cent of GDP; this leaves significant room for increased foreign investment in Israel to approximately US$2 billion per year (Zilberfarb, 1994, p. 92). Therefore, barring drastic changes in Israel's economic outlook, it seems that foreign investment will continue to flow to Israel.

NOTES

1. The effect is significant at the 10% level. Unless otherwise noted, significance in this chapter refers to a level of 5%.
2. The surveys of Aharoni (1966) and Basi (1963) seem to have notably influenced subsequent authors. See also Root and Ahmed (1978, p. 74).
3. For a detailed review of the concept of political risk, see Kobrin (1979). See also Kobrin (1978), pp. 113–17.

4. But see Kobrin (1979, pp. 31–2) for a defense of the use of stock data.
5. 'Rebellion' included variables representing both planned and spontaneous rebellion against government authority; a measure of government reaction (purges); and an indicator of the type of regime most likely to be associated with political violence.
6. 'Government instability' covered executive changes; cabinet changes; and crises (including constitutional or violent regime changes).
7. 'Subversion' included armed attack and guerrilla warfare (planned quasi-military action against the regime).
8. The others were 'turmoil' (protest demonstrations, riots) and 'internal war' (deaths from domestic violence, armed attacks, guerrilla warfare).
9. These are the *only* extra variables significant at 10%.
10. For a more detailed description of the derivation of this index, see Levis (1979, p. 63).
11. It took into consideration 'the effectiveness of the legislative process, the nature of the office nominating process, the existence of parliamentary pluralism, the government's structure and the parties' legitimacy' (Levis, 1979, p. 62).
12. Reuber *et al.* (1973, pp. 51–2) found a weak but positive relationship between aid and foreign direct investment flows.
13. It is predominantly this type of political event that was used in the earlier studies.
14. See Nigh (1985, pp. 14–15) for a description of the source data.
15. Two-year lag models found only internation political events to be significant.
16. Two-year lag models found none of the dimensions of political events to be significant.
17. Nigh (1985, pp. 8–9) formally demonstrated the inappropriateness of pooling developed and developing country data.
18. See Nigh (1986, p. 104) for a suggested explanation of this result.

REFERENCES

Agmon, T., *Political Economy and Risk in World Financial Markets* (Lexington, MA: Lexington Books, 1985).

Agodo, O., 'The Determinants of US Private Manufacturing Investments in Africa', *Journal of International Business Studies*, Winter (1978), pp. 95–107.

Aharoni, Y., *The Foreign Investment Decision Process* (Boston, MA: Harvard University Press, 1966).

Ashenfelter, O. A., 'Estimating the Effect of Training Programs on Earnings', *Review of Economics and Statistics*, 60, February (1978), pp. 47–57.

Ashenfelter, O. A. and Card, D., 'Using the Longitudinal Structure of Earnings to Estimate the Effect of Training Programs on Earnings', *Review of Economics and Statistics*, 67 (1985), pp. 648–60.

Bank Leumi Le-Israel, *Israel Country Risk* (Tel-Aviv: Bank Leumi Le-Israel, September 1994).

Bank of Israel, *Monitoring Survey on Foreign Currency*, 1993 (in Hebrew).

Bank of Israel, *Monitoring Survey on Foreign Currency*, 1994 (in Hebrew).

Bank of Israel, *Monitoring Survey on Foreign Currency*, 1995 (in Hebrew).

Bank of Israel, *1995 Report* (in Hebrew).

Bank of Israel, *1996 Report* (in Hebrew).

Basi, R. S., 'Determinants of United States Private Direct Investments in Foreign Countries', Printed Series No. 3 (Kent State University, Bureau of Economic and Business Research, 1963).

Bennet, P. D. and Green, R. T., 'Political Instability as a Determinant of Direct Foreign Investment in Marketing', *Journal of Marketing Research*, 9 (1972), pp. 162–86.

Blank, S., *Assessing the Political Environment: An Emerging Function in International Companies* (New York, NY: The Conference Board, 1980).

Euromoney, September 1982–95.

Frey, B. S. and Schneider, S., 'Economic and Political Determinants of Foreign Direct Investment' (University of Zurich: Institute of Empirical Economic Research, 1983).

Goldsmith, A. A., 'Political Freedom and the Business Climate: Outlook for Development in Newly Democratizing States', *Social Science Quarterly*, 75, 1 (1994), pp. 115–24.

Graham, E. M. and Krugman, P. R., 'The Surge in Foreign Direct Investment', in K. A. Froot (ed.), *Foreign Direct Investment* (Chicago, IL: University of Chicago Press, 1993), pp. 13–36.

Green, R. T. and Cunningham, W. H., 'The Determinants of US Foreign Investment: An Empirical Examination', *Management International Review*, 15 (1975), pp. 113–20.

Ha'aretz, 'Growth of 146% in Foreign Investments in Israel to $2.2 Million in '95', *Ha'aretz*, 8 April 1996, p. C2 (in Hebrew).

Haendel, D., *Foreign Investment and the Management of Political Risk* (Boulder, CO: Westview Press, 1979).

Healy, P. M. and Palepu, K. G., 'International Corporate Equity Associations: Who, Where, and Why?', in K. A. Froot (ed.), *Foreign Direct Investment* (Chicago: University of Chicago Press, 1993), pp. 231–54.

Howell, L. D. and Chaddick, B., 'Models of Political Risk for Foreign Investment and Trade', *Columbia Journal of World Business*, (Fall 1994), pp. 70–91.

Institutional Investor, March and September issues from 1982–95.

Kedar, Y. and Meltz, G., 'Last Night Standard and Poor's Raised Israel's Credit Rating to A', *Ha'aretz*, 10 December 1995, p. C1 (in Hebrew).

Kleiman, E., 'Peace and Commerce With Neighbors', *Economic Quarterly*, April (1994), pp. 32–43 (in Hebrew).

Kobrin, S. J., 'When Does Political Instability Result in Increased Investment Risk?', *Columbia Journal of World Business*, Fall (1978), pp. 113–23.

Kobrin, S. J., 'Political Risk: A Review and Reconsideration', *Journal of International Business Studies*, 10, Spring/Summer (1979), pp. 67–80.

Levis, M., 'Does Political Instability in Developing Countries Affect Foreign Investment Flow?: An Empirical Examination', *Management International Review*, 19 (1979), pp. 59–68.

McCulloch, R., 'New Perspectives on Foreign Direct Investment', in Froot, *Foreign Direct Investment*, pp. 37–56.

Nachshon, A., 'We Are the World' (1993), *Yediot Aharonot* ('Seven Days' supplement), 15 (1995), p. 16 (in Hebrew).

Nagi, P., *Country Risk* (London: Euromoney Publications, 1984).

Nigh, D., 'The Effect of Political Events on US Direct Foreign Investment: A Pooled Time-Series Cross-Sectional Analysis', *Journal of International Business Studies*, 16, Spring (1985), pp. 1–17.

Nigh, D., 'Political Events and the Foreign Direct Investment Decision: An Empirical Examination', *Managerial and Decision Economics*, 7, June (1986), pp. 99–106.

Peres, S., 'And Even If Not Miraculous, It's Good Enough', *Ha'aretz*, 3 April 1996, p. B2 (in Hebrew),

Raddock, D. M., *Assessing Corporate Political Risk* (New Jersey: Rowman & Littlefield, 1986).

Reuber, G. L. with Crookell, H., Emerson, M., and Gallais-Hamonno, G., *Private Foreign Investment in Development* (Oxford: Clarendon Press, 1973).

Root, F. R. and Ahmed, A. A., 'The Influence of Policy Instruments on Manufacturing Direct Foreign Investment in Developing Countries', *Journal of International Business Studies*, 9, Winter (1978), pp. 81–93.

Root, F. R., and Ahmed, A. A., 'Empirical Determinants of Manufacturing Direct Foreign Investment in Developing Countries', *Economic Development and Cultural Change*, 27, July (1979), pp. 751–67.

Saguy, M., 'New Standard for Financial Disclosure', *Globe*, 17 October 1995, p. 47 (in Hebrew).

UNCTAD, *World Investment Report 1994: Transnational Corporations, Employment and the Workplace* (New York, NY: UN Publications, 1994).

UNCTC, *The Determinants of Foreign Direct Investment: A Survey of the Evidence* (New York, NY: UN Publications, 1992).

Yellnick, Z., 'International Year', *Ma'ariv* ('Business' supplement), 29 December 1995, p. 9 (in Hebrew).

Zilberfarb, B.-Z., 'The Effects of the Peace Process', *Israel Affairs*, 1, 1 (1994), pp. 84–95.

8 The Peace Process and the Internationalization of Internal Legal Arrangements

MENACHEM HOFNUNG

With the signing of the historic agreement between Israel and the PLO in September 1993, most attention was drawn to the international, symbolic, and security aspects of Israel's willingness to recognize the PLO as a legitimate representative of the Palestinian people and to allow the establishment of the Palestinian Authority. From a legal perspective, attention was drawn to the emergence of a new legal entity and to the way in which that would affect the Palestinian residents and Israeli settlers in the territories occupied by Israel since 1967. Israeli legislation concerning affairs within the 'Green Line' (the pre-1967 borders) was regarded as unaffected by the agreement. It will be maintained here, however, that a major consequence of the agreements between Israel and both the Palestinians and Jordan is the emergence of significant international constraints on the drafting of internal Israeli legislation, which will permanently affect the nature of internal Israeli law.

Lawmaking is considered one of the basic attributes of a sovereign state. In this sense, limitations imposed on others' capacity to enact and amend laws freely, without paying much attention to external constraints, can be regarded as an expression of independence and autonomy. In the Oslo and Cairo agreements of 1993 and 1994, Israel insisted on limiting the legislative powers of the elected institutions of the Palestinian Authority (hereafter PA) for the purpose of maintaining a clear demarcation between an independent state that can enact and amend laws without external intervention, and an entity with limited autonomy that can enact secondary legislation, subject to the approval of the primary legislator—i.e., the Israeli military commander of the area (Benvenisti, 1994, p. 300). What went unnoticed were the implications of the international agreements for internal Israeli legislation. The agreements with the PLO constitute a bold initiative to form a new, not fully independent, political entity, which is closely tied to Israel, especially in economic and security matters. The international commitments undertaken in the agreement in fact impose new limits on the range of internal options available to the Knesset, while at the same time increasing the options for cooperation and interdependence in external ties, especially with the Arab world. In this sense, the Oslo and Cairo agreements with the Palestinians and, to a lesser extent, the peace agreement with Jordan in 1994 entail a twofold change in legal arrangements within Israel: they impose practical, informal limitations on the legislative options open to the Knesset in several policy areas, mainly in economic matters; and they extend Israeli law (by agreement) into areas where there is no effective Israeli control.

Even if the peace process does not proceed at the pace initially anticipated, its effects on Israel's legal domain are likely to be felt for a long time. Attempts to pass laws or implement unilateral policies for the purpose of creating irreversible 'facts' in disputed areas are no longer regarded by the international community as internal Israeli affairs. Unilateral measures or legal initiatives that disregard this new reality are likely to meet considerable domestic and external resistance and may lead to harsher reactions than in the period before 1993.[1]

THIRTY YEARS OF ISOLATION

Beginning in 1948, the continuous state of war between Israel and its immediate neighbors brought about the economic and cultural isolation of the Jewish state within its geographical region. This isolation was such that in drafting Israeli legislation, little account was taken of neighboring countries. With the state itself considered illegitimate, Arab countries did not pay much attention to its legislative acts. For their part, Israeli policymakers tended to view regional affairs in terms of coping with external threats and ensuring the existence of the Jewish state. When considering internal legal arrangements, more attention was paid to security-related issues than to considerations of possible future cooperation (Hofnung, 1996, pp. 73–86).

Israel's long isolation in its immediate area was not much eased after the signing of the peace treaty with Egypt. Although Israeli tourists began to appear in Cairo's markets and some Israeli companies were able to establish semiofficial business ties in Egypt and other Arab countries, direct and open economic ties were almost nonexistent. The combination of an ongoing state of war with the other neighboring Arab countries, the occupation of the territories conquered in 1967, and the Arab economic boycott prevented Israel from joining regional and international agreements. This isolation made Israel less dependent on international cooperation with respect to both its policy decisions and its legislative initiatives. In fact, certain laws were enacted with the explicit purpose of establishing irreversible facts in regard to the legal status of Arab refugees and their property (Hofnung, 1996, pp. 101–23). In the early 1980s, two laws—the Basic Law: Jerusalem, Capital of Israel, and the Golan Heights Law—were enacted with the intention of granting formal and irreversible status to the annexation of East Jerusalem and of the Golan Heights, respectively (Rubinstein, 1996, pp. 87–91). In the occupied territories new legislation was enacted, with an eye not to granting the entire population the rights and norms valid in Israel, but to applying Israeli laws to the settlers only. First, in 1984 the justice minister was given the power to change the supplement of the 'Extension of Validation of Emergency Regulations (Judea and Samaria and Gaza—Jurisdiction of Offenses and Legal Assistance)' by issuing an order with the approval of the Knesset Committee on Constitution, Law and Justice. The supplement to those regulations contained a list of laws applicable to Israeli residents of the territories. This meant that the justice minister was given the power (subject to the committee's approval) to make the entire Israeli statute book applicable to Israeli settlers in the West Bank and Gaza.[2] Second, an 'Israeli resident' was so defined as to include only Israeli citizens, and Jews who were not Israeli citizens.[3] In addition, by legislation of the military commander, political and civil rights enjoyed in Israel were granted to Israeli residents of Jewish settlements in the territories.[4] This legislation, although drawing protests from the Palestinian population and from human rights organizations, was implemented unilaterally in neglect of domestic and external pressures.

THE AGREEMENTS WITH THE PA AND JORDAN

The series of agreements between Israel and the PLO/PA and Jordan brought about a significant change in Israel's relations with Arab and many other countries (this trend is also tied to regime changes in most communist countries). Although the peace agreement with Egypt was a milestone insofar as the largest Arab country had recognized and established diplomatic relations with Israel, other Arab countries did not follow suit. This state of affairs was changed through the agreements with the PA and Jordan. The provisions of the agreement with Jordan include termination of the state of war, the determining of agreed-upon borders between the two states, security commitments, full diplomatic relations, and so on. As an immediate consequence of the agreements, Israel was able to upgrade its treaty with the European Union and was invited to join several regional bodies and conventions. From an alien and secluded entity in the Middle East, Israel has turned into an active (though not always welcome) participant in regional affairs. The Arab–Israeli dispute, which was regarded as a zero-sum game of a protracted nature, has moved from a conflict-management phase into conflict-resolution modes (Bar-Siman-Tov, 1994). The new favorable atmosphere opened the way for a considerable upsurge in foreign investments and economic opportunities. However, the opening of new frontiers was accompanied by new, previously unfamiliar constraints on policymaking and legislative initiatives. Mutual cooperation cannot coexist with seclusion and ignorance of other interests in the area. This reality was recognized in drafting the agreements with the PA and Jordan, which include mutual obligations for cooperation and coordination in bilateral and multilateral policy areas. It should be noted that some of these constraints, especially in tax- and customs-related matters, were initiated and put into writing by Israeli policymakers, who recognized the opportunity to use the peace agreements as a catalyst for introducing new internal policies, and for eliminating several protectionist internal policies (by presenting them as required by the agreements).[5]

We shall now analyze the internal legal implications of the agreements with the PA and Jordan according to several variables: application of Israeli law to Israelis living under the jurisdiction of another de facto sovereign; the creation of interdependent economic systems; the establishment of mutual security arrangements;

cooperation in protection of the environment, and the use of natural resources; and infrastructure coordination.

APPLICATION OF ISRAELI LAW TO ISRAELIS UNDER THE JURISDICTION OF ANOTHER SOVEREIGN

A significant aspect of the Cairo agreements of 1994 was the extension of Israeli law (by international agreement) to Israelis residing in or visiting the autonomous Palestinian areas. This provision can be seen as ensuring the individual security of Israelis in those areas, but it can also be interpreted as preserving the special ties to historical territories in which Israel is unable to maintain effective control, but does not want to relinquish all future claims. Therefore, the Cairo agreement, unlike most international agreements, presents a striking imbalance in one party's—i.e., Israel's—favor. Israelis are subject to Israeli law anywhere in the PA areas; Palestinians are subject to PA law only in the autonomous area, and in some cases may be extradited to Israel for offenses performed against Israeli citizens or objects within the area transferred to the PA.

According to the agreement, Israelis are not subject to Palestinian criminal jurisdiction—including criminal law—in the Palestinian territory in which they perform a criminal act, even if their act injures a local resident or disrupts local public order. Minor infractions such as traffic offenses, as well as major infractions such as drug trafficking, damage to property, bodily injury, and murder, are all—if they are committed by Israelis—beyond the jurisdiction of the authority charged with public order and civil defense of the local population, namely, the PA (Wasserstein Fassberg, 1994, p. 339).

Residents of the PA are not similarly exempt from Israeli criminal jurisdiction in Israel, nor are they subject to the protection or regulation of Palestinian law outside the autonomous territories. Israel has the power to arrest non-Israeli persons found in a place, including the PA areas, where Israeli security operations are carried out and who are suspected of having committed an offense there. This is a striking power to possess in a territory that is under the control of another, internationally recognized legal system (Wasserstein Fassberg, 1994, p. 340).

The agreement also contains some provisions that, if fully implemented, open the way for cooperation that is uncommon between two states. Civil judgments issued by either side are supposed to be enforced by the other if the judicial organ issuing the judgment had jurisdiction to render the decision (Annex III, article IV.4) and if enforcement is not contrary to public policy. Judgments are to be executed reciprocally as if they were local judgments. The agreement also specifies procedures for cooperation in criminal cases. Thus far, this cooperation has not been fully implemented because of the long closure and restrictions on movement of Palestinians that were imposed by Israel after a series of bombings in Israeli cities in February and March 1996. However, if implemented, such cooperation would be closer to the practice according to which territorial units in one state (states within the United States; or England, Scotland, and Wales within the United Kingdom) handle, for example, legal-assistance procedures than to what is the norm between independent states (Wasserstein Fassberg, 1994, p. 329).

Arrangements with Jordan that resemble those with the PA are applicable to two areas with special status (Naharayim/Baqura and Zofar/Al-Ghamr). In these two areas, Jordanian sovereignty is recognized, but Israeli law applying to the extraterritorial activities of Israel may be applied to Israelis and their activities (Annex I [b, c]).[6] Although there are special provisions for legal cooperation with Jordan, including a special annex on 'Combatting Crime and Drugs' (Annex III), these are much less detailed than in similar provisions in the agreements with the PA.

THE CREATION OF INTERDEPENDENT ECONOMIC SYSTEMS

In the economic sphere, the impact of the agreements is felt much more on the Palestinian front.[7] With respect to Jordan, small-scale economic relations have been initiated with an eye to building close ties in the future (Arnon *et al.*, 1996, p. 113). The Palestinian economy, however, has been integrated into the Israeli economic system since the late 1960s, so that the agreement with the PLO/PA was based not only on future aspirations, but also on past experience and on a transfer of authorities from the Israeli to the Palestinian side.

Although the main political negotiation took place in Cairo, talks on the economic part of the agreement were held in Paris. The Cairo agreement of May 1994 established that when the two agreements (Cairo and Paris) conflict with each other, the Cairo agreement takes precedence. Therefore, all economic provisions are subject to considerations of national security. Here I shall not attempt to describe the entire scope of the economic agreement, but instead will focus on the most important spheres in the context of the main concern of this chapter, the internationalization of internal legal arrangements.

During the economic talks, it was soon agreed that the two economies would maintain close ties and that a physical border would be established between the two entities. Subsequently, as noted by Kleiman (1994, pp. 352–3), who attended the talks, three possible solutions were considered:

1. Common market. At the most integrated end of the options considered, short of a complete economic merger, stood the possibility of a common market. This arrangement, if adopted, would have meant open borders and no limitations on the transportation of both goods and means of production. Merchandise and services, capital and labor would move freely between members of the common market, without incurring customs duties or bureaucratic obstacles. An example of such a common market is, of course, the European Union (Stuenenberg, 1994).
2. Customs union. A more restrictive arrangement was that of a customs union, where free movement of goods but not of means of production, such as labor and capital, would be allowed. A customs union requires not only a common tariff, but also common methods of customs evaluation, standardization, and specifications. Such a customs union existed in the Benelux countries before they became part of the European Community (Kleiman, 1994, p. 353).
3. Free Trade Area agreement (such as NAFTA, which covers Canada, the United States, and Mexico). Such an agreement would limit the free movement of goods to those produced by the contracting parties. It would not extend free movement to goods imported from the rest of the world. Israel has had a free-trade area agreement with the EU since 1975, and with the United States since 1985 (Kleiman, 1994, p. 354).

Israel opposed the first option of a common market because it did not want to commit itself to unrestricted movement of workers from the occupied territories. A common market was not very appealing to the Palestinians, either, because of their desire to distance themselves from Israel. The third option of a free-trade area was looked on favorably by the Palestinians, but not by Israel because it would necessitate strict control of the borders between the PA and Israel.

Therefore, a model built mainly on the second option of a customs union was adopted.

The key provision of the economic agreement is that movement of goods and agricultural products between the two sides will be free (with some exceptions) 'of any restrictions including customs and import taxes' (Articles IX.1 and VIII.1, respectively). To make this provision applicable to Israeli law, the Knesset passed internal legislation for establishing a customs union with the PA.[8]

Without a customs union, the Palestinians would have been able to collect only duties. The borders between Gaza and Israel are so porous that there would be little to collect. There is no better proof of this porousness than the sharp 45 per cent increase, during the first year of PA rule, in car thefts from Israel to 'slaughterhouses' in Gaza, Jericho, and the West Bank where they are stripped for spare parts or resold to local inhabitants (*Ha'aretz*, 9 May 1995).

The implementation of the agreement in internal Israeli legislation imposed a number of formal limitations on Israeli economic policy decisions and secondary legislation.[9] These limitations also entail, in my view, informal but considerable restrictions on the Knesset's power to amend economic legislation, because choosing certain options without the consent of the Palestinians may amount to a breach of the agreement and may significantly influence policy-making within the PA.

Taxation

The open-borders principle brought to the fore the problem of taxation. Tax differentials, unless offset by other considerations, provide incentives for buyers to shift their purchases from the high- to the low-tax economy (Kleiman, 1994, p. 360). The main indirect tax in Israel, value-added tax (hereafter VAT), is a uniform-rate, multi-stage tax. Sellers at each stage are entitled to set off, against the tax due on their sales, VAT paid on their purchases from others. Consequently, tax saved at one stage increases the tax liability at the subsequent one. Should there be a significant gap between the two economies, it would be difficult to prevent widespread tax evasion by businessmen who might try to exploit the tax differentials.

Therefore, the agreement allows the Palestinian VAT to be no more than 2 per cent lower than the Israeli rate, levied at the same rates on imports as well as on domestic production (Article III.7). Although limits are set on the PA, it is unlikely that Israel would unilaterally change its own VAT rate without first considering the possible bilateral ramifications of such an act and then consulting the PA, since the agreement also provides for overall clearance of VAT between the PA and Israel. The same principle of establishing similar rates applies to purchase-tax rates (Article VI.2).

Imports

Two lists of specific goods are defined in the agreement with respect to imported agricultural products. First, there is a limited quantity of goods with respect to which the PA is to exercise complete discretion over both tariffs and all other conditions of importation. Second, there are a number of products for which the PA can decide the mutual tariff rates but not other aspects, such as standard requirements or licensing (Kleiman, 1994, p. 358). Therefore, on all these goods, the PA's decisions may be (once the price in the PA is lower than in Israel) binding for products imported to Israel as well.

Money Transfers

Because the Israeli economy is much larger than the Palestinian economy, the ramifications of the agreement are felt much more on the PA's side. Because of this imbalance of economic power, Israel's considerations throughout the negotiations were mainly political (excluding the issue of tariffs and the VAT already discussed). Israel regarded future economic prosperity within the PA as essential for curbing the growth of Islamic fundamentalism and political discontent. Therefore, besides the clear interest of protecting the Israeli economy from the possible influence of uneven indirect taxes (VAT and purchase-tax rates), the Israeli negotiating team had to take into consideration the economic agreement's effects on the PA (Gabbay, 1994; Kleiman, 1994).

Although the agreement acknowledges the right of both sides to independently set their direct tax rates, there are exceptions in regard to income tax deducted from salaries of Palestinians employed in Israel and in Israeli settlements in the territories. In both cases, income is generated in Israel and Israel collects the tax on it, but most of the public services consumed by the employees are supplied by the PA, in which their families live. The agreement recognizes this situation by transferring to the PA 75 per cent of the taxes deducted from the income of Palestinians employed in Israel and in Israeli settlements. As of June 1996, Israel had transferred to the PA NIS 1,280 million (about US $420 million) for customs and tax returns ('Israel Foreign Ministry Memorandum,' 11 June 1996; Frisch and Hofnung, 1997).

The formation of a customs union did not bring the PA the gains anticipated in view of the economic advantages stemming from employment opportunities in, and the short geographical distance from, Israeli population centers (Angrist, 1996, p. 425). Partly because of the closure imposed on the border passages between the PA areas and Israel, opportunities did not materialize. However, other advantages of the Palestinian economy, such as low income tax, were not exploited by Israeli or foreign businessmen for different reasons that are also related to legal issues. The lack of a coherent legal system, and the absence of effective courts that could enforce contracts and payments, has brought an atmosphere of uncertainty with regard to investments. A change in legal conditions may create more opportunities and constrain Israel to either amend its economic policy or coordinate it with the PA, in order to prevent manipulation of differential tax brackets or other loopholes.[10]

MUTUAL SECURITY ARRANGEMENTS

Unlike previous peace agreements, where the main concern was mutual security arrangements for preventing external attacks by one state against the other, the main considerations in the agreements with the PA involve internal security in Israel, in the Jewish settlements, and on the main roads in the territories. One of Israel's preconditions for signing the Declaration of Principles (DOP) was internal security, as expressed in a letter of 9 September 1993 by PLO Chairman Yassir Arafat to Prime Minister Yitzhak Rabin:

> The PLO recognizes the right of the State of Israel to exist in peace and security ... The PLO commits itself to the Middle East peace process, and to a peaceful resolution of the conflict between the two sides ... the PLO renounces the use of terrorism and other acts of violence and will assume responsibility over all PLO elements and personnel in order to assure their compliance.

The Cairo agreement of 4 May 1994 establishes in detail the authority of, and the types and sizes of weapons possessed by, the

Palestinian police force. The most significant issue, however, concerns the elaborate coordination and cooperation mechanisms that were constructed to ensure the withdrawal of Israeli forces from Gaza and parts of the West Bank, to ensure safe movement of thousands of people between Israel and the PA areas, and to prevent terrorist attacks and eruption of hostilities in areas where both Israelis and Palestinians conduct their daily affairs. Unlike the peace agreement with Egypt and the interim agreement with Syria, where clear lines of separation are established between the armies and implementation is assisted by international forces, there are no clear lines between Israeli and Palestinian forces. Moreover, with the exception of Hebron, no international force is involved in maintaining the agreement, and the interim period, which involves areas of shared responsibilities, may continue over several years. Therefore, daily coordination is necessary in implementing and maintaining the fragile agreement. Such coordination may also facilitate further future cooperation with other Arab countries (Karsh and Sayigh, 1994).

The Security Coordination and Cooperation Bodies

Annex I of the Cairo agreement sets up a Joint Security Coordination and Cooperation Committee (JSC) for mutual security purposes. The committee is a forum for dealing with security issues raised by either side, for providing an information-exchange channel, for recommending guidelines, and for providing directives for the District Coordination Offices (DCOs), which operate under the JSC (Annex I, Article II). The Cairo agreement does not say what the security-policy guidelines should include, or what types of security issue should be discussed; it is left to the parties to decide such questions later (Calvo Goller, 1994, p. 264). The regional DCOs, which are staffed with up to six officers from each side, form the daily co-ordinating offices. These DCOs operate 24 hours a day and deal with all matters of a joint nature between the two sides.[11] They are entrusted with coordination between the Israeli and Palestinian headquarters on matters of joint patrols, crossing points and passages, ensuring the flow of traffic on the roads, and dealing immediately with various incidents and complaints.[12]

Other provisions of Annex I deal with specific security arrangements in Gaza and the West Bank; regulation for security reasons of planning, building, and zoning in the PA areas; crossing points; safe

passages between Gaza and the West Bank; security of Israeli settlements and military installation areas; Israeli surveillance of international crossing into the PA; limits on maritime activity along the
Gaza coastline; and security of airspace. The agreement also allows
Israeli forces to take 'engagement steps' that are defined as 'an
immediate response to an act or incident constituting a danger to life
or property' (Article VIII, Para. 9[a]). Not included in Annex I but also
constituting part of the understanding between Israel and the PA, is
coordination on matters of intelligence. On several occasions the PA
security forces, after being informed by Israel, have arrested persons
suspected of planning terrorist attacks on Israeli targets (*Ha'aretz*, 27
June 1996).

Security Arrangements With Jordan

The security arrangements with Jordan are much less complicated
than those with the PA. There is a clearly defined border between the
two countries. Unlike the agreement with the Palestinians, which
grants Israel superior status on various matters, the treaty with Jordan
reflects agreement between equal partners (Banerji, 1995). There is a
mutual commitment of not 'joining or in any way assisting ... with any
coalition, organization or alliance ... with a third party, the objective
of which includes launching aggression or other acts of military
hostility against the other party' (Article 4[4]). Unlike the peace treaty
with Egypt, the treaty with Jordan gives no role to international
forces. The two countries were able to settle all major disputes
without the involvement of a third party (for a different view, see
Zunes, 1995), a factor that is more conducive to further cooperation.

COOPERATION IN PROTECTION OF THE ENVIRONMENT
AND THE USE OF NATURAL RESOURCES

The small geographical area shared by the three entities, combined
with the fact that environmental resources and hazards may not
accommodate international borders, compels the parties to cooperate in the protection and use of such resources (Hirsch, 1994, p. 374).
The parties were quite aware of this situation and the agreements
contain many provisions on environmental and natural-resource
issues. A fundamental principle of international law that is affirmed
in the agreements with Jordan and the PA is that of harm prevention,

according to which states undertake mutual commitments that activities within their own territories will not cause damage to the environment of neighboring states (Hirsch, 1994, p. 378).[13]

Cooperation and Coordination With the PA

Annex II of the Cairo agreement (Protocol on Civil Affairs) gives elaborate prescriptions for cooperation and coordination on all civil matters. The annex establishes a Joint Civil Affairs Coordination and Cooperation Committee (CAC), which is entrusted with ongoing coordination responsibilities between Israel and the PA. Under the central CAC there are regional subcommittees that are authorized to deal with day-to-day civil matters as they arise. Among these responsibilities is coordination in the domain of natural resources and protection of the environment.

One of the most important provisions of the Cairo agreement is the 'veto power' given to Israel with respect to zoning and planning within the PA, according to Article II.32(e) of the Protocol on Civil Affairs.[14] Since the CAC (which Article II refers to) comprises an equal number of representatives from Israel and the PA, this provision actually grants Israel a veto power with respect to public planning by the PA. This power, however, is not absolute, since objections must be related to land use and are subject to the international-law principle of good faith.

Other provisions of the agreement deal with coordination in such matters as maintaining nature reserves, as well as managing water and sewage systems.[15] Although the Palestinians depend on Israel for a steady supply of drinking water, lack of cooperation in this area may cause considerable problems within Israel. Unauthorized drilling of water, especially in the West Bank, could severely affect water reserves in Israel; likewise, Palestinian failure to take sufficient care of their sewage systems could cause severe environmental hazards in Israel. The payoffs for cooperation on both sides are much greater than the advantages of acting unilaterally and risking the other side's retaliation.

Cooperation and Coordination With Jordan

The acknowledgment that regional cooperation is necessary is clearly demonstrated in Article 6(3) of the treaty with Jordan: 'The parties recognize that their water resources are not sufficient to meet their needs. More water should be supplied for their use through various methods, including projects of regional and international cooperation.' In other words, both countries explicitly agree that the current situation is a zero-sum game, in which any attempt to transfer water from one party to the other may result in immediate water shortage for the transferring party. Nevertheless, Israel undertook to help Jordan in obtaining three distinct quantities of water (short-, medium-, and long-term projects), each totaling 50 million cubic meters of water. The first allocation is to come from water resources already utilized by Israel, the other two from joint cooperation in developing storage facilities and finding new sources (Reisner, 1995, p. 9). For its part, Jordan agreed that Israel be allowed to operate and use 15 wells in its territory in order to supply water for the Israeli settlements in the Arava area (Article IV of Annex II).

INFRASTRUCTURE COORDINATION

Both the agreement with the PA and the peace treaty with Jordan contain provisions on the extensive coordination of infrastructure issues between the parties. Spheres of coordination range from natural resources, such as water, land, gas, and petroleum, to initiated projects, such as electricity, telecommunications, sewage, and roads.

Infrastructure Coordination with the PA

Most of the provisions for infrastructure coordination between the PA and Israel are found in Annexes II and IV of the Cairo agreement. Annex II, article II, dealing with the transfer of powers and responsibilities of the Israeli civil administration, contains a range of provisions on control and management of infrastructure resources that 'shall be transferred to the Palestinian Authority in the Gaza Strip and the Jericho Area', such as fisheries, land registration, government and absentee land and other immovables, and gas and petroleum. These provisions encompass such issues as licensing, agricultural permits, and general powers and responsibilities pertaining to the afore-mentioned spheres.

Annex II, Article II.B, also addresses a range of initiated infra-structure issues, such as electricity, public works, telecommunications, and planning and zoning, all of which require coordination between the parties. In the Jericho area the PA is to buy electricity from the Jerusalem Electric Company, and in Gaza from the Israel Electric Company (IEC), while undertaking not to interfere with IEC supply of electricity to the areas of Jewish settlement such as Gush Katif and Kfar Darom. In the electromagnetic sphere, the available frequencies for television and radio transmission are specified and each side commits itself not to interfere with the other's trans-missions (Article II.B.29).

Article VIII of Annex IV, the Protocol on Economic Relations, deals with agricultural issues, and provides for cooperation on standards and regulations concerning animal health, animal products, and plants. All of these provisions are related to the broader aspects of economic coordination and integration between the parties, and are indicative of the extent to which the Gaza–Jericho agreement establishes a wide range of coordinated spheres of activity between the PA and Israel.

Israeli–Jordanian Understandings on Infrastructure

The peace treaty between Jordan and Israel deals with numerous issues of infrastructure coordination. Among these are transporta-tion and roads; telecommunications; energy-related issues (includ-ing cooperation in such matters as solar energy and the establishment of interconnecting electric grids in the Eilat–Aqaba region); develop-ment of the Rift Valley in economic, environmental, energy-, and tourist-related matters; and joint development of the Eilat–Aqaba region (for implementation steps, see Kliot, 1997).

Such coordination may take years to implement, if it is achieved at all. The important issue, however, is that an agreement containing such mutual commitments was next to impossible before the peace process with the Palestinians began. Unlike on the Palestinian front, cooperation with Jordan has continued after the Likud's accession to power, as is evident from the signing of a transportation agreement according to which the Jordanian airport in Aqaba will serve as an international airport for Eilat (*Yediot Aharonot*, 30 May 1997).[16]

CONCLUSION

The ultimate rationale behind the agreements with the Palestinians and Jordan was the vision of a 'New Middle East', where the state of war between the nations would terminate and regional cooperation and coordination would be established.[17] This vision did not materialize at the pace that was anticipated. Cooperation and coordination, especially with the Palestinians, almost came to a halt after the decisive victory of right-wing parties in the Israeli elections of May 1996 and the establishment of a Likud-led government.[18] Because of the extended closure since March 1996, the Palestinian economy has suffered substantial losses and the standard of living has sharply declined (especially in Gaza). On the Israeli side, there is considerable disappointment over what is considered insufficient adherence to the agreement, especially regarding the commitments to abolish the Palestinian Covenant and to fight terrorism. Still, it appears that what has been achieved thus far will affect Israeli lawmaking in the long run.

Despite all the difficulties associated with implementing the agreements, a significant portion of their provisions is being carried out by the respective parties. Although another portion is not being implemented, the parties are well aware of their mutual undertakings. A search of the Israeli *Book of Laws* reveals more than 50 laws that make direct references to the agreements with the PA and Jordan. These laws refer to an even larger body of amendments in other existing laws that are affected by the agreements. In other words, in implementing Israel's internal legislation, an ever-increasing portion is affected by the requirements of coordination and cooperation with the PA and Jordan. This legislation deals with such matters as integrated tax systems, monthly transfers of money to another political entity because of mutual economic arrangements, elections to a foreign legislative assembly under Israeli surveillance (and on Israeli soil, i.e., in East Jerusalem), ongoing coordination on security affairs, and so on. Israel has moved from a situation of isolation within the region to one of either full or partial diplomatic ties with most countries in the Middle East.

The agreements, when more fully implemented, may be interpreted as harming Israel's sovereignty. This claim may have some basis, because Israel has assumed such commitments as granting safe passage through its territory, coordinating in deciding tax and customs rates, releasing prisoners convicted of murder, and other bilateral obligations in regard to its agreements with Jordan and the PA. Such practices, very common between developed, friendly countries, are uncommon in the history of Israel and its immediate neighbors. The trade-off may be one of less sovereignty and more cooperation, coordination, and interdependence. There is probably no better indication of the rewards for regional cooperation than the sharp increase in foreign investments in Israel since the signing of the DOP with the PLO in September 1993.[19] Many internal changes require immediate coordination because they affect not only Israel's international commitments, but also the lives and businesses of thousands of individuals and companies who are engaged in daily economic activity with Israelis.

The peace process may move back and forth between hope and despair, negotiations and crises, but it seems that in the learning process of living together in the same area, the legal steps already taken are paving the way to future cooperation and coordination, built not only on aspirations, but also on the everyday experience of implementing the provisions of the agreements as entrenched in the internal legislation of the respective parties.

NOTES

1. Consider, in this respect, the riots after the decision of the Likud-led government to open the Western Wall tunnel in September 1996, and the international community's reaction to the decision to build a new Jewish neighborhood at Har Homa in East Jerusalem.
2. The laws made applicable to Jews living in the territories were: the Entry into Israel Law (1952); the Security Service Law (Consolidated Version) (1959); the Bar Association Law (1961); the Income Tax Ordinance; the Population Registry Law (1965); the National Law (Consolidated Version) (1968); the Psychologists Law (1977); the Registration and Enlisting of Equipment for the IDF Law (1981).
3. Regulation 6B(a) reads: 'For purposes of the legislation mentioned in the schedule, the term "resident of Israel" or any other term regarding Israeli residency appearing therein, will be deemed to include a person who lives in the area and who is an Israeli citizen or who is entitled to become an Israeli citizen under the Law of Return, 1950, and who, if he lived in Israel, would come within that term.'
4. The Management of Municipal Councils (Judea and Samaria) Order (No. 892) (1981), *Collection of Proclamations, Orders and Appointments* (C.P.O.A. 1982), p. 864, (1984), pp. 12, 170; the Management of Regional Councils (Judea and Samaria) Order (No. 783) (1979), C.P.O.A. (1981), pp. 88, 122, 200, C.P.O.A. (1982), pp. 450, 866, 878; Jurisdiction of Rabbinical Courts (Judea and Samaria) Order (No. 981) (1982), C.P.O.A. (1983), p. 58; Security of Educational Institutions (Judea and Samaria) Order (No. 817) (1980), C.P.O.A. (1981), pp. 258, 348. See also Drori (1980, 1981).
5. Interview with Yoram Gabbay, Director of Israel Revenue Administration, 10 and 13 August 1994.
6. Law of Implementation of the Peace Treaty between the State of Israel and the Hashemite Kingdom of Jordan (1995), Article 3.
7. The volume of trade with the PA was US$2 billion in 1996, compared with US$14 million with Jordan for that year (*Ha'aretz*, 2 July 1997).
8. Implementation of the Agreement on Gaza Strip and Jericho Area Law (Law Amendments) (1994); Implementation of the Interim Agreement on the West Bank and Gaza Strip Law (Law Amendments) (1996).
9. Law of Implementation of the Agreement Concerning the West Bank and Gaza Strip (Judicial powers and other instructions) (Legislative amendments) (1996); Law of Implementation of the Agreement Concerning the Gaza Strip and Jericho Area (Economic arrangements and miscellaneous instructions) (Legislative amendments)

(1994); Law of Implementation of the Agreement Concerning Preparatory Transfer of Authorities to the Palestinian Authority (Legislative amendments and miscellaneous instructions) (1995).

10. An example of such a tax loophole was reported in the daily *Ha'aretz*. An article related that businessmen had imported Gillette shaving razors through Israel to the PA, paid the purchase tax, and used the different income tax levels in Israel and the PA to sell the razors in Israel, thus making a considerable profit (*Ha'aretz*, 4 April 1997).

11. For the enforcement of coordination methods through the DCOs, see H.C. 6757/95 *Haffez v. Military Commander of Judea and Samaria* (yet unpublished, decision given on 11 February 1996).

12. See, e.g., H.C. 6757/95 *Hirbawi v. Commander of IDF*. In this case the Israeli High Court of Justice ruled that any arrest of a resident of the PA areas by the IDF should immediately be reported to the DCO.

13. See also, on this matter, Principle 21 of the United Nations Conference on the Human Environment ('Stockholm Declaration') (1972); Principle 2 of the Rio Declaration on Environment and Development.

14. Article II.32(e) of the Protocol on Civil Affairs reads: 'If Israel considers such a plan to be inconsistent with the terms of the Agreement, … it may, within thirty (30) days, … bring it for consideration by a special subcommittee. … The Palestinian Authority shall respect the recommendation of the subcommittee. Pending the completion of such a consideration process, … the planning procedures shall not be finalized.'

15. For a Palestinian view of water allocation, see Elmusa (1993, 1995).

16. The agreement stipulates that a joint Israeli–Jordanian company will provide ground services for the airport. The agreement also contains the option to include Egypt in the management and use of the airport.

17. For an argument that the peace agreements cannot solve the basic economic problems, and only far-reaching changes in policies can extricate the region's Arab states from stagnation, unemployment, and poverty, see Kanovsky (1995).

18. See, in this regard, the decision of Arab foreign ministers who convened in Cairo after the Israeli government's decision to start a housing project at Har Homa in East Jerusalem. The resolution recommended that members of the Arab League freeze relations with Israel by closing their offices there, renewing the Arab boycott on Israel, and banning multilateral peace negotiations (*Ha'aretz*, 31 March 1997).

19. Foreign investment in Israel jumped from US$504 million in 1992 to US$756 million in 1993, fell slightly to US$626 million in 1994, and made a quantum leap to US$1,911 million in 1995 and US$2,355 in 1996 (data supplied by the Israel Central Bureau of Statistics).

REFERENCES

Angrist, J., 'Short-Run Demand for Palestinian Labor', *Journal of Labor Economics*, 14 (1996), pp. 425–53.

Arnon, A., Spivak, A., and Weinblatt, J., 'The Potential for Trade Between Israel, the Palestinians and Jordan', *World Economy*, 19 (1996), pp. 113–34.

Banerji, A.-K., 'The Israeli–Jordanian Peace Treaty: Jordan's Long Quest for Security and Identity', *Strategic Analysis*, 17 (1995), pp. 1,419–30.

Bar-Siman-Tov, Y., 'The Arab–Israeli Conflict: Learning Conflict Resolution', *Journal of Peace Research*, 31 (1994), pp. 75–92.

Benvenisti, E., 'Responsibility for the Protection of Human Rights

Under the Interim Israeli–Palestinian Agreements', *Israel Law Review*, 28 (1994), pp. 297–317.

Calvo Goller, K., 'Legal Analysis of the Security Arrangements Between Israel and the PLO', *Israel Law Review*, 28 (1994), pp. 236–67.

Drori, M., *Local Government, Democracy, and Elections in the Area of Judea and Samaria: Legal Aspects* (Jerusalem: Institute for Federal Studies, 1980) (in Hebrew).

Drori, M., 'Organization and Municipal Structure of the Israeli Settlements in Judea and Samaria: Legal Aspects', *City and Region*, 4 (1981), pp. 28–45 (in Hebrew).

Elmusa, S. S., 'Dividing the Common Palestinian–Israeli Waters: An International Water Law Approach', *Journal of Palestine Studies*, 22 (1993), pp. 57–77.

Elmusa, S. S., 'Dividing Common Water Resources According to International Water Law: The Case of the Palestinian–Israeli Waters', Natural Resources Journal, 35 (1995), pp. 223–42.

Frisch, H. and Hofnung, M., 'State Formation and International Aid: The Emergence of the Palestinian Authority', *World Development*, 25, 8.(1997), pp. 1,243–55.

Gabbay, Y., 'The Custom and Tax Agreement: Israel and the Palestinian Authority' Unpublished paper (1994) (in Hebrew).

Hirsch, M., 'Environmental Aspects of the Cairo Agreement on the Gaza Strip and the Jericho Area'. *Israel Law Review*, 28, 2–3 (1994), pp. 374–401.

Hofnung, M., 'States of Emergency and Ethnic Conflict in Liberal Democracies: Great Britain and Israel', *Terrorism and Political Violence*, 6, 3 (1994), pp. 340–65.

Hofnung, M., *Law, Democracy and National Security in Israel* (Aldershot, UK: Dartmouth, 1996).

Kanovsky, E., 'Middle East Economies and Arab–Israeli Peace Agreements', Israel Affairs, 1 (1995), pp. 22–39.

Karsh, E., and Sayigh, Y., 'A Cooperative Approach to Arab–Israeli Security', *Survival*, 36 (1994), pp. 114–25.

Kleiman, E., 'The Economic Provisions of the Agreement Between Israel and the PLO', *Israel Law Review*, 28 (1994), pp. 347–73.

Kliot, N., 'The Grand Design for Peace: Planning Transborder Cooperation in the Red Sea', Political Geography, 16 (1997), pp. 581–603.

Reisner, D., 'Peace on the Jordan', *Justice*, 4 (1995), pp. 1–10.

Rubinstein, A. and Medinah, B., *Constitutional Law of the State of Israel,*

5th ed (Jerusalem and Tel Aviv: Schocken, 1996) (in Hebrew).

Singer, J., 'Aspects of Foreign Relations Under the Israeli–Palestinian Agreements on Interim Self-Government Arrangements for the West Bank and Gaza', *Israel Law Review*, 28 (1994), pp. 268–96.

Stuenenberg, B., 'Decision-Making Under Different Institutional Arrangements: Legislation by the European Community', *Journal of Institutional and Theoretical Economics*, 150 (1995), pp. 642–69.

Wasserstein Fassberg, C., 'Israel and the Palestinian Authority: Jurisdiction and Legal Assistance', *Israel Law Review*, 28 (1994), pp. 318–46.

Zunes, S., 'The Israeli–Jordanian Agreement: Peace or Pax Americana?', *Middle East Policy*, 3, 4 (1995), pp. 57–68.

9 The Role of the Media in Shaping Israeli Public Opinion

CHANAN NAVEH

During the night of 20–21 August 1993, Uri Savir and Abu Ala signed the original Israeli–Palestinian Declaration of Principles in one of the rooms of an official Norwegian guest house near Oslo. The general terms of this agreement were leaked to the press and were first published in the Israeli newspaper *Yediot Aharonot* two days later. The publication of this news was one of the key factors that set the public internal environment (or public opinion) in which Israeli decision-makers have acted since 1993.

It seemed at first that the peace process received large public support, but the decisions involved were controversial and even at its peak the support did not exceed two-thirds of the Israeli public. During this process, the Israeli media hardly supplied the government with the tools to deepen public support or, even more important, to gain legitimacy for its policy. The goal of this chapter is to explore whether and how the Israeli media has related to the issue of legitimacy and public support during the peace negotiations since January 1993. The chapter will scrutinize the media's role as a public mood-setter and as a component of the foreign policy environment that decisionmakers had to take into account.

The analysis will deal, throughout, with four components that are involved in the legitimacy process: the specific nation-state under consideration (Israel) and its media environment; the leadership in that state and its use of the media; the media as a political participant with its specific needs and characteristics; and the public in the state, especially its attitudes toward the media and toward the peace process.

In dealing with these components, certain questions will be discussed: Did the media use its professional tools to secure legitimacy for the government's policy? Did the media foster a reality that was supportive or inimical to the process? Did the government and the opposition have equal access to the media? Finally, what was the meaning and relevancy of the battle—played out in the context of the media—for legitimacy and public support for the process?

PEACE PROCESSES AND THE MEDIA—THEORY

The Search for Legitimacy for the Peace Policy

When leaders in democracies formulate new directions in foreign policy, they have to work hard to gain public support. Public support for leaders increases in times of international crisis, when patriotic feelings run high (Brody, 1994, p. 212). Public opinion affects foreign policy to the extent that foreign policymakers perceive support or opposition to their policies (Cohen, 1973, p. 26).

But to be truly effective, public opinion, defined as 'those opinions held by private persons which governments find it prudent to heed' (Powlick, 1995, p. 428), must take the form of public legitimacy for foreign policy, especially if that policy entails new processes and, in particular, if these are shifts from war to peace. Bar-Siman-Tov has added the dimension of legitimacy to the international relations literature, pointing out that the need for legitimacy is especially crucial in the case of protracted conflicts where leaders have decided to make tangible concessions in shifting from war to peace.

> Mobilization of legitimacy is requisite not only to the effective formulation and implementation of a peace policy, but also to enhance decision makers' self-confidence in the peace policy, to maintain their desired identity images, and to improve their own performance in the peace process. The decision makers must achieve a fundamental, stable and comprehensive national consensus, encompassing substantial proportions of ruling elites, competitive elites, interest groups, and public opinion. (Bar-Siman-Tov, 1994, p. 4).

Moreover, legitimacy is seen as essential especially during the phases of formulating the peace policy, signing of the peace treaty, and, finally, implementation (Bar-Siman-Tov, 1994, pp. 5–7). The process of acquiring legitimacy involves an internal political contest, one of whose objectives is to gain control over the political environment.

The Media and Legitimacy for Peace Policy

How do governments and leaders gain support and legitimacy for nonconsensual foreign policy, and what affects the process of gaining such support? It is clear that political elites and opinion leaders play important roles in framing the public's response to uncertain international events. Whether such elites publicly interpret a crisis as a result of policy failure or, conversely, support the government's position will affect whether the public will rally behind the government. A rally will last as long as the government's tacit or explicit support-coalition persists (Brody, 1994, p. 212).

Bar-Siman-Tov suggests that the process of legitimization is formal as well as informal. The formal dimension involves legal and constitutional processes in such institutions as party, parliament, and government; the informal dimension, which has both political and nonpolitical aspects, is necessary to the formal one. Bar-Siman-Tov also describes means employed by decisionmakers to legitimate peace policies, such as symbols, language, rituals, and so on (Bar-Siman-Tov, 1994, pp. 8–17). But among these means and mechanisms he does not include the media, which is one of the main tools in the process of mobilizing public support (Aggestam, 1996, pp. 7–8; Cohen, 1986, p. 5).

Public opinion is multifaceted, with no one public 'voice' operating wholly independently of any other. Public opinion and foreign policy interact in complex ways. Elites act as both influencers and receptors of public opinion on foreign policy; elected representatives (as well as interest groups) also express views (Cohen, 1986, pp. 8, 66); the public itself expresses itself directly through demonstrations, letters, and opinion polls. Finally, the news media acts as a transmitter of information, and foreign policy officials regard it as a reflection of public opinion (Cohen, 1973, pp. 106–11; Bennett, 1994, pp. 31–3; Powlick, 1995, pp. 428–9).

Let us now consider the role of the media in terms of media environment and of the ways in which government makes use of the media in pursuing its policy goals.

Media Environment

The mechanisms used by the media to gain legitimacy for foreign policy, especially peace policy, depend on a variety of media dimensions that compose the media environment. This environment is global on the one hand, and relates to the international media, but it is also internal insofar as specific media aspects are typical of specific states. We turn now to an overview of some general components and functions of the media environment.

Political-communication regime
The relations between the state and the media span a continuum from authoritarian to libertarian (Lambeth, 1995, pp. 4–11). These relations are sometimes divided into four categories: the authoritarian, Soviet, social-responsibility, and libertarian. To these, two more categories may be added: developmental (i.e., Third World type) and democratic-participant (McQuail, 1994, pp. 127–31; Lambeth, 1995, pp. 14–16). These categories help define the political-communication regime of a given state.

Communication policy
A government's communication policy refers to such issues as: promoting competition and pluralism of the media, minimizing regulations, preventing cross-ownership, allocation of broadcasting frequencies, protecting copyrights, and so on (Baldwin *et al.*, 1996, pp. 301–52). Both the political-communication regime and communication policies are also relevant at the global level, with many parallels to the internal level (Frederick, 1993, pp. 244–66; Baldwin *et al.*, 1996, pp. 301–52; Zacher and Sutton, 1996, pp. 127–80).

Economic setting of the media
Most of the modern mass media (internally and globally) is motivated by profit considerations. More specifically, seven key factors determine the economic setting of the media (Bagdikian, 1987, pp. 4–10; Herman, 1995, pp. 82–3; Mosco, 1996):

1. Advertising is the main source of income.
2. Media organizations tend to merge into large corporations.
3. Media organizations are, with increasing frequency, bought out by nonmedia corporations.
4. These corporations are often part of multinational global corporations.
5. The corporations tend to become media monopolies.
6. These media monopolies try to increase their audiences by using the most modern technologies.
7. The corporations have strong political and other ties with governments.

Media channels and organizations
The combination of the above dimensions of media environment (communication regime, communication policy, and economic setting) sets the background for the fourth dimension: the existence of various communication channels, from newspapers, radio, and television to modern interactive technologies, at the state and international levels (McQuail, 1994, pp. 12–21; Winston, 1995; Baldwin *et al.*, 1996; Friedland, 1996; Merrill and Ogan, 1996).

Typical media functions
Finally, the media affects foreign policy decisionmaking by its professional performance. Lasswell (1971, p. 85), in his pioneering discussion, distinguished three functions of the media: surveillance of the environment; correlation of the parts of society in responding to the environment; and transmission of the social heritage from one generation to the next. Later, two functions were added to the list (McQuail, 1994, pp. 78–9), namely, entertainment and mobilization.

In this multifaceted media environment, the leadership and the public interact. In such interaction, all of the above-mentioned dimensions are relevant, but three of the media functions are most relevant: the informative, correlative, and mobilizing. In performing these functions, the reporters inform the public about the international, foreign, and security events; journalists provide background and interpretation (correlative); and in its third key role, the media can provide support to the established authority and its norms, especially in times of crisis or during a peace process.

In the process of influencing public opinion about the government's peace policy, the media can create an environment that will either support or oppose the policy. By using its professional journalistic tools, the media may construct a reality, that is, create the environment to which the leaders and the public relate in this political process. Here the mass communication channels constitute both the input variable, influencing the foreign policymaking process, and an output framework to which the leaders must refer in making their decisions. This dual effect of the media can be thought of in terms of agenda-setting and framing.

Agenda-setting
Late in the 1940s, Lazarsfeld and Merton (1971) described the media's status-conferral function:

the mass media confer status on public issues, persons, organi-zations, and social movements. Common experience as well as research testify that the social standing of persons or social policies is raised when these command favorable attention in the mass media ... The mass media bestow prestige and enhance the authority of individuals and groups by legitimizing their status (pp. 560–1).

This indicates the media's importance as a source of legitimacy for any kind of policy, including foreign policy, and particularly for a peace process that involves shifts from war and conflict to conciliation.

This perspective was much further developed by Cohen (1963), when he introduced it to the field of foreign policy in his classic book on the role of the media in the foreign policymaking process. His ideas are pertinent:

It is here, in the description of the political environment and the suggestion of the policy alternatives that give the best promise of managing the environment, that we shall find the press playing such an important role in current thinking about foreign policy. This 'map making' function of the press is so central to the foreign policy field that a few words of elaboration may be appropriate ...

For the most of the foreign policy audience, the really effec-tive political map of the world—that is to say, their *operational* map of the world—is drawn by the reporter and the editor, not by the cartographer ...

The press ... may not be successful much of the time in telling people what to think, but it is stunningly successful in telling its readers what to think *about*.

The last paragraph is regarded in the communication literature as the basis for the more developed 'agenda-setting approach', which is mostly associated with McCombs (McCombs and Shaw, 1972; McCombs, 1981). McCombs stated that 'while the mass media may have little influence on the direction or intensity of attitudes, it is hypothesized that *the mass media set the agenda for each political campaign, influencing the salience of attitudes toward the political issues'* (McCombs and Shaw, 1972, p. 177). In other words, the salience of an issue in the mass media influences its salience among the audience

(McCombs, 1981, p. 126; Rogers and Dearing, 1994). This perspective can be summed up in four hypotheses (McQuail, 1994, pp. 356–7):

- Public debate is represented by salient issues (an agenda for action).
- The agenda derives from a combination of public opinion and political choice.
- Mass-media news and information reflect the content and order of priority of issues.
- This representation of issues in the mass media exerts an independent effect on the issue.

The agenda-setting approach can be applied not only to the informative and interpretive functions of the media, but also to its mobilization and entertainment functions. Here the media can be described as mood-setting, and as a creator of the 'imagined foreign policy environment'. The process involves an ongoing competition among proponents of different perspectives, to gain the attention of the media professionals and, through them, the public and policy elite (Dearing and Rogers, 1996, p. 6).

Framing

The media constructs the reality (and helps in achieving legitimacy or forfeiting it) with another tool called framing. This technique is important, since any political conflict centers on the struggle over interpretive frames (Wolfsfeld, 1993, p. xiii; 1997a, pp. 13–35). In this process the media transforms the nature of events through 'formats', which constitute ideological or value perspectives, in which the media focuses on 'story lines', symbols, and relevant stereotypes (Entman, 1991; Entman and Rojecki, 1993; Entman and Page, 1994; Iyengar and Simon, 1994, p. 171). The evidence indicates that individuals' views of national issues are altered by the way in which television news frames them (Iyengar, 1994, p. 141). Therefore, in the competition over media frames some relevant factors should be analyzed, such as the use of loaded modifiers; the ways in which the political actors are referred to; and nuances of the use of language (e.g., in headlines) (Roeh and Nir, 1993, pp. 178–80; Wolfsfeld, 1997a, p. 49).

News values

What are the criteria that lead editors to include items concerning war, peace, or any other foreign-policy events in the news? Do journalists follow rules in making such decisions, or do they act spontaneously? The truth lies somewhere in between; scholars refer to the relevant criteria as news values (Galtung and Ruge, 1970; Larson, 1984; Westerstahl and Johansson, 1994).

The following seem to be the main criteria or news values in selecting an event and making it a news item:

- Ideology as the basic orientation of the news editor.
- The event must be new and surprising.
- The event should involve the dimension of importance, or from the international perspective, should involve the powerful global elite, in terms of countries and leaders.
- Events that are violent or can be defined as negative will get better coverage.
- The event must be relevant to the nation whose media covers it, and it must be accessible to coverage.
- Finally, journalists prefer an event that is recognizable in terms of former news patterns.

Foreign-policy events and processes that satisfy these criteria will be regarded as news. War qualifies; so do shifts from conflict to cooperation. Such news events will usually be at the top of the agenda set by the media, and they will be framed by the specific frame relevant to the event, the issue, and the international actor(s) involved. Thus the media sets the environment of the foreign policy process, and within this media environment the decisionmakers must seek to gain support and legitimacy for their policy.

The Use of the Media by Governments in Foreign Policy

A government may use the media by regulating the flow of information, as an aspect of controlling the political environment (while competing with the opposing political powers). When governments are able to take control of events and enjoy a high degree of consensus, the role of the news media will be dependent and supportive. But when a government loses control over the political environment, the media becomes independent and critical (Wolfsfeld, 1997a, p. 25; 1997b, pp. 30–4).

The first mechanism of the interaction between the media and foreign policymakers is the domestic politicization of foreign-policy decisions. When television anchorpersons are perceived as opinion leaders, the policy officials attempt to gain their support for policies. The second mechanism is the media's acceleration of diplomatic processes, by providing immediate information on events to all policy officials before the official and diplomatic communication channels provide it. The third mechanism, used by leaders, is to shift policy focus to the main decisionmaker (O'Heffernan, 1991, pp. 62–7); the fourth is to adapt to the media environment setting that is relevant to the specific process and utilize it for policy purposes.

Here, the leaders use the media in order to keep options open and at the same time to build consensus. The media, by setting policy agendas and stimulating popular support for policies, provides the tools for leaders to assert control. Moreover, the leader's staff can utilize the media to deliver specific messages to specific audiences (Gergen, 1991, pp. 55–6; O'Heffernan, 1991, pp. 62–7, 105–12; 1994, p. 242). In addition, the media's role as promoter of public debates on policy issues can be used as a tool to gain support (Cohen, 1986, pp. 8, 66; Rosenfeld, 1991, p. 251; Entman and Page, 1994, pp. 83–4).

Even successful peace processes need media support. In these processes, the media can become a foreign policy tool for the actors involved, who may utilize the aspects of the media that compose both the internal and external media environments. Here, the leaders must recognize the relevant media characteristics: the political-communication regime of their own state, its communication policy, its political-economy setting of the media, and its typical media channels and organizations. Second, the decisionmakers must know the media itself: its typical functions, its role in agenda-setting, its framing capability, and the terms of its news values. Third, the leaders must be aware of the international-global media setting, including its channels and organizations, its functions, and its news values. All these factors will enable the leaders to best utilize the media for support and legitimacy.

THE MEDIA IN ISRAEL, 1992–96

We shall now apply these theoretical aspects to the role of the media in Israel, specifically to its ability to help legitimize the controversial peace policy conducted by the Rabin–Peres governments. First, we shall give an overview of the Israeli media environment; subsequently, we present research results on the linkages between the Israeli public's political views and its attitudes toward the media.

The Media Environment

Foreign-policy decisionmaking takes place within the media environment; we now consider the media environment in Israel during the peace process in 1992–96. We shall address only the internal-state dimensions.

The political-communication regime

Israel is a democracy, and during the above-mentioned period the government changed hands twice through elections. The media in Israel has performed its functions in democratic patterns since the mid-1960s (Galnoor, 1985, pp. 352–69). During the 1990s, the relations between the government and the media in Israel have usually been close to the libertarian pole of the political-communication spectrum, though with complications. Caspi and Limor (1992) regard the Israeli political-communication model as a mixed model that incorporates characteristics of various theories mentioned earlier. Caspi and Limor summarized the Israeli model in the early 1990s, but since then a communication revolution has taken place in Israel and the map of the media has changed almost totally.

First, television cables were introduced mainly during that period, and by mid-1996 reached more than 60 per cent of the households in the country (Y. Katz, 1996a, pp. 78–81). Second, on 4 November 1993 the second television channel, financed solely by advertisement, began to broadcast. Third, the map of the printed press changed: the socialist newspapers *Davar* and *Al-Hamishmar* closed, as did the independent newspaper *Hadashot*, while the Orthodox-religious press blossomed (Liebes *et al.*, 1996, pp. 12–15). Fourth, new regional radio stations (up to 18) began to broadcast, and were added to by dozens of private 'pirate' stations operating all over the country (Limor, 1996, p. 55). Finally, overall, competition based partly on profit considerations became a strong motivating force in the media's performance (Mosko, 1996, pp. 4–7; Tikochinski, 1996, pp. 4–9; Lachman-Messer, 1997; Limor, 1997).

These developments have intensified the mixed nature of the Israeli political-communication model. In keeping with Caspi and Limor's observations (1992, pp. 134–43), it still consists of some typical authoritarian patterns (especially in the security area), some developmental patterns (e.g., the national issue of immigration), and some social-responsibility patterns. But with the communication revolution of the 1990s, the nature of the Israeli media has predominantly conformed to the libertarian model.

The communication policy

Did the Israeli leaders formulate a communication policy at all during that period, and was it compatible with the mixed communication regime? The Knesset, combining government and Knesset members' initiatives, passed laws allowing the almost complete competition and pluralism of the electronic media (Negbi, 1995, pp. 174–81; Katz, 1996, pp. 73–81). During the long legislative process, some cross-ownership was averted, broadcasting frequencies were allocated, and public control was set through the Cable Council and the Second Authority Council. These laws were added to the existing formal structure of controls in the Israel Broadcasting Authority (IBA) (Rogel and Schejter, 1995).

To these communication policy characteristics should be added the laws dealing with the media and the freedom of the press, together with Supreme Court decisions that set the norms and rules of this communication environment (Negbi, 1995; Segal, 1996).

The political-economy setting of the Israeli media

The Israeli communication revolution of the 1990s changed the media's political-economy setting completely. As we saw, from 1992 to 1996 television cables reached over 60 per cent of households, with total revenues during these years of approximately US$735 million (while US$400 million were invested in infrastructure).[1]

The second television channel, as noted, began broadcasting in November 1993, and by the end of 1995 had reached revenues of about US$150 million, with maximum viewing ratings of 4 per cent of the households in Israel (*Second Television and Radio Authority Annual Report*, 1995).

In 1995 the IBA budget reached US$180 million, with 60 per cent of income from annual fees, 33 per cent from radio advertisement and television sponsorship, and 7 per cent deficit.[2] Among the newspapers, *Yediot Aharonot* has the largest distribution, with an average of 60 per cent of Israelis reading it. In 1994, *Yediot Aharonot*'s annual revenues from selling newspapers and advertisement space reached over US$250 million. *Ma'ariv* is second, with sales that reach about 25 per cent of the Israeli public, and sales and advertisement revenues in 1994 coming to US$90 million (Limor, 1997).[3]

During the 1990s, the Israeli media seems to have been most strongly motivated by profit and business calculations. The general media trends mentioned in the theoretical section are hardly relevant at this stage, because the Israeli communication market is small, and the external market is not yet influential since the majority of Israeli media products are in Hebrew.

Media channels and organizations in Israel
The media in Israel is mapped by the political-communication regime, the communication policy, and the political-economy setting (Caspi and Limor, 1992; Avraham, 1993; *Second Television and Radio Authority Annual Report*, 1995; Liebes *et al.*, 1996; Lachman-Messer, 1997; Limor, 1997). The various outlets include a variety of television channels, radio networks, and printed newspapers, as well as state-of-the-art multimedia technologies (for details, see Appendix A).

The Israeli Public and the Media in Israel, 1992–96

Can the Israeli media provide a framework for mobilizing domestic support for foreign policy? This depends on media consumption in the country, and on the Israeli public's attitudes toward the media—issues that will form the focus of this section.[4]

The Israeli citizen as a news addict
First, let us attend to the myth that every Israeli devotes a great deal of time to printed, television, and radio news.

Eighty-two per cent of the public read a newspaper more than twice a week; of them, 51 per cent read *Yediot Aharonot*, 22 per cent *Ma'ariv*, 11 per cent *Ha'aretz*, and 3 per cent *Globes*.[5] These and earlier-cited findings suggest why, in 1995, *Yediot Aharonot* was declared a media monopoly by the Ministry of Industry and Trade.

Some 86 per cent of the population watch television news regularly, though not necessarily daily. Of them, 49 per cent watch Mabat, the main news broadcast on Channel 1, 44 per cent watch the main news bulletin on Channel 2, and only 3 per cent watch the news on foreign channels.

The distribution among radio listeners in Israel is more complex. Twenty-eight per cent tune in to the Kol Israel news network, 20 per cent to the Galei Tzahal main network, 11 per cent to various regional stations, and 8 per cent to the Kol Israel pop network. It is believed that about 7 per cent listen to Channel 7; the listener rate of the pirate stations is unknown (Limor, 1996). All of these stations and networks broadcast news almost every hour, so that the Israeli radio listener is indeed continually exposed to news.

Do Israelis trust the media?
Table 9.1 was compiled from various surveys (Diskin, 1997; Shvakim-Panorama, 1997).[6] It shows that the most popular medium is the radio, followed by television, while the level of satisfaction with newspapers is much lower.

Table 9.1: Israelis' Ratings of the Different Media (%)

Satisfaction	Certainly yes	Yes	Maybe	No	Certainly not	No opinion
Newspapers	4.5	27.5	38	18.8	8.3	2.9
TV	7.7	44.0	30.5	10.9	3.5	3.4
Radio	14.4	49.3		29.8	6.5	

Table 9.2 (Shvakim-Panorama, 1997)[7] shows that in times of violence and crisis, Israelis trust television the most, with radio second, and the press hardly trusted.

Table 9.2: Israelis' Trust of Different Media During Violent Events and Crises (%)

	Press	TV	Radio	All the same	None
War and terrorism	7.4	48.1	33.6	7.9	3.0
Political crises	14.1	44.0	25.0	8.7	8.2

It can be concluded that television news should be the most preferred medium for gaining public support in general, and especially in times of stress and crisis. The attitudes toward the press seem to reflect some of the general hostility toward the media in Israel.

General attitudes toward the media in the peace process
Various surveys have focused on how Israelis perceive the media and its coverage of the peace process. Some surveys dealt with very specific attitudes; the most comprehensive was done by Diskin (1997) as part of the Leonard Davis Institute project (see note 4). The following are some of the findings:

- Fifty-three per cent of respondents believed they received enough information about the peace process from the media; 23.3 per cent said the information was insufficient; 14.9 per cent believed it was excessive (Teleseker Institute, 1995).
- Some 51.2 per cent believed that the media's coverage of the peace

process was fair and objective; 36.8 per cent gave the opposite response (Teleseker Institute, 1995).

- Seventy-six per cent of respondents believed that the media was not objective toward the Netanyahu government; only 13 per cent believed it was, and 11 per cent were undecided (Katz, 1996b).

Political attitudes and the media [8]

The most important findings show that about a third of the Israeli citizens who voted for Netanyahu in the 1996 elections do not trust the print media, compared with only a fifth of Peres voters. Among Netanyahu supporters, almost 20 per cent do not trust the television news (more than three times the Peres supporters).

These findings are similar to those concerning the voters' opinions in terms of the outcomes of the 1992 and 1996 elections. A right-wing tendency correlates with very low trust of the Israeli press and only slightly higher trust of television, whereas left-wingers tend to rely on the media, mainly television. As for the religious and Arab sectors, whereas the Jewish religious and especially the ultra-Orthodox (i.e., *haredi*) voters generally strongly object to the media, the Arab voters distrust the press but regard television as reliable.

Similar linkages emerge between attitudes toward security and peace and the attitudes toward the media. People who give high priority to security and do not support peace at any price tend to distrust the media, compared with holders of the opposite attitudes. Opinions about removal of settlements, relinquishing the Golan Heights and the Jordan Valley, or dividing Jerusalem show very similar correlations.

Overall, the Israeli public trusts the television news much more than the printed press, but this does not mean full trust and large groups do not believe what they see on television either. The Rabin government was based on a left-wing coalition, and its policy involved various territorial and political concessions. The surveys clearly show that people who opposed this policy also regarded the press and television as less than reliable. Thus, the people whom the government most needed to persuade about the peace process tended to distrust the media. If the government had aimed to use the media in order to achieve legitimacy, the printed press could not have been an effective tool, and even the television news would have been inadequate.

Before examining the actual media reporting during the 1992–96 peace process, it should be noted that during that period the media provided an environment of a mixed political communication regime and a complex media map; it was in this environment that the Israeli leaders had to make foreign-policy decisions.

The findings presented below focus on the media as one of the main factors that Israeli decisionmakers must take into account. We shall consider the media's roles as an agenda- and mood-setter in the context of the 1992–96 peace process. It will emerge that the media was involved more with the public's than with the leaders' agenda, and that it took part in shaping public opinion during that period.

THE MEDIA AND THE PEACE PROCESS (1992–96): CASE STUDIES

We shall focus on specific events that occurred since the signing of the Oslo 1 agreement in September 1993, and on the behavior of the media in its agenda-setting function. During this period, the media developed specific patterns of reporting the events, placing them on the public agenda, and creating a communication environment to which decisionmakers had to relate.[9]

The Peace Process, 1992–96

On the night of 20–21 August 1993, the Oslo agreement was initialized, and over the next three weeks it was approved by the Israeli government. The Declaration of Principles was finally signed on 13 September 1993 in Washington. These agreements were, of course, achieved through secret negotiations as a back channel to the formal Washington negotiations, which proceeded from the Madrid Conference and were completely open and public, with press conferences, leaks, publications, and use of spokespersons. The media played an important role there as a signaling tool, so that the Washington talks had a strong public-relations element (Aggestam, 1996, pp. 18–19). The Oslo channel was initiated because of the inadequacies of the official negotiations in Washington. Secrecy was regarded as an essential element of the Oslo channel, enabling exploration of the other party's 'red lines' of concessions, the determination of preferences, the search for new ideas, and the avoidance of domestic criticism and time pressures. Indeed, once the agreement was made public, it was criticized on both the Israeli and Palestinian sides (Aggestam, 1996, pp. 27–9).

Subsequently, intensive negotiations led to the Cairo agreement or 'Gaza and Jericho First' (4 May 1994), and its implementation during the following months (Bar-Siman-Tov, 1996). During the latter half of 1994, the negotiations focused on the accord with Jordan, culminating in the Israeli–Jordanian peace treaty (26 November 1994). Then the Palestinian issue (together with fruitless negotiations with the Syrians) again took center stage, and further intensive negotiation yielded the Oslo 2 agreement on 28 September 1995.

Each of these agreements was followed in Israel by another process, namely, that of gaining the formal approval of the Knesset. The peace process with Jordan won broad public legitimacy (89–91 per cent; Bar-Siman-Tov, 1996, p. 96), but the process with the Palestinians was controversial, and formal approval by the Knesset did not legitimize the agreements either for the parliamentary opposition or extraparliamentary groups. These groups protested by demonstrating and by demanding some sort of referendum (Bar-Siman-Tov, 1996, pp. 86–7; 1997). Let us now consider how these events were reflected in some specific cases of treatment by the media.

Coverage and Reporting

During the peace negotiations, various topics were covered by the media.

Peace negotiations

The first case study dealt with the coverage of the Israeli–Palestinian peace process (Oslo 1 and Oslo 2) and of the Israeli–Jordanian peace negotiations by *Yediot Aharonot*.

The findings reveal that *Yediot Aharonot* dealt with these events differently. It covered the Oslo 1 agreement very intensively from late August to mid-September 1993. During that period, the process was always on the front page and received an average of 10 on a salience scale of 1–10. The Oslo 2 process, however, involved prolonged months of public negotiations, during which it was not always the main topic in the news. Even in the last month of the negotiations it received a very low salience score in *Yediot Aharonot*, and only once, the day after the signing in Washington (29 September 1995), was rated 10. During that month (September 1995) as a whole, the Israeli–Palestinian negotiations were rated in *Yediot Aharonot* as 2.5–3.5, and on the signing day as 5.7.

The coverage of the peace negotiations with Jordan was similar to the coverage of the Oslo 2 process in *Yediot Aharonot*. During the period of July–November 1994, on five days in which key events occurred, the negotiations with Jordan were rated 10; the last two of these events occurred on 25–26 November, when the peace treaty was signed in the Arava. The salience of the rest of *Yediot*'s coverage of the Israeli–Jordanian peace process was rated mostly low.

It seems that the 'historic' events were accorded major news value in *Yediot Aharonot*, but not so much the processes surrounding these events. *Yediot* made the environment 'historic' only for short periods of time, which were not sufficient for the government to utilize them to mobilize support and legitimacy.

Public demonstrations

During the peace negotiations with the Palestinians, the opponents of the process held major demonstrations, mainly in the summer and fall of 1995 (before Rabin's assassination). In the second case study, the coverage of these demonstrations by *Yediot Aharonot* and *Ma'ariv* was analyzed. The findings show that during a period of three months, *Yediot* printed 234 reports on these events, or 21 per cent of its total news coverage, and *Ma'ariv* published 259 reports on them, or 19 per cent of its total news coverage.

Of the opinions expressed in the reports, the government received 36 per cent of the share, the established right-wing opposition 26 per cent, and the extraparliamentary opposition 8 per cent (balanced reporting accounted for 21 per cent, and impartial experts 9 per cent). Altogether, then, during July–October 1995, the anti-Oslo attitudes received as much coverage in *Yediot* and *Ma'ariv* as the pro-Oslo opinions. In such a media environment, the government clearly could not rely on the press as a tool for gaining legitimacy.

Changing the Palestinian Covenant

Another case study focused on coverage by two newspapers, *Yediot Aharonot* and *Ha'aretz*, of the issue of changing the Palestinian Covenant during January–May 1996.

The findings revealed that despite the symbolic importance of the issue, it received the highest salience score (10) in both newspapers only once, on the day after the Palestinian National Council resolution (April 1996). Otherwise, the issue received low coverage. During a period of 125 days, *Ha'aretz* reported on the issue 77 times, almost twice as much as *Yediot*. As for articles offering commentary on this issue, *Ha'aretz* printed 19 articles (23 per cent of coverage), *Yediot* 15

(36 per cent of coverage). Most of the articles were mobilizing in nature, but in *Ha'aretz* about half of them supported Prime Minister Peres's position that the Covenant had already been abrogated, whereas in *Yediot*, surprisingly, only one article out of 15 accepted this position. On this issue it seems that *Ha'aretz* acted as a mobilizing tool for the government (it is read, however, mainly by left-wingers who already support the peace policy); *Yediot*'s record here was anomalously one-sided.

Overall, then, the printed press gave high salience to the Oslo 1 agreement, and considerably less to the Israeli–Jordanian peace process, the Oslo 2 process, and the Palestinian Covenant issue. At the same time, the newspapers gave considerable salience to the antigovernment demonstrations, and hence could not serve as a legitimacy tool for the government.

Terrorist attacks
It is believed that the media coverage of the winter 1996 terrorist bombings was one of the factors that changed public opinion in Israel leading up to the May 1996 elections. In this case study, the coverage in *Yediot* and *Ma'ariv* of two other major terrorist attacks was analyzed: the bombings of Bus No. 5 on Dizengoff Street in Tel-Aviv (19 October 1994) and of the military bus station at Beit Lid (22 January 1995).

The findings in Table 9.3 show that during two three-day coverage periods (20–22 October 1994 and 23–25 January 1995), the salience patterns in the two papers were similar, starting from a very high score, diminishing, and almost disappearing (on the fifth day after the Bus No. 5 explosion, both in *Yediot* and *Ma'ariv*, the salience score was 0.5 or lower).

Table 9.3: Salience Patterns of Coverage of Two Terrorist Attacks
(Salience Score: 0–10)

	Bus 5			Beit Lid		
Days	1	2	3	1	2	3
Ma'ariv	9.7	4.4	2.7	9.2	6.1	2.3
Yediot	7.5	2.2	1.6	8.0	5.4	2.5

Clearly, on such occasions where there is a high casualty toll, the media coverage is high and the events are high on the public agenda. In such times of crisis, Israelis tend to trust the media as a source of information. But the events in themselves were not favorable to the peace process, and the government could hardly utilize these situations to gain support for its peace policy, which seemed responsible for the terrorist attacks.

Wolfsfeld, in analyzing press reports during sample days from 27 August 1993 to 5 May 1994 (Wolfsfeld, 1997a, pp. 96–7), found that in general the peace process was the main topic of the press as it fulfilled its functions of surveillance, coverage, and reporting during that period. News of the peace process superseded almost any other event or process except the terrorist attacks, which were the other side of the coin. Further analysis of this period should focus on how the press performed the function of correlation, and whether the press was used as a mobilizing factor for the different competing parties during the process.

Agenda-Setting by the Media

Radio as a mood-setter

The preceding case studies reflected the agenda-setting role of the printed press in performing the coverage and reporting function. We turn now to the role of radio broadcasts, specifically music programming on Kol Israel (Voice of Israel) and Galei Tzahal (the military network), in creating the mood as an aspect of agenda-setting. The working hypothesis was that these stations change the pattern of music programming in response to major news events, such as terrorist attacks or breakthroughs in the peace process.

The theoretical basis of this hypothesis lies in the international relations notion of the 'state in siege'. In a 'state in siege', most of the population believes that the international environment poses a threat to their existence (Bar-Tal, 1983, 1991). The leadership and public of such a state may react with various mobilization strategies. Here the media joins in the mobilizing function, and radio stations tend to support morale by, among other things, broadcasting music with national themes.

Using the data supplied by AKUM (the Israeli Association of Composers and Writers), this hypothesis was tested. Music programs of three radio stations were studied: Reshet Bet and Galatz, which are news stations, and Reshet Gimel, which is a music and pop station. Programs were analyzed in the context of three 'peace' events: the Oslo 1 ceremony; the Washington declaration with Jordan; and the opening of the Arava terminal between Israel and Jordan. The same procedure was used in the context of three terrorists attacks: the Hebron massacre; the kidnapping and murder by terrorists of Shalom

Wachsman; and the Bus No. 5 bombing in Tel-Aviv. The findings showed that on three 'neutral, regular' days, for all three radio stations an average of 40 per cent of the songs broadcast in their music programs were Israeli songs. Table 9.4 shows the percentages of Israeli songs played by the three stations on the days of the special events.

Table 9.4: Percentages of Israeli Songs Played by the Three Networks on
Days of Major Peace and Terrorist Events
(Compared With a 40% Rate on 'Regular' Days)

Event	Reshet Bet	Galatz	Reshet Gimel
Oslo 1	80	40	No change
Washington declaration	70	n.i.	No change
Arava terminal	60	No change	No change
Hebron massacre	No change	No change	No change
Wachsman	60–70	n.i.	No change in percentage of songs, but change in nature—more 'sad' music
Bus No. 5	90	No change in percentage of songs, but change in nature—more 'sad' music	No change in percentage of songs, but change in nature—more 'sad' music

The findings suggest that the radio stations, in terms of increasing the amount of nationally oriented music, played only a partial role in setting the national mood during these events. This mood-setting function was observable only for Reshet Bet, which is connected to Kol Israel's newsroom. The other stations did not change the type of song played during these events, and only in some cases changed the mood. Since the findings show no overall effect, there is no justification in seeing the radio-music channels as agenda-setters of the public. Whether such partially mood-setting roles hinder or help decisionmakers when they need support and legitimacy for their policy is a question for further research.

Right-wing media organs
The media map in Israel includes two right-wing organs, the newspaper *Hatsofeh* and the Channel 7 radio station. The first part of this case study analyzed samples of the commentaries broadcast on

Channel 7 and found blatant antigovernment propaganda. The sample, which included some of the station's typical commentators (such as E. Haetzni and Professor H. Weiss), shows that the attitudes expressed in the broadcasts toward Arabs, Palestinians, and the Rabin government were highly negative-stereotyped, sometimes to the point of demonization. The commentaries also expressed highly Jewish-ethnocentric attitudes that were xenophobic toward the Palestinians.[10]

The second part of the case study analyzed *Hatsofeh* on a day-to-day basis from September 1995 to May 1996. The findings revealed strong, stereotyped group-thinking, demonstrated by anti-Arab expressions, demonization of the image of Yassir Arafat, antipeace-process coverage and attitudes, and delegitimization of the Rabin–Peres government. As the organ of the National Religious Party, *Hatsofeh* demonstrated these images and expressions while fulfilling the main media functions. In its informative function, it played up reports that were favorable to the party line and gave these the largest headlines; 'negative' information was very much played down. Reports on important events were mixed with commentary. Finally, in the correlating role, *Hatsofeh* carried only opinions of supporters of the party line.

These findings about the right-wing media clearly indicate that the Rabin government had little or no possibility of influencing the right. *Hatsofeh* and Channel 7 were read or listened to by the majority of the peace-process opponents, and at the same time this public was highly critical of the other media organs and was not influenced by them, even though, as shown earlier, they hardly contributed to legitimizing the process.

The 'peace' and 'disaster' frames

Wolfsfeld (1997a), in analyzing the framing of the peace process in two newspapers, *Ha'aretz* and *Yediot Aharonot*, compared two frames—the 'chance for peace', which was put forward by the Rabin government, and the 'national disaster', which was promoted by the right-wing opposition—and found that neither side was able to dominate public discourse. In the early part of the process, the political breakthrough strengthened the 'peace' frame, but when the terrorist attacks began they strengthened the 'disaster' frame. Wolfsfeld believes, however, that the settlement movement had significant success in promoting its frames to the Israeli news media (Wolfsfeld, 1997a, pp. 122–3).

The various case studies surveyed here indicate that the government could not have made much use of the media, which had different frames and opinions at the top of its agenda and even set moods and agendas in reaction to terrorist attacks. We turn now to the question of whether the Rabin government actually attempted to use the media to gain legitimacy.

DID THE GOVERNMENT TRY TO USE THE MEDIA?

Israeli leaders hold critical attitudes toward the media. As Rabin (1994, pp. 12, 20) stated:

> I believe that the first television channel needs to be balanced. It is impossible constantly to bring to the screen and the microphone the extremism of the settlers without any balance from the other side … The extremists are not many, but they get media exposure out of proportion to their numbers, only because they express themselves extremely.

Yet even Rabin, with the cooperation of his media adviser Eitan Haber, used the media to promote his policies. Haber, who produced and conducted some of the peace ceremonies during 1993–95 (Oslo 1, the Cairo agreement, the agreements with Jordan in Washington and in the Arava, and Oslo 2), made them characteristic media events (Dayan and Katz, 1992). Haber has acknowledged (in an interview with K. Inbar, 28 August 1997) adding biblical phrases at the end of each of Rabin's peace ceremony speeches. Haber has also described how Rabin was aware that the whole world was watching these events. In the Knesset debates during the peace process, Haber notes, Rabin used his speeches to convey his views to the Israeli public. He also did this in connection to specific events when he appeared in the media (after the Beit Lid terrorist attack, after the Wachsman killing, etc.).

Although Haber describes a 'media attentive' attitude in Rabin's office, other leaders involved in the peace process were less interested in using the media. Peres described the pre-Oslo, Washington talks with the Palestinians as an ongoing peace conference in which public opinion played too great a role; he felt that Oslo, in contrast, offered a channel for holding discrete and substantive negotiations (Peres, 1993, pp. 16–36).

According to another participant in the negotiations, Yossi Beilin, Peres was aware of the need to prepare public opinion for the developments (Beilin, 1997, pp. 83, 118). Beilin believes a mistake was made in neglecting to explain to the public where things were leading. He suggests that a combination of the Declaration of Principles (DOP) itself together with an information campaign could have altered the public's reaction (Beilin, 1997, p. 16).

During the Norwegian negotiations, at any rate, the parties invested much in maintaining secrecy. The Israeli negotiators felt that the secrecy of the talks safeguarded them against American, Syrian, and internal Israeli pressures. This, they believed, enabled informality, which in turn fostered the exploration of the parameters of a possible agreement and eased the psychological climate (Makovsky, 1996, pp. 129–35).

It is interesting to compare these attitudes with the way in which participants in the Madrid talks perceived the role of the media. Yossi Achimeir (1997), who was Prime Minister Shamir's media adviser in Madrid, described it as a media event, a ceremonial affair that provided a stage for press conferences and media reports, with Binyamin Netanyahu and Hanan Ashrawi competing for the media's attention. Achimeir asserts that all the members of the delegations acted as spokespersons, eager to deliver the messages of their respective sides (Achimeir, 1997, pp. 49–51).

Elyakim Rubinstein was head of the Israeli delegation to the negotiations with the Jordanians and Palestinians in Washington, which resulted from the Madrid Conference, but he was excluded from the Oslo process. Rubinstein (1997) too, an experienced negotiator since Camp David in 1978, described the Madrid Conference as a media event that gave the sides opportunities to express whatever they wanted to the public. Another participant, the Foreign Ministry official Eytan Bentsur (1997), mentioned the important role of the media in the Madrid Conference and praised the way in which the Americans, especially Secretary of State James Baker, made use of the media. He makes hardly any mention, however, of use of the media by the Israelis.

This ignoring of the media's role in the process is typical of the Israeli decisionmakers' ambivalent attitude toward the media during this period; they acknowledged it as a fact, but did not try to make the best of it. Shimon Shiffer (1997), the political correspondent of *Yediot Aharonot* who revealed the Oslo agreement, stresses that there is no culture of relations between the Israeli decisionmakers as information providers and the media, and charges the officials with mendacity. Even after *Yediot* announced the DOP in a lead headline, Shiffer claims, Peres denied its existence when asked about it. On the other hand, Shiffer blames the Israeli media for failing to expose the process because of a mistaken assumption that the Israeli government under Rabin would not negotiate directly with the PLO (Shiffer, 1997, pp. 67–71).

THE PUBLIC'S ATTITUDE TOWARD THE PEACE PROCESS

Finally, we turn to Israeli public opinion. Did the Israeli public support the peace process during the period under consideration? The level of support can be gauged by using data from various polls and surveys, though it is not easy to assess the media's effect on this attitude. Table 9.5[11] shows that public support for the Oslo process fluctuated between 43 per cent and 61 per cent during 1993–96. The changes of attitude occurred mainly after important events, and this may indicate that the reporting of an event caused these changes; there is no evidence, however, that the media was the only factor in shaping these opinions.

Table 9.5: 'Do You Support the Peace Process With the Palestinians?'

Event	Year	Time of poll	% of supporters of Oslo process
Washington negotiations	1993	Jan.	46
Before Oslo 1 details published		29 Aug.	53
After Oslo 1 details published		31 Aug.	53
After signing of Oslo 1		14 Sept.	61
		19 Nov.	48
	1994	Jan.	60
After Gaza–Jericho agreement		June	59
After Arafat's arrival in Gaza		Aug.	55
After peace with Jordan		Nov.	48
	1995	Jan.	43
		May	49
After signing of Oslo 2		Oct.	47
After Rabin assassination		End of Nov.	58
After terrorist bombing	1996	March	51
After Sharm-el-Sheikh summit		April	56
Before elections		May	53
After elections		June	48
Netanyahu government in office		July	51

CONCLUSIONS

The main conclusion that has emerged is that the conditions were not suitable for the Rabin government to use the media to gain legitimacy for its policy. This conclusion was reached by analyzing the media environment in Israel, the ways in which the Israeli leadership tried to use the media, the specific needs of the media, and by assessing the relevant opinions of the Israeli public.

During 1992–96, the media environment in Israel was highly competitive, influenced in its professional decisions mainly by business considerations, and characterized by a 'new journalism' mode in its news coverage. The press was dominated by one popular newspaper, *Yediot Aharonot*; the state television channel was superseded by the new commercial television channel.

Israel being a democracy, it is difficult to mobilize the media to support the government and its policy in any case. In crisis situations, however, the media manifested responsibility and was ready to be mobilized for the state and even the government. The Oslo peace process, however, was ongoing and controversial, and there was no reason for the media to express only the government's attitude and disregard the opponents of the process. Indeed, the media gave much salience to the views and events staged by the parliamentary and extraparliamentary opposition; the inquiries into agenda-setting and framing show that the anti-Oslo attitude received large coverage in the media. The media also set moods by means of televised 'disaster marathons', choice of music on the radio, or color photographs in the press. This mood-setting was oriented much more to the public than to the government, and it was very difficult for the Rabin government to transmit opposing messages in these situations.

Moreover, parts of Israeli society did not trust the media, especially the printed press. This mistrust was strongest among the opponents of the government and its policy. Therefore, even if the government could have used the media to marshal support for its policy, the people who most needed to be influenced would have been impervious to what they considered the 'hostile' media.

Finally, the Rabin government did not even aim at using the media to legitimize its policy. The original Oslo negotiators preferred the secret channel, but even when the DOP was signed and more than 60 per cent of Israelis expressed support, the government did not invest efforts in maintaining this support. With the exception of the signing ceremonies and major events, no systematic method was developed for gaining the media's attention through the surveillance and correlation functions, or through relating to the news values of the journalistic community.

On the theoretical plane, several conclusions emerge. In peace processes, the role of the media varies according to the different stages. In the initial, predecisional stage, negotiations are often carried out secretly in back channels, legitimacy is not yet needed, and therefore the media usually has little or no role. In the second stage, where peace policy is formulated, the talks usually become public, and here the media may play a major role in securing legitimacy. The above-mentioned variables, such as the media environment, the media's agenda-setting, public attitudes toward the media, and the leadership's ability to use and even manipulate the media, are now significant. During this period, the media may serve as a source of information for the public as well as the negotiators, it may have a catalyzing effect by speeding up the process, and it may even influence the parties by presenting agendas and frames of reference.

In the third stage, that of the signing of the peace treaty, breakthroughs are revealed, and the media gives intensive coverage. Peace ceremonies are usually media events, and the media, by the way in which it presents the events, the leaders, and their policies, plays the main role in gaining legitimacy and public support. In these situations, leaders also use the media to acquire public (internal and external) support and legitimacy.

Finally, in the implementation stage, the media again performs as during the second, formulating stage, giving critical and professional coverage to the events, though this does not necessarily ensure legitimacy.

Overall, we have seen that during 1992–96, the Israeli leaders did not succeed in gaining media support, and thus legitimacy, for their peace policy at its various stages. The theoretical insights that have emerged from this chapter should be applied to other attempted processes of shifting from conflict to reconciliation, such as the Vietnam peace negotiations in the 1970s, the Israeli–Egyptian peace process, the Northern Ireland peace talks, or the reconciliation processes in former Yugoslavia.

Acknowledgment

I would like to thank the students of my seminars on 'The Media and Foreign Policy', held at the International Relations Department of the Hebrew University and at the Political Science Department of Tel-

Aviv University. I am also grateful to Einat Mahleb for her research assistance.

Aviv University. I am also grateful to Einat Mahleb for her research assistance.

APPENDIX A: MEDIA CHANNELS AND ORGANIZATIONS IN ISRAEL

Television

- Israel Broadcasting Authority (IBA). Channel 1 and Channel 3 (information, mobilization, and entertainment).
- 2nd Channel. Three broadcasting franchises: Keshet, Reshet, and Telad (mainly entertainment and information).
- Cable. Five franchises in 31 regions. Up to 50 channels are available in the average package. Most channels deal only with entertainment; some supply information. Cable gives the Israeli public access to global media networks such as CNN, Sky, BBC, MTV, as well as Arab, Russian, and various European channels.

Radio

- Kol Israel. Four internal networks in Hebrew (Aleph, Bet, Gimel, Kol Hamusika), one internal and Middle Eastern network in Arabic, one internal network in Russian, one global short-wave network (in various languages), one regional network, one regional station in Haifa, and some regional educational stations. Most stations are informative in nature, but they also have mobilization and entertainment roles.
- Galei Tzahal (the military network). One general station, one service station for drivers (mainly information, mobilization, and entertainment).
- Second Television and Radio Authority. Fifteen regional radio stations, all over the country. These stations were established as sources of regional information, and their broadcasts are mostly entertainment.
- Channel 7. A political right-wing station. It is located at a West Bank settlement, and is privately owned. It is totally mobilized to the settlers' cause, and fulfills informative and entertainment functions in this context (Limor, 1996).
- Pirate radio stations. Approximately 40 pirate radio stations all over the country, on a regional basis. Some stations are totally

mobilized and offer Orthodox-religious programs, others broadcast to the Arab population, others play Oriental music (entertainment and mobilization functions) (Limor, 1996).

Newspapers (dailies)

- *Yediot Aharonot* (information and commentary).
- *Ma'ariv* (information and commentary).
- *Ha'aretz* (information and commentary).
- *Globes* (information and commentary).
- *Hatsofeh* (information, party opinion, commentary).
- *Yated Ne'eman* (information, party opinion, commentary).
- *Vesti* (Russian-language; information, commentary, some mobilization).
- *Jerusalem Post* (English-language; information and commentary).

Local newspapers (Avraham, 1993; Caspi and Limor, 1998, pp. 30–1)

- *Ha'aretz-Schocken* network (information and commentary).
- *Yediot Aharonot* network (information and commentary).
- Local/private/commercial newspapers.
- Various religious local newspapers (opinion, commentary, information).

Multimedia technologies

For these technologies, the most important function is the informative; but they also offer entertainment as well as opinion and commentary.

- *BitNet*: the interuniversity computer network (the first Internet provider).
- *Private Internet providers* (e.g., Netvision, Kavei Zahav, IOL).
- *State Internet providers* (through the Bezek telephone corporation).
- Development of infrastructure for the use of *direct broadcast satellites,* mainly for the Israeli communication satellite *Amos*.

APPENDIX B: DISKIN SURVEY:
MEDIA AND POLITICAL ATTITUDES

Diskin (1997) conducted public opinion surveys (before and after the 1996 elections) as part of the larger Davis Institute project (see note 4). In these surveys, four basic questions focused on the media: what newspaper(s) do you read; what television channel(s) do you watch; what is your attitude toward the newspaper(s); what is your attitude toward the television channel(s)? These questions were crossed with all other parts of the survey, and the results are shown in Tables B1–B12.

Table B1: What the Public Reads and Watches (%)

	Channel 1	Channel 2	Other TV
Yediot Aharonot	41	55	1
Ma'ariv	37	44	22
Ha'aretz	54	17	4

Table B2: 'Do You Trust the Media?' (%)

Media	Trust	Do not trust
Yediot Aharonot	40	24
Ma'ariv	28	28
Ha'aretz	41	24
Channel 1	56	12
Channel 2	60	13
Other TV	35	9

Table B3: 'For Whom Did You Vote for Prime Minister?' (%)

	Trust print media	Do not trust print media	Trust TV	Do not trust TV
Netanyahu	26	33	42	19
Peres	41	19	60	6

Table B4: Voting for Knesset Parties—1992 Elections (%)

Party	Trust print media	Do not trust print media	Trust TV	Do not trust TV
Moledet	54	45	45	36
Tzomet	23	42	39	22
Likud	34	29	56	15
NRP	32	32	39	17
Torah	–	57	20	70
Shas	25	56	67	20
Labor	42	20	65	10
Meretz	34	22	66	5
Mada (Arab)	39	17	67	–
Hadash (Communist)	30	20	62	–
Progressive List (Arab)	37	27	55	18

Table B5: Voting for Knesset Parties—1996 Elections (%)

	Trust print media	Do not trust print media	Trust TV	Do not trust TV
Moledet	11	53	24	41
Likud (Gesher, Tzomet)	29	32	50	16
NRP	29	29	42	22
Torah	–	40	–	80
Shas	38	50	38	50
Labor	45	15	70	7
Meretz	33	26	57	7
Mada (Arab)	29	21	48	8
Hadash (Communist)	29	24	57	5
Aliyah	13	50	39	35
Third Way	35	19	35	41

Table B6: 'What is Your Attitude About Israel's Security?' (%)

	Trust print media	Do not trust print media	Trust TV	Do not trust TV
Security right-wing	28	35	45	21
Security left-wing	37	21	64	7

Table B7: 'Do You Believe Peace is Very Important?' (%)

	Trust print media	Do not trust print media	Trust TV	Do not trust TV
No	18	44	23	40
Yes	35	27	57	12

Table B8: 'Do You Support Removal of Settlements for Peace?' (%)

	Trust print media	Do not trust print media	Trust TV	Do not trust TV
No	25	33	40	23
Yes	38	21	63	6

Table B9: 'Do You Believe in the "New Middle East"?' (%)

	Trust print media	Do not trust print media	Trust TV	Do not trust TV
No	22	39	31	18
Yes	37	24	60	9

Table B10: 'Do You Support Giving Up the Golan Heights for Peace?' (%)

	Trust print media	Do not trust print media	Trust TV	Do not trust TV
No	32	30	47	18
Yes	32	25	63	8

Table B11: 'Do You Support Giving Up the Jordan Valley for Peace?' (%)

	Trust print media	Do not trust print media	Trust TV	Do not trust TV
No	31	30	47	18
Yes	35	25	64	8

Table B12: 'Do You Support Dividing Jerusalem for Peace?' (%)

	Trust print media	Do not trust print media	Trust TV	Do not trust TV
No	34	29	50	17
Yes	28	30	59	9

NOTES

1. Data were compiled by the author for a course on 'Political Communication', taught at Tel-Aviv University during 1993–97.
2. Data (see note 1) based mainly on Teleseker Institute (1997).
3. Economic data on the Israeli media were compiled by the author for the same course; the information regarding *Ha'aretz* was insufficient.
4. The sources for the displayed information (both text and tables) are two surveys on media consumption in Israel. The most useful survey was done by Diskin (1997) as part of a Leonard Davis Institute project that also included the present study. The survey was done in May 1996 (N=1,064) and in July 1996 (N=1,087) and included two questions on media consumption. The other source is Teleseker Institute (1997) (N=2504).
5. See note 4.
6. For Table 1, too, Diskin was the basic source for the findings, but other surveys were used as well: a survey conducted by Katz (December 1996; N=1,250); a Teleseker Institute survey (June 1995; N=405); two surveys conducted by the Shvakim-Panorama Institute (January 1997; N=560).
7. The Shvakin-Panorama survey gave only four categories: certainly trust, fairly trust, fairly not, completely not.
8. Here the main findings of the Diskin (1997) survey will be presented and analyzed.
9. The agenda-setting role of the media was distinguished by analyzing the salience of the appearance of the events in the media (press and television). The more salient the coverage, the higher the place in the agenda. The salience factor was developed mainly by using Galtung and Ruge's (1970) news criteria.
10. For the meaning of these images, see Elitzur (1986).
11. The table was compiled from various polls and surveys (Arian, 1995, 1996; Ben-Meir, 1995; Diskin, 1997; Tami Steinmetz Center, 1997).

REFERENCES

Achimeir,Y., 'Media Considerations of the Likud Government (1990–1992) and the Madrid Peace Conference', Lecture presented at the symposium on 'Spokesmanship in the Service of Peace in the Middle East', Bar-Ilan University, 13 May 1997.

Aggestam, K., 'Two-Track Diplomacy: Negotiations Between Israel and the PLO Through Open and Secret Channels', Davis Papers on Israel's Foreign Policy, No. 53 (Jerusalem: The Leonard Davis Institute for International Relations, Hebrew University of Jerusalem, November 1996).

Arian, A., 'The Peace Process and the Terror: Conflicting Trends in Israeli Public Opinion in 1995', Memorandum No. 45 (Tel-Aviv: Jaffee Center for Strategic Studies, Tel-Aviv University, February 1995).

Arian, A., 'Israeli Security Opinion: February 1996', Memorandum No. 46 (Tel-Aviv: Jaffee Center for Strategic Studies, Tel-Aviv University, March, 1996).

Avraham, E., *The Media in Israel: Center and Periphery Coverage of the Development Towns* (Breirot, 1993) (in Hebrew).

Bagdikian, B. H., *The Media Monopoly*, 2nd edn (Boston: Beacon Press, 1987).

Baldwin, T., McVoy, F. D., and Steinfield, C. (eds), *Convergence* (Sage, 1996).

Bar-Siman-Tov, Y., *Israel and the Peace Process, 1977–1982: In Search of Legitimacy for Peace* (New York, NY: State University of New York Press, 1994).

Bar-Siman-Tov, Y., 'The Transition From War to Peace: The Complexity of Decision Making: The Israeli Case' (Tel-Aviv: Tami Steinmetz Center for Peace Research, Tel-Aviv University, 1996).

Bar-Siman-Tov, Y., 'Peacemaking in Israel as a Two-Level Game', Lecture presented at the conference on 'The Role of Domestic Politics in the Foreign Policymaking of Democratic Societies' (Jerusalem: Leonard Davis Institute for International Relations, Hebrew University of Jerusalem, 10 December 1997).

Bar-Tal, D., 'The Massada Syndrome: A Case of Central Belief', Discussion Paper No. 3 (Tel-Aviv: International Center for Peace in the Middle East, 1983).

Bar-Tal, D., 'Siege Mentality in Israel: Understanding Psychological Bases of the Israeli–Palestinian Conflict', Discussion Paper No. 12 (Tel-Aviv: International Center for Peace in the Middle East, 1991).

Beilin, Y., 'Touching Peace' (Tel-Aviv: *Yediot Aharonot*, 1997) (in Hebrew).

Ben-Meir, Y., 'Public Opinion in Israel: Israel and the Palestinians: Issues for the Final Settlement', Research Paper No. 6 (Tel-Aviv: Jaffee Center for Strategic Studies, Tel-Aviv University, 1995).

Bennett, W. L., 'The News About Foreign Policy', in W. L. Bennett and D. Paletz (eds), *Taken by Storm: The Media, Public Opinion and U.S. Foreign Policy in the Gulf War* (Chicago, IL: University of Chicago Press, 1994).

Bentsur, E., 'The Road to Peace Crosses Madrid' (Tel-Aviv: *Yediot Aharonot*, 1997) (in Hebrew).

Brody, R., 'Crisis, War, and Public Opinion', in W. L. Bennett and D. Paletz (eds), *Taken by Storm: The Media, Public Opinion and U.S. Foreign Policy in the Gulf War* (Chicago, IL: Chicago University Press, 1994).

Caspi, D. and Limor, Y., *The Mediators: The Mass Media in Israel, 1948–1990* (Tel-Aviv: Eshkolot-Am Oved, 1992) (in Hebrew).

Caspi, D. and Limor, Y. (eds), *Mass Media in Israel* (Tel-Aviv: Open University of Israel, 1998) (in Hebrew).

Cohen, B., *The Press and Foreign Policy* (Princeton, NJ: Princeton University Press, 1963).

Cohen, B., *The Public's Impact on Foreign Policy* (New York, NY: Little, Brown, 1973).

Cohen, Y., *Media Diplomacy* (London: Frank Cass, 1986).

Dayan, D. and Katz, E., Media *Events: A Live Broadcasting of History* (Harvard, IL: Harvard University Press, 1992).

Dearing, J. and Rogers, E. M., *Agenda Setting* (Thousand Oaks: Sage, 1996).

Diskin, A., 'Voters' Attitudes Before and After the June 1996 Elections', Unpublished draft (Jerusalem: Leonard Davis Institute for International Relations, Hebrew University of Jerusalem, 1997).

Elitzur, J., 'Images in Conflict Situations: Four Basic Concepts', in D. Zacks (ed.), *Israel and Its Arab Neighbors* (Van Leer Institute, 1986) (in Hebrew).

Entman, R., 'Framing US Coverage of International News', *Journal of Communication*, No. 41 (1991).

Entman, R. and Page, B., 'The News Before the Storm'. in W. L. Bennett and D. Paletz (eds), *Taken by Storm: The Media, Public Opinion and U.S. Foreign Policy in the Gulf War* (Chicago, IL: Chicago University Press, 1994).

Entman, R. and Rojecki, R., 'Freezing Out the Public: Elite and Media Framing of the US Anti-Nuclear Movement', *Political Communication*, No. 10 (1993).

Frederick, H., *Global Communication and International Relations* (Belmont, CA: Wadsworth, 1993).

Friedland, L. A., 'Electronic Democracy and the New Citizenship', *Media, Culture and Society*, 18, 2 (1996).

Galnoor, I., *Steering the Polity: Communication and Politics in Israel* (Tel-Aviv: Am Oved, 1985) (in Hebrew).

Galtung, J. and Ruge, M., 'The Structure of Foreign News', in

J. Tunstall (ed.), *Media Sociology* (London: Constable, 1970).

Gergen, D., 'Diplomacy in a Television Age: The Dangers of Tele-democracy', in S. Serfaty (ed.), *The Media and Foreign Policy* (New York: St Martin's, 1991).

Halevi, A., 'The Image of the Palestinians', Survey conducted by the Statistics Consulting Unit, Haifa University, for Kol Israel, 8 September 1995.

Herman, E., 'Media in the U.S. Political Economy', in J. Downing, A. Mohammadi, and A. Sreberny-Mohammadi (eds), *Questioning the Media*, 2nd edn (Thousand Oaks, CA: Sage, 1995).

Iyengar, S., 'Television News and Citizens' Explanations of National Affairs', in D. Graber (ed.), *Media Power in Politics*, 3rd edn (Washington, DC: Congressional Quarterly Press, 1994).

Iyengar, S. and Kinder, D., *News That Matters* (Chicago, IL: University of Chicago Press, 1987).

Iyengar, S. and Simon, A., 'News Coverage of the Gulf Crisis and Public Opinion', in W. L. Bennett and D. Paletz (eds), *Taken by Storm: The Media, Public Opinion and U.S. Foreign Policy in the Gulf War* (Chicago, IL: University of Chicago Press, 1994).

Katz, Y., 'The Development of Cable Television in Israel and Its Linkage to the Social-Political System', *Patuach*, 3 (1996a) (in Hebrew).

Katz, Y., 'Public Opinion Towards the Media in Israel', Bar-Ilan University Institute for Communal Research, School of Education (conducted in December 1996b).

Lachman-Messer, D., 'The New Communication Map in Israel', *Dvarim Achadim*, No. 1 (Spring, 1997).

Lambeth, E. B., 'Global Media Philosophies', in J. C. Merrill (ed.), *Global Journalism*, 3rd edn (White Plains, New York: Longman, 1995).

Larson, J., *Television's Window on the World: International Affairs Coverage on the U.S. Networks* (Norwood, NJ: Ablex, 1984).

Lasswell, H., 'The Structure and Function of Communication in Society', in W. Schramm and D. Roberts (eds), *The Processes and Effects of Mass Communication*, 2nd edn (Urbana: University of Illinois Press, 1971).

Lazarsfeld, P. and Merton, R., 'Mass Communication, Popular Taste and Organized Social Action', in W. Schramm and D. Roberts (eds), *Processes and Effects of Mass Communication*, 2nd edn (Urbana: University of Illinois Press, 1971).

Liebes, T., Peri, Y., and Grabelski, T., 'Where Does the Real Influence

Exist?: Communication and Alternative Communication in the 1996 Elections in Israel', *Kesher*, No. 20 (November, 1996) (in Hebrew).

Limor, Y., 'The Stormy Wave of Pirate Radio in Israel', *Kesher*, 19 (May, 1996) (in Hebrew).

Limor, Y., '"The Little Prince" and "the Big Brother": The Media Industry in Israel in an Era of Change', in D. Caspi (ed.), *Communication and Democracy in Israel* (Tel-Aviv: Van Leer Institute and Hakibbutz Hameuchad, 1997) (in Hebrew).

Makovsky, D., *Making Peace With the PLO: The Rabin Government's Road to the Oslo Accords* (Boulder, CO: Westview Press, 1996).

McCombs, M. E., 'The Agenda Setting Approach', in D. D. Nimmo and K. R. Sanders (eds), *Handbook of Political Communication* (Beverly Hills: Sage, 1981).

McCombs, M. E. and Shaw, D. L., 'The Agenda Setting Approach: Function of the Media', *Public Opinion Quarterly*, 36, 2 (1972).

McQuail, D., *Mass Communication Theory*, 3rd edn (London: Sage, 1994).

Merrill, M. and Ogan, C., 'The Internet as a Mass Medium', *Journal of Communication*, 6, 2 (1996).

Mosco, V., *The Political Economy of Communication* (London: Sage, 1996).

Mosko, Y., 'Protection: Why Do Israeli Newspapers Sponsor Events?', *Ha'ayin Hashevi'it*, No. 6 (November–December, 1996) (in Hebrew).

Negbi, M., 'Freedom of the Press in Israel: The Legal Aspect' (Jerusalem: Jerusalem Institute for Israel Studies, 1995) (in Hebrew).

O'Heffernan, P., *Mass Media and American Foreign Policy* (Norwood, NJ: Ablex, 1991).

O'Heffernan, P., 'A Mutual Exploitation Model of Media Influence in U.S. Foreign Policy', in W. L. Bennett and D. Paletz (eds), *Taken by Storm: The Media, Public Opinion and U.S. Foreign Policy in the Gulf War* (Chicago, IL: University of Chicago Press, 1994).

Peres, S., *The New Middle East* (Steimatzky, 1993) (in Hebrew).

Powlick, P., 'The Sources of Public Opinion for American Foreign Policy Officials', *International Studies Quarterly*, 39 (1995).

Rabin, Y., Interview, in *Yearbook of Journalists* (Tel-Aviv: Journalists Association, 1994).

Roeh, I. and Nir, R., 'Reporting the *Intifada* in the Israeli Press', in A. Cohen and G. Wolfsfeld (eds), *Framing the Intifada* (Norwood, NJ: Ablex, 1993).

Rogel, N. and Schejter, A., *The Nakdi Document: Guidelines for Broadcasting News and Current Affairs* (Jerusalem: Israel Broadcasting Authority, 1995).

Rogers, E. and Dearing, J., 'Agenda-Setting Research: Where Has It Been, Where Is It Going', in D. Graber (ed.), *Media Power in Politics*, 3rd edn (Congressional Quarterly Press, 1994).

Rosenfeld, S., 'In the Gulf: The Wars of the Press', in S. Serfaty (ed.), *Media and Foreign Policy* (St Martin's, 1991).

Rubinstein, E., 'Peace Diplomacy: Between Disclosure and Concealment', Lecture presented at the symposium on 'Spokesmanship in the Service of Peace in the Middle East', Bar-Ilan University, 13 May 1997.

Second Television and Radio Authority Annual Report, 1995.

Segal, Z., *Freedom of the Press: Between Myth and Reality* (Tel-Aviv: Papyrus, 1996) (in Hebrew).

Shvakim-Panorama Ltd, Marketing—Research and Polls, Strategic Planning. Surveys conducted on 5–7 January, 12–14 January, 1997. Published on Kol Israel—Reshet Bet (Israeli Public Radio), 7, 14 January 1997.

Shiffer, S., 'The Oslo Accords: The Failure: How Did We Miss It?', Lecture presented at the symposium on 'Spokesmanship in the Service of Peace in the Middle East', Bar-Ilan University, 13 May 1997.

Tami Steinmetz Center for Peace Research, 'The Peace Index: Results of the Project, June 1994–October 1997' (Tel-Aviv: Tami Steinmetz Center for Peace Research, Tel-Aviv University, 1997).

Teleseker Institute, 'Survey: Opinions Regarding the Media and Peace Process in Israel' (conducted in June 1995).

Teleseker Institute, '1997 Media Planning Survey', For the Israeli Advertisers Association, and published in the major Israeli newspapers (conducted in November 1996) (1997).

Tikochinski, J., 'What Is Your Business: The Economic Interests of the Three Newspapers in Israel', *Ha'ayin Hashevi'it*, No. 5 (September–October, 1996) (in Hebrew).

Westerstahl, J. and Johansson, F., 'Foreign News: News Values and Ideologies', *European Journal of Communication*, 9 (1994).

Winston, B., 'How Are Media Born and Developed?', in J. Downing, A. Mohammadi and A. Sreberny-Mohammadi (eds), *Questioning the Media*, 2nd edn (Thousand Oaks, Sage, 1995).

Wolfsfeld, G., 'Framing Political Conflict', in A. Cohen and G. Wolfsfeld (eds), *Framing the Intifada* (Ablex, 1993).

Wolfsfeld, G., *Media and Political Conflict: News From the Middle East* (Cambridge: Cambridge University Press, 1997a).

Wolfsfeld, G., 'Fair Weather Friends: The Varying Role of the News Media in the Arab–Israeli Peace Process', *Political Communication*, 14, 1 (January–March 1997b).

Zacher, M. and Sutton, B., *Governing Global Networks: International Regimes for Transportation and Communications* (Cambridge: Cambridge University Press, 1996).

10 The Unique Approach to Military–Societal Relations in Israel and Its Impact on Foreign and Security Policy

MOSHE LISSAK

Since its establishment, Israel has experienced, on the one hand military confrontations and, on the other, discussions of cease-fire arrangements and armistices, diplomatic negotiations, political–military arrangements, and peace talks. This historical experience required the political leadership and the military command to fashion, from the very outset, a well-established pattern of relations. Although the principles of this model have not changed, particularly that of the subordinate position of the military with regard to the political system, quite a few changes have occurred in their inter-pretation and implementation. This is particularly true concerning the influence of the patterns of relations between the two elites on the shaping of foreign and security policy.

Although the emergence of a certain model was perhaps not by chance, it is not difficult to imagine other possible alternatives. For example, the need to survive under the conditions of military–political siege experienced by the inhabitants of Israel over many long years could have led to the growth of a military elite with an ethos strongly emphasizing strength and heroism, codes of extreme nationalism, and far-reaching political ambition. Yet the Israel Defense Forces (IDF) never followed this path as an organization; indeed, it drew back from such cultural codes. Nevertheless, the unique conditions under which the Israeli security system was formed left their stamp on Israeli society.

This influence is tangible in many areas, such as education, communication, and economy, but particularly in the area of political activity, which centers on the subject of the security of the state. Many army officers, both on active duty and retired, have participated in such activity. Awareness of the dangers of politicization of the armed forces and the consequent militarization of the civilian sector is deeply rooted in the history of the Yishuv (the prestate Jewish community). More specifically, during this period there was a fear that the political-military organizations (Etzel and Lehi) would continue their activities even after independence was declared. Consciousness of the danger of politicization found expression in the IDF Ordinance of 1948, one of the first laws adopted by the provisional government. This law states that the oath of allegiance to the IDF refers to the state, its laws, and its duly constituted authorities.[1] The concept of duly constituted authorities was specifically intended to thwart partisan-political involvement in the young army that might have stemmed from the loyalty of various security personnel to their parties in the prestate period.

In practice, during the period of the Yishuv, politicization extended to all aspects of public life, particularly defense. It is therefore not surprising that the attempt to remove political-partisan influences from the IDF brought about the two main political crises that occurred in the first months of the state's existence—that in the wake of the Altalena incident, and that following the disbanding of the separate command of the Palmach.[2] Ben-Gurion's insistence on preventing at all costs even a hint of political autonomy in the IDF ensured that it would remain a single, undivided army in terms of its unqualified commitment to the political leadership of the state. This insistence was particularly directed toward the former members of the Etzel and Lehi—organizations with a tradition of refusing to accept the authority of the elected democratic institutions of the Jewish community during the period of the Yishuv. Although the Palmach did not have such a tradition, the nearly uniform political identification of the Palmach commanders with the leftist Mapam Party was a thorn in the side to Ben-Gurion. This was one of the main reasons that brought him, first of all, to disband the independent staff of the Palmach, and thereafter also to disband all of its brigades.[3]

One may assume that, had peace agreements been signed with the Arab states immediately following the War of Independence, all this would have become a rather marginal question, not much more important than in other democratic societies. However, the fact that the War of Independence was not the last war, and that Israel experienced six additional wars (the Sinai Campaign of 1956, the Six Day War, the War of Attrition, the Yom Kippur War, the Lebanon War, the war over the security zone in southern Lebanon, not to mention countless security incidents between the wars), meant that issues of security and of related diplomatic activity remained high on the public agenda. By the nature of things, the relations between the IDF command and the diplomatic-political level were intensely and increasingly discussed by the press, the electronic media, and the academic community.[4]

BOUNDARIES BETWEEN THE MILITARY AND CIVILIAN SECTORS

Anyone examining the history of military–government and military–societal relations in Israel will find, along with features shared with other countries, a number of unique characteristics. This is particularly so in comparison to other democratic societies. The uniqueness of military–societal relations in Israel has had many manifestations in the political, economic, social, and cultural areas. These may perhaps best be described by analyzing the boundaries and the interactions that took shape over the years between the security system in general, and the IDF in particular, and the various civilian sectors. Nevertheless, neither the unique characteristics nor those common to other societies were ever static; the patterns that emerged during the formative years of the state gradually changed. Presumably, this pace of change will accelerate if a postwar era is indeed established in the Middle East.

At the beginning of its path, the sovereign state of Israel established its own unique tone that deviated to a certain degree from what was prevalent in other democratic societies. This deviation, however, gradually diminished as the common denominator between Israel and other democratic states expanded. What then was the uniqueness of Israel, and how did its normalization find expression?

Our point of departure is the nature of the boundaries and interactions between the military and the civilian sectors. To begin with, the issue of these boundaries needs to be set in a broader framework—namely, that of different institutional boundaries in general. This is one of the classic subjects that engage modern social scientists. Thus, for example, sociologists and political scientists like to describe the social history of societies undergoing social change, among other things, as the history of processes of structural and functional differentiation.[5] These processes generally bring in their wake changes in the location and nature of various institutional boundaries, such as that between the political and economic domains, or between the political and the cultural. The pace of change of these boundaries will of course depend, on the one hand, on the strength of the pressures exerted on them and, on the other, on their power of resistance. With all their much-vaunted conservatism, even professional armed forces respond to external and internal pressures and to the need to redefine the nature of the boundaries of the military system, the division of tasks, and the characteristics of interactions between it and the civilian system.

Luckham distinguishes three kinds of boundaries between the military and the civilian system: integral (impenetrable) boundaries; permeated boundaries; and fragmented boundaries. Luckham also suggests two central criteria for the distinction between different kinds of boundaries: the degree of supervision over military personnel at different levels in their contacts with the nonmilitary environment; and the degree of blurring between goals and frameworks of the military sector on the one hand and of the civilian sector on the other.

On the basis of these criteria, a military system may be defined as having an integral boundary if the following condition obtains: 'the interchange between persons holding roles at various levels of the military hierarchy and the environment is under the control of those with responsibility for setting the operational goals of the armed forces, that is the higher command'. Boundaries are permeated 'to the extent to which there is complete fusion both in respect of goals and of organization between the possessors of the means of violence and other social groups'. The boundary is fragmented if 'in a military with distinctive military format and goals—the interactions of holders of military roles with holders of civilian roles escape the control of the military elite in a way that impairs its freedom to interact with the political and social environment as a single entity in a consistent way'.[6]

In the latter situation, certain sections of the boundaries tend to be integral, whereas others tend to be more permeable. This typology is admittedly highly schematic and abstract, but is still useful as a basis for speculation; moreover, the general characteristics are translatable into more specific operative characteristics.[7] In order to clarify these concepts, one needs to relate to a central aspect of this issue, which Luckham hardly deals with—namely, the issue of institutional linkages or meeting points between the military system and various sectors of the civilian system. These situations of linkage or meeting exist even when the boundaries are integral; all the more so if the boundaries are completely permeable or fragmented. Situations of meeting are frequently institutionalized in one way or another, but in part they are also nonestablished and somewhat esoteric. In every society there are certain meeting points, at different levels. A small number of meeting points indicates a high level of integrity of the boundaries; a large number of meeting points suggests more permeated or fragmented boundaries.

Several questions arise in this context, which may be adequately answerable only by means of empirical research. Thus, for example, one needs to ask: Who are the participants in a meeting (politicians, officials of executive authorities, representatives of the public, etc.)? What is the degree of institutionalization of the situations of meeting? What is the status of the participants in the meeting and, particularly, who has the right of veto in case of disagreements—the civilian partner or the military one? What are the rules of the game (competitive, conflictual, or consensual)? In what domain is the meeting conducted (civilian or military)? Finally, the central question is: What is the degree of basic ideological-normative agreement in relation to the nature of the boundaries and their various attributes? In other words, what is the degree of authoritativeness in the area of national security doctrine and of the central social ethos?

We cannot attempt here to answer all of these questions in the Israeli context, nor can we engage in an extensive, systematic comparison with the norms prevalent in other democratic societies. Instead, we shall consider certain central features of the Israeli 'case'. We may note, to begin with, that the boundaries between the two sectors within Israeli society are more varied and complex, and the situations of encounter between representatives of the defense establishment and the general population more numerous, than might be thought at first glance. It should also be pointed out that the concept 'defense system' refers in this context to those serving in the standing and conscription army, the reserves, employees of the Defense Ministry, and those working in the intelligence community. This paper will nevertheless deal only with the IDF, and not with any other system of the defense establishment.

In the Israeli context, one may identify at least seven central meeting points (each one of which carries over into other contexts) between the military and civilian sectors: the political network; the economic network; the educational and cultural networks; the professional network (research and development); the social network; the public opinion and communication network; and the symbolic network. Within the framework of these general categories, we can identify with relative ease dozens of meeting points with reasonable levels of institutionalization. In the majority of meeting points (albeit with differing frequencies), the military participants in the meeting are members of the military staff on active duty, and not civilians working in the security apparatus. In other words, in these meeting points the explicitly military (uniformed) component, having veto power, is in practice the dominant participant, at least in quantitative terms.

MEETING POINTS BETWEEN THE MILITARY AND CIVILIAN SECTORS

Even from this schematic presentation, it emerges that the interactions between the military and civilian sectors are conducted at a variety of meeting points, both on the individual and institutional levels. The most salient meeting point on the micro level is that of compulsory military service, as dictated by the Law of Security Service. It is superfluous to elaborate on how this service affects the life of the individual, beginning with the limitations imposed on his freedom of movement and expression during a certain period (including the period of reserve duty), the taking of personal risks, and the economic implications.[8] Together with this, military service is accompanied (or at least was in the past) by various social rewards, including rewards of status, and most important of all an honorable ticket of entry into civilian society.[9]

The permeability of boundaries between the military and the civilian realms is not limited to the life of the individual. In terms of the overall influence of military–societal relations, the permeability of the boundaries is particularly important on the institutional level, relating as it does to the functioning of the political-democratic system under circumstances of ongoing violent conflict. It should be noted in this context, as we shall see below, that, despite the partial permeability of the boundaries, there did not develop in Israel a 'garrison state'[10] but what is referred to in the literature as 'a nation in arms' or, in the Israeli version, 'a nation in uniform'. This term refers to a society in which there is extensive cooperation of civilians in the military effort and partial permeability of the boundary between the two sectors. The model of a 'nation in arms' assumes the existence of a permeable boundary and a wide variety of meeting points between the military and civilian sectors, far more so than in the model of the 'garrison state'. As a result, there is a discernable phenomenon of 'civilianization of the military' in a partial sense, as well as 'militarization' of the civilian sector. This leads to a weakening of the military-security apparatus relative to the civilian sector.

Nevertheless, the boundaries are not permeable in an overall or comprehensive way, such that the boundary lines between the two systems could be defined as fragmentary, in Luckham's terminology. This means that, as opposed to those areas in which the military sector is quite independent, there also exist areas in which civilian involvement is relatively high. However, there are also areas in which the accepted rules of the game give legitimacy to involvement of the army in civilian activity, as well as areas where the military's involvement is seen as improper or undesirable. From the viewpoint of institutional analysis, there is particular interest in arrangements that facilitate extensive involvement of the military sector in the shaping of foreign and defense policy. This encompasses such activities as national intelligence evaluation, conducting negotiations on cease-fire agreements and peace treaties—from Rhodes through the implementation of the Oslo agreements—and the administration of the military government until 1966 in Israel and after 1967 in the territories conquered during the Six Day War.[11]

In examining the institutional significance of the phenomena of civilianization of the military on the one hand and militarization of the civilian sector on the other, one needs to consider the perspective of role expansion of the military system.[12] The advantage of this perspective is that it allows the raising of questions about the area of national security, in which military involvement is seen as legitimate. The expansion of the military may have two different manifestations, examples of which may also be found in Israel: an increase in the involvement of the military level in all that pertains to policy formulation and decisionmaking in matters of national security; and direct implementation activities of the army, such as in the area of education and socialization of soldiers. In Israel, changes have occurred over the years, some of which point toward role expansion and others toward role contraction. Thus, for example, extensive role expansion took place in the economic or military–industrial area following the

Yom Kippur War, but in recent years this interaction has been greatly reduced.[13]

In other areas as well, which go beyond the explicitly military, phenomena of alternating role expansion and contraction have occurred over the years. Thus, changes have taken place in the scope of the army's educational activity, largely reflecting the approaches of various chiefs of staff to the IDF's priorities. Chief of Staff Rafael Eitan significantly expanded the activities of providing basic education to 'marginal youth'.[14] On the other hand, during his period, the cultural and entertainment activities of the army as a whole were reduced. The large army troupes were disbanded and the activity of Gadna (the Youth Brigade) was also curtailed. At the beginning of his term as chief of staff, Ehud Barak also sought to restrict, if not entirely eliminate, several 'civilian' activities of the IDF; he cut back considerably the activities of the army radio station, Galei Tzahal, and closed several of the periodicals published by the Defense Ministry and the IDF. Because of heavy public pressure, however, Barak's success in these measures was very limited.

One of the more sensitive areas of contact between the military and civilian sectors, particularly from the political viewpoint, is that of the mass media. The general tendency during the 1950s and 1960s was toward role expansion: the setting up of the army radio network; the establishment of an IDF magazine (*Bamahaneh*) and of various other magazines, as well as a publishing house (Ma'arakhot); and performances of army troupes before civilian audiences. During the 1970s and 1980s, however, the scope and weight of this role expansion were reduced relative to its civilian counterparts. This phenomenon may be explained in terms of budget limitations on the one hand, and a decrease in the army's prestige, especially after the Yom Kippur War, as well as an erosion in the national consensus about security, on the other. This refers especially to the issue of the legitimacy of elective wars. The erosion in consensus, especially following the Lebanon War, led to particular sensitivity about the messages conveyed by the IDF in those media subject to its influence, as a result of which these messages became more vague in their meaning.

All this went hand in hand with a reduction in the security establishment's involvement in the area of civilian communications (press and television) by means of military censorship. This reduction was only carried out after much controversy between the press and the censor. Generally speaking, these disputes led to a softening of the censorship under pressure from the media. This was particularly noticeable after the Yom Kippur War, when the press repeatedly violated the censor's instructions.[15] The critical attitude of the press and its willingness to defy the IDF reached their height during the Lebanon War, when the military correspondents of the daily papers became the vanguard of criticism of the purposes and conduct of the war. Among many other examples, a striking one was the Bus 300 incident, which took place during the period of the intifada, and in which security personnel were photographed by a reporter as they led a captured terrorist away to be killed.[16]

Thus, further modifications now occurred in the initially vague boundaries between these two sectors. Certain boundary lines, such as in the security–political area, became more permeable, whereas others, as in the cultural area, became less so.

All these processes took place within the framework of rules of the game that were more or less accepted by both the civilian and military elites, and by civilian public opinion. The system of norms that took shape in this context may be described as the dominant security–political culture in Israel, which remained unchallenged over the years. Only with the weakening of the national consensus about the use of military force as a solution to political problems, and the decline in prestige that the security establishment underwent in the wake of the Yom Kippur War and the Lebanon War, did voices of protest begin to be heard against these norms.

Academic researchers played an active role in this criticism. Their critique covered a broad area: beginning with discussion of the glaring faults in Israeli democracy resulting from the close connection between security policy and governmental, legal, and social arrangements, and ending in the attempt to adduce as much evidence as possible about the militaristic nature of Israeli society. The faults in Israeli democracy, especially those stemming directly or indirectly from the need to deal with ongoing, existential questions of security, were examined in a series of studies; a typical example is that of Yaniv.[17] Among these shortcomings, all of which he attributes to the interrelations between security problems and the functioning of the governmental and social systems, Yaniv cites the low civilian status of Israeli Arabs, and even more so of Arabs of the 'territories', who completely lacked even the civilian status of Israeli Arabs;[18] restrictions on the 'public's right to know' about various activities of the IDF, and also about certain security conceptions;[19] the partial politicization of the IDF, especially during the Ben-Gurion period; and the faults in the judicial system and in the quality of the rule of law in light of the existence of a dual, if not triple, system of law in the 'territories'.[20]

Phenomena of involvement of the military in political-security decisions on the one hand, and of connections between political parties and military personalities on the other, thus reflected the two aspects of the issue of the permeability of boundaries between the political and military systems. At times, the same phenomenon operated in both directions. On the one hand, the involvement of former senior officers in political decisions influenced policy by means of the professional knowledge and doctrines they brought with them from the IDF; on the other, it helped the political system reduce its dependence on the professional advice of serving officers.

The arrangements based on involvement of the military in decisionmaking processes, and the phenomenon of civilianization within the military establishment, are likewise manifested in the nature of the interrelations between the military and civilian elites, which has been described as 'partnership among elites'.[21] This term implies several different aspects, some of which are not unique to Israel, but have already been noted by students of military–state relations in other democratic states since the Second World War. The practice of close official and unofficial contact between the senior military staff and individuals and groups in the political elite led, in most Western democracies, to proximity and convergence between the elites.[22] There nevertheless still exists a difference between Israel and other Western states in terms of the extent and intensity of cooperation between the elites, resulting from those factors that made Israel the representative case of a 'nation in arms'. Compared with military elites in other democratic countries, the Israeli military elite has a more important status in society and greater political involvement in security matters. The most recent example of this is the substantial military involvement in discussions with representatives of the Palestinian Authority about implementation of the Oslo agreements. At the same time, there is a strong tendency among the civilian elites toward involvement in issues of national security, especially through their extensive contacts with the military elites within the framework of shared social networks.

These social networks are not limited to the connections between officers in active duty and functionaries in the political and administrative establishments with whom they come into contact during the course of their duties, but also involve social contacts that create a circle of informal acquaintances.[23] One of the results of these contacts is the adoption, at least in part, of civilian points of view, particularly among officers who are close to the end of their military service—that is, at the zenith of their military careers. Given the relatively early retirement age, many officers are assimilated into the civilian realm following their demobilization, while continuing to maintain contacts with military personnel on active duty. Moreover, at times the demobilized officers continue to hold senior command functions in the reserves. The complex social networks serve as a source of exchange of information, and contribute to the convergence of attitudes and conceptual systems between the military and civilian elites.

Nevertheless, the cooperation between the military and civilian elites does not mean that the boundaries between them are entirely permeable. It is based on rules of the game that define, on the one hand, the legitimate realms of military involvement in activities of a civilian nature and, on the other, the dimensions of the military's professional autonomy, preventing excessive involvement of the civilian sector in what occurs in the IDF.

IS ISRAEL A MILITARISTIC SOCIETY?

The unique development of Israel's political-security culture in its early years, and especially its formation after the Six Day War, have led to attempts to describe Israeli society as a militaristic one. The arguments of those who take this position may be summarized in the words of Ben-Eliezer, who asserts that the concept of a 'nation in uniform' is no more than a camouflage for the concept of militarism. According to him, a 'nation in uniform' is a cultural notion used by the political and military elites to provide justification for political problems and to mobilize the entire population for war.

> A 'nation in uniform' is based on a confusion among individual, family, society, nation and state; on the creation of a militaristic culture for the society as a whole, and not only for the army; and on the fashioning of a reality that negates the distinction between wartime and peacetime. This blurring of boundaries is the tool with which one makes wars.[24]

According to Ben-Eliezer, this culture originated during the Yishuv period, was cultivated to an extent by the Palmach, and crystallized and was institutionalized during the early years of the state. The most striking features of this culture are, in his view, the glorification of the army and of war, the demonization of the enemy, and the banalization of the conflict, as well as phenomena of nationalism, machoism, and rituals for the fallen.[25] Ben-Eliezer draws comparisons with military cultures that in their day have characterized Japan, Prussia, Jacobin France, and Czarist Russia. Kimmerling, who shares this point of view, defines Israeli militarism as 'cognitive militarism',[26] that is, a situation in which military considerations almost always take priority over political, economic, or ideological ones. The broad public accepts this military mind-set as almost self-evident without thinking too much about its long-term implications.

These arguments, however, are mistaken, and one may note several faults in their conceptual framework.[27] The main error of these sociologists' approach is that they ignore a central feature of militaristic societies. Here we need to distinguish between necessary conditions, without which it is impossible to describe any society as militaristic, and sufficient conditions. The presence of sufficient conditions, in addition to the necessary conditions, enables one to make more or less definitive judgments about the militaristic nature of a given society. The necessary conditions include, first of all, the existence of a highly offensive security doctrine: that is, a military doctrine that is part of an overall doctrine of security, and that is based on the explicit desire for territorial expansion unrelated to self-defense and the tactical or strategic need to make a surprise attack. Nevertheless, such a policy, even if continued over a protracted period of time, is not a sufficient indicator of a society's distinctly militaristic nature. It must be accompanied by normative-ideological justifications and an ethos that are substantially unrelated to the country's objective strategic situation. The connection of these justifications to any concrete threats posed by an enemy, even if he does not conceal his wish to obliterate the country, must likewise be very tenuous.

Yet even if these conditions do exist, to rely on this dimension alone in proving the militaristic nature of a given state is shortsighted and one-dimensional. One also needs to consider whether some further necessary conditions exist, specifically, whether the military establishment constitutes a source of inspiration and authority (formal and informal) for the political decisionmakers and, even more important, whether the army also constitutes an overall reference point for the society as a whole, or at least for central groups within it.

In such a society, one will find a great degree of glorification of war and heroism, together with extreme chauvinism; in other words, the army will constitute the supreme formative factor and regulator of social norms in most institutional areas: political, economic and, of particular importance, in culture and lifestyle. This regulation is primarily unidirectional; moreover, there is an almost complete absence of powerful countercultures in civilian society. Such overall regulation is extremely rare; it existed to a considerable extent in Prussia and in imperial Japan.

There can also be cases of partial and limited regulation of only one or two areas. This will generally involve the political-partisan area, within which various manipulations are performed, including those related to internal and external security policy. Such a situation does not require significant overflow into other areas—economic, cultural, or social—which continue more or less to maintain autonomy, based on their own normative operative principles. In such a case, it is highly doubtful whether the society in question may be called militaristic.

Here we should again mention what we noted about military–civilian relations in Western democracies: a certain blurring of the boundaries between the military and civilian establishments is not unusual, and has existed both in various historical contexts[28] and in modern societies, particularly since the Second World War. The old formal distinctions—for example, among various civilian and military executive authorities—do not always meet the test of reality. Such is the case in Israel; the very fact of such blurring is an insufficient condition for the emergence of militarism. The matter also depends, as mentioned, on the military's capacity for regulation and other characteristics, such as the nature of the social networks.

In addition to ignoring this central characteristic, many of the studies attempting to describe Israeli society as militaristic suffer from additional weaknesses, the most important of which are the lack of sufficient historical perspective and the failure to distinguish between tendencies of a militaristic coloration and totally opposite tendencies. A further weakness is that the studies refrain from comparative study of other factors likely to have a greater impact than military–societal relations on the shaping of civilian society, such as the magnitude of immigration, social composition, economic growth or decline, changes in the political culture, and various other factors.

Thus, the following conclusions emerge from this discussion. One may not rely on analysis of foreign and defense policy alone, particularly in light of the fact that in the Israeli case it has not been uniform or consistent. Even if a certain degree of 'militarization' does exist in one area, this does not necessarily imply significant penetration into other areas. It is impossible to speak of the military elite as being all of one piece; one must examine and test various gradations within it. For example, it is a fact that, following their retirement from active duty, senior IDF officers have placed themselves along the entire breadth of the political spectrum, from extreme left to extreme right. All of this indicates that there are strong 'antibodies' in Israeli society that act, covertly or overtly, against the militarization of society.

Paradoxically, the ideological–political fissures that have beset Israeli society from its earliest days have also served as the strongest antibodies. Israeli pluralism is a rare achievement, even if one considers only the Jewish sector; the more so if we add the Arab sector, which is likewise deeply divided. Ideological rifts in themselves do not necessarily constitute antidotes to the development of militarism; also important are the different sides to the controversies and over what they disagree. But we must also take into account the structures of the cleavage or cleavages: is one dealing with a dichotomous, polar cleavage between two camps having totally different political cultures, with an almost unbridgeable psychological, cultural, and social gap between them? Such a situation is loaded with explosive force, liable to deteriorate into acts of violence and public disorder.[29] In such a case, the involvement of the armed forces is quite likely. On the other hand, when the split is not dichotomous or polarized, the likelihood of military involvement is low, even when there are sharp outbreaks of verbal and even physical violence. From a structural viewpoint, a nonpolar division means that, notwithstanding the existence of extreme camps on the right and the left, there are any number of intermediary shades within the political–ideological map, among which there is partial overlap.[30] In other words, the ideological–political distance between those camps that lie between the radical groups is not that great; there is a good possibility of dialogue and adherence to agreed rules of the game. Such a situation is much more likely when the intermediate camps also constitute the majority of the population.

Such has been the situation within Israel, at least since the electoral turnabout of 1977. Before that time the issue of the ideological–political split was less significant, since one large party, Mapai (the forerunner of today's Labor Party), enjoyed political hegemony. Mapai served as an axial party, without which it was impossible to compose any alternative government.[31] Following Labor's return to power in 1992, it seemed that the ideological–political split focusing on the implementation of the Oslo agreements might develop symptoms of a dichotomous, unbridgeable rift. That this did not happen is evidently attributable to the sobering of the body politic in regard to verbal and physical violence—with the exception of extreme religious groups such as Kach, Kahane Chai, and messianic and Kabbalistic groups—in the wake of the assassination of Yitzhak Rabin. Hence, the basic conditions needed for bringing the army into the sharp public controversy were never created. Israeli society continues to function according to the above-discussed formulas; that is, a dipolitical map with partial overlap among the camps. Moreover, the balance of electoral forces has meant that all past governments, and evidently also those to be elected in the future, must be coalition governments.[32] This means that, at least since 1967, there has been no firm consensus in Israeli society on basic issues of national security. The number of security conceptions and approaches, and the ways of expressing them in public discourse, have been almost as great as the number of parties and ideological streams.

Another antibody, related to the former and no less important, is that of the pluralism within the IDF itself, particularly among the senior staff. This situation did not exist during the 1950s and 1960s, but developed during the later years, and the tendency toward conceptual heterogeneity within the IDF on the issue of the types of solution to the Jewish–Arab conflict seems to have continued. Although the heterogeneity among the senior staff does not precisely reflect that among the civilian public, it is sufficiently broad so that the IDF General Staff and senior officers rarely formulate a unified position on any substantive military-strategic issue. There are numerous examples of this; it suffices to again mention the fact that retired officers who go into politics are found at almost every shade of the spectrum.[33] In other words, the military could not have become a supreme arbitrator of the Israeli 'belief system' because it has no clear-cut belief system of its own.[34]

The fact that these tendencies failed to develop seems connected to another phenomenon—namely, the existence of numerous situations of interaction between the IDF and civilian frameworks. Although such meeting points exist in every society, they are very salient in Israel and are, in part, unique to it. These meeting points are ubiquitous, some of them institutionalized and some not; they may be found, as mentioned, on the senior levels of both the military and civilian hierarchies.

This situation does not indicate, as some scholars have suggested, a symbiosis between the IDF and the political elite, with a unified, militant security outlook. The actual situation is far more complex: in these meeting points a dialogue takes place, sometimes harmonious, but often sharply disputatious, and almost always resolved according to decisions of the prime minister and the government.

A striking example of this disharmony was the criticism during late 1996 by central political figures, including Prime Minister Netanyahu, of excessive involvement by generals in the diplomatic process. This criticism reached its height in condemning the contacts between some of the generals and opposition leaders.

A completely different category of antibodies is found in the system of relations between Israel and the Diaspora, especially in the United States. The American Jewish community, with the exception of a portion of its Orthodox component and certain organizations participating in the President's Council, belongs to the most liberal wing of the American political map. This community's support of and identification with Israel since its founding had diverse roots: religious, ethnic, cultural, the Holocaust, and so on. There is no doubt, however, that the democratic political culture that developed in Israel was a source of pride and identification. One may assume that had the American (or West European) Jewish community seen Israel as a militaristic society, a significant portion of the Jewish intellectual elite and organizational leadership would have found themselves in a difficult position concerning relations with Israel. The same considerations apply to Israel's relations with various other democratic states.

SUMMARY AND FUTURE TRENDS

In the first section, we posed several questions about future trends in military–societal and military–administrative relations in Israel, and the degree to which some of their unique characteristics may dissipate in a postwar age. Before dealing with these issues, let us summarize what we have said so far.

Israel, though it was involved in a violent and protracted conflict, never behaved like a society under siege and never turned into a 'garrison state'. Despite a constant mood of emergency, democratic patterns of life prevailed. Paradoxically, it was precisely the partial involvement of the military sector in those activities of the civilian sector pertaining to the realm of national security that facilitated the survival of the democratic rules of the game and of the routines of civilian life. The process of partial convergence of the military system and the civilian system, both by partial 'militarization' of the civilian sector and by controlled civilianization of the military sector, prevented the army from becoming a separate force in value conflict with the civilian elites. However, these very characteristics, which led to a low probability of de facto domination by the military of the civilian systems and its becoming the supreme regulator of the country's belief system, made the Israeli policymaking system vulnerable to the manipulations of the security establishment or parts of it.

All this took place during the 'Age of Wars', an epoch of violent conflict with the Arab world. What will happen if we enter a postwar age? To answer this, we need to return to the central question posed at the beginning of this chapter: will the unique features of the above-described interrelations between the security and civilian domains remain as they were? And if a change occurs, as it doubtless will, what direction will it take? Will Israel proceed on the path of 'normalization' (according to the standards prevalent in Western democratic states)? What are the possible scenarios in this context, and what will be the implications of one or another change for Israeli society, especially for its myths and ethos of security? A detailed prognosis is not feasible; it is still difficult even to discern the policy of the government elected in 1996 toward the full implementation of the Oslo agreements. What may be done, and this too with caution, is to suggest certain possible directions of development.

To begin with, the very entrance into the age of peace entails a sharp ideological–political struggle. Its extreme and even violent nature has already been seen in the assassination of Yitzhak Rabin. Schematically speaking, two possible scenarios may result from completion of the peace process with the Palestinians and the Syrians, one more pessimistic, the other more optimistic.

The pessimistic scenario could emerge insofar as the movement toward final arrangements with the Palestinians and the Syrians will involve extensive evacuation of the settlers. It will likewise relate to compromises of one sort or another about the status of Jerusalem. Such things may happen even after the right-wing victory in the 1996 elections. In such situations, the probability of violent acts by groups on the extreme right, particularly those belonging to the fundamentalist-religious wing, is high, including further attempts at attacks on political leaders or opposition figures. The danger here involves not only expressions of hatred or violent acts, but also the deep scars that will be left in Israeli society. Such scars will heal, if at all, only over a very long period of time. Until that happens, the political atmosphere will be ugly and the rift between the political camps will widen.

The more optimistic scenario will occur if the final arrangements include reasonable solutions to the question of the settlements, to the status of Jerusalem, and to the establishment of permanent borders and security arrangements, solutions that a large portion of the public will accept and be able to live with. Such arrangements will succeed, in no small measure, in uprooting the destructive potential of the present situation. The danger to the democratic rules of the game will diminish, and the scars left by the peace arrangements will be less severe and capable of healing faster.

Second, one needs to consider the changes currently taking place within the IDF itself, which in the near future will gain further momentum. These changes are seen, first of all, in the quantitative contraction of the security system and its manpower in light of the real decrease in the defense budget. The order of forces of the IDF is becoming smaller and its economic-security offshoots (e.g., the military-defense industries) are also shrinking. All these and other factors (such as an excess of certain types of manpower) will require: the implementation of plans for structural changes in the quantitative balance between the professional standing army on the one hand and the regular army, and reserve divisions, on the other; significant changes—namely, reduction—in the extent of the 'civilian' functions of the IDF (such as education and culture); and an increasing focus on the standing army and a more selective regular army, together with reduction of the civilian tasks performed by the IDF. Such changes will likely affect the nature of the boundaries between the IDF and the civilian realm, both on the institutional and symbolic-cultural levels. The Israeli governments, for their part, will confront several difficult dilemmas:

1. To what extent will conscription to the regular army become more selective and elitist, and will this endanger the social–national goals of conscription to the IDF—i.e., the enabling of broad sections of the population to have the experience of army service? So far, this experience has been considered the most honorable

entrance ticket to civilian society. If army service ceases to play that role, will it be necessary to change the goals of military service and to find means of strengthening the motivation for it?[35]

2. Insofar as the burden of reserve duty will fall primarily on a selective group of combat soldiers and officers, a decision must be made between giving appropriate rewards to those carrying this burden or running the risk of increasing avoidance of reserve duty.

3. Regarding the permanent army, a choice will need to be made between several means of preserving an order of forces suitable for members of the permanent army, in light of the sharp competition for this quality manpower with the civilian markets. The debate that has been waged for several years about the salary, perks, and retirement conditions for the regular army does not bode well in this area.

The strengthening of the historical tendency away from role expansion and toward withdrawal inward, while contracting its civilian roles, is likely to harm the IDF's educational activities in particular, such as those conducted by soldier-teachers; the special programs for youths from disadvantaged homes; the scope of activity of Galei Tzahal (the army radio station); the activity of the Gadna Youth Corps and the Nahal (units stationed for certain periods on kibbutzim); the *hesder* yeshivas (combining army service and religious studies); and the immigrant-absorption projects. Nevertheless, certain quasi-civilian functions may also be strengthened. For example, the academic *atudah* (allowing postponement of regular military service until after the BA) and university education (the Talpiyot project) frameworks are likely to receive greater support than in the past, in order to retain quality manpower in the permanent army for longer periods of time, thereby assuring the quality of officers in a situation of competition with the civilian realm. On the lower level of manpower, the tendency to create situations of national service for those otherwise exempt from army service may also be strengthened. This framework may even include Israeli Arab citizens, who for various reasons will seek integration into Israeli society through obtaining this entrance ticket, albeit one of lower status than that provided by service in the IDF.

All these potential processes, insofar as they are realized, will certainly lead to substantial changes in Israel's security ethos, whose beginnings may already be felt today. It is not yet clear what shape these changes will actually take, but one may reasonably conjecture that the tendency will not be toward strengthening the militaristic ethos, but toward considerable loosening of what has unjustly been called the religion of security. One may likewise conjecture that the great symbiosis between the military and the civilian sectors will continue to dissipate. Only a severe regression in the conditions of national security as a result of the failure of the peace process is likely to revivify and strengthen the militaristic tendency.

NOTES

1. Z. Ostfeld, *An Army Is Born* (Tel-Aviv: Ministry of Defense, 1994), p. 104 (in Hebrew).
2. On the Altalena affair, see U. Brenner, *Altalena: A Political and Military Study* (Tel Aviv: Hakibbutz Hameuchad, 1978) (in Hebrew); on the Palmach, see A. Shapira, *The Army Controversy, 1948: Ben-Gurion's Struggle for Control* (Tel Aviv: Hakibbutz Hameuchad, 1985) (in Hebrew); Y. Gelber, *Why the Palmach Has Been Dissolved* (Tel Aviv: Chen, 1986) (in Hebrew).
3. Gelber, *Why the Palmach Has Been Dissolved*, Ch. 15–16.
4. M. Lissak, '"Critical" Sociology and "Establishment" Sociology in the Israeli Academic Community: Ideological Struggles or Academic Discourse', *Israel Studies*, 1 (1996), pp. 247–93.
5. M. Lissak, 'Boundaries and Institutional Linkages Between Elites: Some Illustrations From Civil–Military Relations in Israel', in G. Moore (ed.), *Research in Politics and Society: A Research Annual*, 1 (1985), pp. 129–48.
6. A. R. Luckham, 'A Comparative Typology of Civil–Military Relations', *Government and Opposition*, 6 (1997), pp. 17–18.
7. Ibid.
8. M. Lissak, 'Convergence and Structural Linkages Between Armed Forces and Society', in M. L. Martin and E. Stern (eds), *The Military, Militarism and the Polity* (New York: The Free Press, 1984), pp. 50–62.
9. D. Horowitz, 'The Israel Defence Forces: A Civilianized Military in a Partially Militarized Society,' in R. Kolkowicz and A. Korbonski (eds), *Soldiers, Peasants and Bureaucrats* (London: G. Allen and Unwin, 1982), pp. 77–106.
10. H. Laswell, 'The Garrison State', *American Journal of Sociology*, 46, 4 (1941), pp. 455–68.
11. D. Horowitz and M. Lissak, 'Democracy and National Security: An Ongoing Confrontation', *Contemporary Jewry*, 4 (1987), pp. 42–6 (in Hebrew).
12. M. Lissak, *Military Roles in Modernization: Civil–Military Relations in Thailand and Burma* (Beverly Hills, CA: Sage, 1976), Ch. 1.
13. A. Mintz, 'The Military–Industrial Complex', in M. Lissak (ed.), *Israeli Society and Its Defense Establishment* (London: Frank Cass, 1984), pp. 110–11; S. Cohen, 'The IDF and Israeli Society: Towards Reduction of IDF Functions?', in M. Lissak and B. Knei-Paz (eds), *Israel Toward the Year 2000: Society, Politics and Culture* (Jerusalem: Magness, 1996), pp. 215–32 (in Hebrew).
14. M. Gal, 'The Integration of Soldiers Into the IDF From Weak, Underprivileged Social Groups', *Ma'arakhot*, 283 (1983), pp. 36–44 (in Hebrew).
15. P. Lahav, 'The Press and National Security', in A. Yaniv (ed.), *National Security and Democracy in Israel* (Boulder, CO: Lynne Riennet, 1993), pp. 173–96; Y. Limor and H. Nussek, 'Military Censorship in Israel', *Leipziger Jahrbuch zur Buchgeschichte*, 5 (1995), pp. 281–302.
16. M. Hofnung, *Israel: Security Needs vs. the Rule of Law* (Nevo, Jerusalem, 1991), pp. 271–6 (in Hebrew).
17. A. Yaniv, 'An Imperfect Democracy', in Yaniv, *National Security*, pp. 227–39.
18. S. Smooha, 'Part of the Problem or Part of the Solution? National Security and the Arab

Minority', in Yaniv, *National Security*, pp. 105–28.

19. Lahav, 'Press and National Security'; M. Negbi, *Paper Tiger: The Struggle for Press Freedom in Israel* (Tel-Aviv: Siftiat Poalim, 1985) (in Hebrew).
20. M. Shamgar, 'Legal Concepts and Problems of the Israeli Military Conquest: The Initial Stage', in M. Shamgar (ed.), *Military Government in the Territories Administered by Israel, 1967–1980: The Legal Aspect* (Jerusalem: Hebrew University, 1982), pp. 13–16; Hofnung, *Israel: Security Needs*, pp. 281–92.
21. Y. Peri, *Between Battles and Ballots: Israeli Military in Politics* (Cambridge: Cambridge University Press, 1983), pp. 172–4; Y. Peri, 'Political–Military Partnership in Israel', *International Political Science Review*, 2, 2 (1981), pp. 303–15.
22. M. Janowitz, 'Armed Forces in Western Europe: Uniformity and Diversity', *Archives Europeenen de Sociologie*, 6, 2 (1965), pp. 225–37; C. C. Moskos, 'Armed Forces and American Society: Convergence and Divergence?', in C. C. Moskos (ed.), *Public Opinion and the Military Establishment* (Beverly Hills, CA: Sage, 1971), pp. 271–92; J. Van Doorn, *The Soldier and Social Change* (Beverly Hills, CA: Sage, 1975), pp. 98–100.
23. D. Maman and M. Lissak, 'The Impact of Social Networks on the Occupational Patterns of Retired Officers: The Case of Israel', *Forum International*, 9 (1990), pp. 279–308; D. Maman and M. Lissak, 'Israel', in C. Danopoulos and D. Watson (eds), *The Political Role of the Military: An International Handbook* (Westport, CT: Greenwood, 1996), pp. 223–33.
24. U. Ben-Eliezer, *The Emergence of Israeli Militarism, 1936–1956* (Jerusalem: Drit, 1995), pp. 51–65 (in Hebrew).
25. Ibid., p. 61.
26. B. Kimmerling, 'Patterns of Militarism in Israel', *Archives Europeenen de Sociologie*, 34 (1993), pp. 199–202.
27. Lissak, '"Critical" Sociology'.
28. Luckham, 'Comparative Typology'; M. Lissak, 'Modernization and Role Expansion of the Military in Developing Countries: A Comparative Analysis', *Comparative Studies in Society and History*, 14, 3 (1967), pp. 233–56; Lissak, 'Boundaries', pp. 129–48.
29. D. Horowitz and M. Lissak, *Trouble in Utopia* (Albany, NY: State University of New York Press, 1989), pp. 32–6.
30. Ibid., pp. 33–9.
31. Ibid., Ch. 4.
32. Ibid.
33. Y. Peri and M. Lissak, 'Retired Officers in Israel and the Emergence of a New Elite', in G. Harries-Jenkins and J. Van Doorn (eds), *The Military and the Problem of Legitimacy* (London: Sage, 1976), pp. 175–92.
34. Y. Peri, 'The Impact of Occupation on the Military: The Case of the IDF, 1967–1987', in I. Peleg and O. Seliktar (eds), *The Emergence of a Binational Israel: The Second Republic in the Making* (Boulder, CO: Westview, 1989), pp. 143–50.
35. D. Horowitz and B. Kimmerling, 'Some Social Implications of Military Service and the Reserve System in Israel', *Archives Europeenen de Sociologie*, 15 (1974), pp. 262–76; E. Lomsky-Feder, 'Youth in the Shadow of War—War in the Light of Youth: Life Stories of Israeli Veterans', in V. Weeus et al. (eds), *Adolescence, Careers and Cultures* (Berlin, 1992), pp. 405–7.

Index